God With Us

An Introduction to the Old Testament

W9-AZC-786

God With Us

An Introduction to the Old Testament

Stephen J. Lennox

TRIANGLE PUBLISHING ®
Marion, Indiana

God With Us: An Introduction to the Old Testament
Stephen J. Lennox

Second Edition

Direct correspondence and permission requests to one of the following:

E-mail: info@trianglepublishing.com
Web site: www.trianglepublishing.com
Mail: Triangle Publishing
            Indiana Wesleyan University
            1900 West 50th Street
            Marion, Indiana 46953

The *Chicago Manual of Style* is the preferred style guide of Triangle Publishing.

Published by Triangle Publishing
Marion, Indiana 46953

ISBN: 978-1-931283-37-3

All Scripture quotations, unless otherwise indicated, are taken from the *Holy Bible, New International Version ®. NIV ®*. Copyright © 1973, 1978, 1984 by International Bible Society. Used by permission of Zondervan. All rights reserved.

Scripture quotations marked NLT are from the *Holy Bible, New Living Translation,* copyright © 1996, 2004. Used by permission of Tyndale House Publishers, Inc., Wheaton, Illinois 60189. All rights reserved.

Scripture quotations marked RSV are taken from *The Holy Bible: Revised Standard Version,* copyright © 1946, 1952, 1971 by the Division of Christian Education of the National Council of the Churches of Christ in the U.S.A.

Scripture quotations marked CEV are taken from *The Holy Bible: Contemporary English Version,* copyright © 1995 by The American Bible Society. Used by permission. All rights reserved.

Scripture quotations marked NJB are taken from *The Holy Bible: The New Jerusalem Bible*. Biblical text copyright © 1985 by Darton, Longman & Todd Ltd and Doubleday, a division of Bantam Doubleday Dell Publishing Group, Inc.

Copyright © 2003, 2009 by Triangle Publishing. All rights reserved. No part of this publication may be reproduced, stored in a retrieval system, distributed, or transmitted in any form or by any means: electronic, mechanical, photocopy, recording or any other, except for brief quotations in printed reviews and as permitted under United States Copyright Act of 1976, without prior written permission of the publisher.

Cover design: Jim Pardew
Graphic design: Gary Phillips
Original illustrations: Eric Wieringa

Printed in the United States of America

Contents

Acknowledgments

I have many people to thank for their help in the preparation of this book. I am grateful to Nathan Birky, Publisher of Triangle Publishing, and Provost, Dr. David Wright, for envisioning this book and inviting me to write it. I am also grateful to Indiana Wesleyan University for granting me a sabbatical leave during which the book took shape. Mrs. Bonita Wuertley assisted me with manuscript preparation, as did one of my students, Miss Angie Hinton. Thanks to my Old Testament Survey classes who improved the book by their excellent feedback. Of course, I am especially grateful to my wife, Eileen, and to my kids, Abby and Ethan. Their patience, support, and encouragement are irreplaceable.

I would like to dedicate this book to Dr. David A. Dorsey, Professor of Old Testament at Evangelical Theological Seminary. He has been a source of wise counsel since I first sat under his instruction at Evangelical, even to the preparation of this volume. It was Dr. Dorsey who showed me the importance of asking what a passage teaches about God. More importantly, he has provided a wonderful model of a warm-hearted, humble scholar.

Stephen J. Lennox

How to Use This Book

I have written this book for the newcomer to the Old Testament, someone without any knowledge of the Bible or whose knowledge is sketchy. Those who know their way around this material but don't quite understand how it all fits together may also find this book useful. I have tried to avoid complicated issues and in-depth discussions.*

In the first five chapters, I introduce the Old Testament, pointing out the reasons why this material deserves careful study (chapter 1) and how to read for maximum understanding (chapters 2–5). The remaining twenty chapters detail the individual books of the Old Testament, presented in chronological order. Each chapter begins with suggestions for how to read that particular kind of literature **(light blue box)**. Then I summarize the content of the book or books under consideration. Scattered throughout this summary are **gray boxes** in which I discuss particularly puzzling passages. Each chapter concludes with a "Book at a Glance" box **(bold blue outline)** that summarizes relevant information in chart form.

Important to the makeup of chapters 6–24 are the questions at the end of the chapters. The application questions are intended to help you apply what you've learned about God from that chapter. The study and discussion questions are to help you progress in understanding. If you are studying this book as part of a class, some of these questions will lend themselves to interesting discussions.

Ideally, you should read the chapter first, then read the Old Testament material under consideration in that chapter. If you cannot read all the biblical material, at least read the passages I suggest. However, don't let this book become a substitute for reading the Bible. By reading both this book and the Bible, and by answering the assigned questions, I believe you will gain a good understanding of the Old Testament's content and themes and will learn to apply this knowledge to your life.

---

* Those looking for this kind of treatment should consult one of the following:
Bill T. Arnold and Bryan E. Beyer, *Encountering the Old Testament: A Christian Survey* (Grand Rapids, Mich.: Baker, 1999) Andrew E. Hill and John H. Walton, *A Survey of the Old Testament* (Grand Rapids, Mich.: Zondervan, 1991).

It is one of the most influential books in the history of the world. Millions of people around the world consider it sacred. Yet the Old Testament is little known, little read, and little appreciated. I want to change that. I want you to share my love, my admiration, my fascination for this literature. I want you to have the confidence to open its pages and read for your own enjoyment and personal growth. I want you to become better acquainted with the loving God whose shadow falls on every page.

Stephen J. Lennox

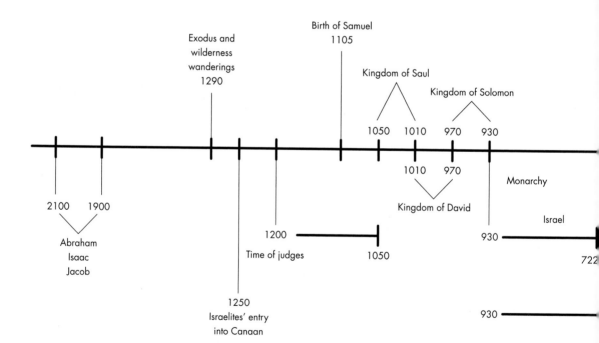

Birth of Samuel
1105

Exodus and
wilderness
wanderings
1290

Kingdom of Saul

Kingdom of Solomon

1050   1010   970   930

2100   1900

1010   970

Abraham
Isaac
Jacob

Monarchy

Kingdom of David

Israel

1200   930

Time of judges   1050   722

1250
Israelites' entry
into Canaan

930

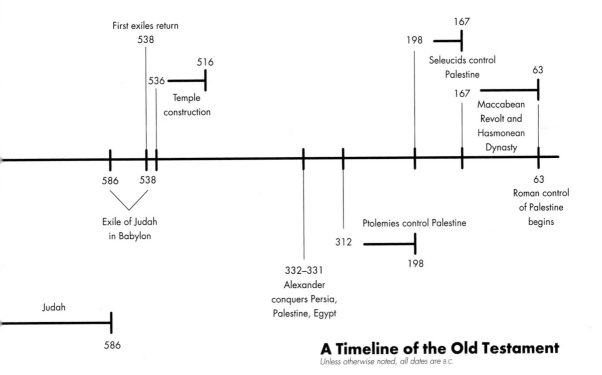

First exiles return
538

516

536

Temple
construction

167
198

Seleucids control
Palestine

63

167

Maccabean
Revolt and
Hasmonean
Dynasty

586   538

63
Roman control
of Palestine
begins

Exile of Judah
in Babylon

Ptolemies control Palestine

312

198

332–331
Alexander
conquers Persia,
Palestine, Egypt

Judah

586

A Timeline of the Old Testament
Unless otherwise noted, all dates are B.C.

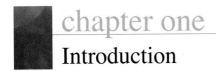

chapter one

Introduction

WHAT IS THE OLD TESTAMENT?

Jews simply call it the Bible,[1] but most know it by its Christian name: the Old Testament. Jews and Christians agree it is the Word of God. That is, they believe it to be more than a book written by humans about God. They believe God inspired the human authors to write about himself.

This inspiration was not the same as what William Shakespeare or John Milton experienced; those great authors never claimed to speak the words of God. However, the Old Testament authors made precisely this claim, and Jesus himself agreed they were correct. God inspired these authors but did not dictate the Bible to them like a boss dictates a letter to a secretary. If the authors were just God's secretaries, the entire Bible would sound the same, like one long letter from God. In fact, the books that make up the Old Testament do *not* sound alike. Each one reflects the personality and purpose of its human author. Somehow, God inspired each author to write exactly what He wanted him to say, but in a way that perfectly fit that author's own personality and goal.

Tertullian, a church leader from Africa who lived from A.D. 160 until about A.D. 220, was one of the first people to refer to the Jewish Bible as the Old Testament.[2] By using the title "Old Testament," he wanted to emphasize that the Jewish Bible was Part One—the earlier or older part of a two-part work. Part One describes how God worked through the Jews to prepare for the coming of Christ. By testament, Tertullian meant something like arrangement or agreement. Part Two—the New Testament—tells about Jesus' life, how He died and rose from the dead.[3] It also describes how the early church continued what Jesus began.

The Old Testament is actually a collection of thirty-nine books.[4] Almost all were written in the Hebrew language with a small portion in Aramaic, a related language.

בְּרֵאשִׁית בָּרָא אֱלֹהִים אֵת הַשָּׁמַיִם וְאֵת הָאָרֶץ׃

Genesis 1:1

The earliest book, probably Genesis, was written between 1400 and 1200 B.C. The latest books to be written were probably 1 and 2 Chronicles, composed about 400 B.C. That means the Old Testament was written over a span of eight hundred years. Relating that span of time to our understanding today, we have only to remember that eight hundred years ago a very different kind of English language was spoken and the printing press had yet to be invented.

Like a library, the Old Testament contains different types of literature written by many different authors. It includes poems, stories, laws, proverbs, songs, family records, and sermons, not always neatly arranged. Few of the books identify their authors, and those authors we know about represent many occupations from every level of society.

The Jews probably realized almost immediately that some of this material was God's Word. For some books the process took a little longer. Scholars agree that by 400 B.C., at the latest, Jews considered the Pentateuch—Genesis, Exodus, Leviticus, Numbers, and Deuteronomy—as sacred Scripture. Most of the historical and prophetic books were recognized as

Scripture by 200 B.C. The rest of the Old Testament was validated by 100 B.C. The early church, without any controversy, adopted the Jewish Bible as Part One of its Scriptures.[5]

WHY IS THE OLD TESTAMENT IGNORED?

If you have seldom or never read the Old Testament, you are not alone. Many Christians avoid it like a trip to the dentist. Why do so few read a book that so many agree is so important?

A Matter of Relevance

Many find it irrelevant, like outdated software. They don't see it as necessary to their spiritual lives. After all, why would they need to know a long list of names or the ancient law against wearing two kinds of fabric in the same piece of clothing? Unable to grasp the significance of the Old Testament, they ignore it and develop their knowledge of God almost exclusively from the New Testament. Occasionally they pay a visit to the Old Testament, mostly to learn how it predicted the coming of Jesus or for peace and quiet in the Psalms. Those of this mind-set might include a reading from the Old Testament in a random church service, but few sermons would be based on it. The Old Testament could disappear overnight and many would never miss it.

Those who do try to read the Old Testament find themselves almost immediately overwhelmed by its length—about one thousand pages in most translations. Since this huge amount of material is not arranged chronologically, it is very hard to follow the story from beginning to end. Faced with the task of walking through a large, dense forest without clear paths, many avoid the woods altogether. Those who dare the attempt often lose sight of the forest for the trees. They get lost in the details. Too many rules about sacrifices, too many territorial allotments, too many kings and prophets—it is easy to forget what you came looking for and easier still to lose the big picture.

An Unusual Country

Those who press on find themselves in unfamiliar territory. They read about events that took place more than three thousand years ago among people and in countries they never heard of and whose names they cannot pronounce. Many of us have trouble with history anyway. We don't see its relevance, even when it's our history! Old Testament events transpired in strange, exotic places that are hard to visualize, even for those who watch the Travel Channel. Yet as we read the Old Testament, it is clear that so many of the events detailed were directly impacted by the geography of this unusual land.

In Israel, water is scarce, hills are numerous, and forests are sparse.[6] Unlike ancient Babylon or Egypt, which were nourished by major rivers, this area depends heavily on rainfall. Earthquakes are common and a deep split known as the Rift Valley scars the land. This valley, running north and south, contains the Sea of Galilee, the Jordan River, and the lowest spot on the earth, the Dead Sea. Within this little country, smaller than the state of New Jersey, you can find extinct volcanoes, snow-capped mountains, and two large lakes below sea level. Fertile, green oases stand out against bone-dry, barren hills. This is a very unusual place indeed!

An Unusual Culture

Even more confusing than the ancient history of a foreign land is the strange culture we meet in the Old Testament. We're not used to a man having several wives or to women who are okay with that. We're bothered by the group-oriented culture that stifles individuality. We're surprised that they believe in a supernatural world and take this belief seriously.

In those areas of the world that have retained this culture, such as parts of Africa today, the Old Testament is more easily understood and embraced. However, those of us in different cultures often become offended by what we find in the Old Testament. We cringe at the hundreds of passages that describe violence, especially when God is the one being violent. We are offended by examples of patriarchalism, the dominance of men over women. I know one

MAP 1 Physical Map of Palestine

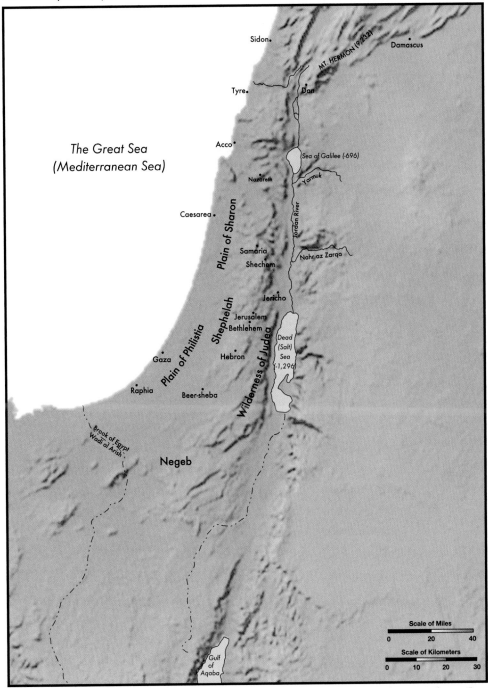

The Great Sea
(Mediterranean Sea)

Sidon

MT. HERMON (9,232)

Damascus

Tyre

Dan

Acco

Sea of Galilee (-696)

Nazareth

Yarmuk

Caesarea

Plain of Sharon

Jordan River

Samaria

Shechem

Nahr az Zarqa

Jericho

Jerusalem

Bethlehem

Dead (Salt) Sea (-1,296)

Shephelah

Gaza

Plain of Philistia

Hebron

Raphia

Beer-sheba

Wilderness of Judea

Brook of Egypt
Wadi al Arish

Negeb

Gulf of Aqaba

Scale of Miles

0   20   40

Scale of Kilometers

0   10   20   30

5

woman who completely rejected the Bible because she thought it embraced patriarchalism. In chapter 3, we'll return to this cultural divide and its implications for reading the Old Testament.

Misused and Distorted

Some ignore the Old Testament because they have seen it misused. Perhaps they heard a sermon that ignored the obvious meaning of a passage or made a passage say something it was never meant to say. I once heard the opening chapter of the book of Ezekiel used to prove the existence of spaceships. This kind of abuse is rightly rejected; unfortunately, the abused text is sometimes rejected as well.

The opposite is also true. Some pastors who use outdated information or scholarship produced on the fringes of respectability dismiss the Old Testament as only a human book about God, rather than God's Word to humans.[7] Sadly, not only the misguided pastor but also his or her parishioners feel justified in ignoring the Old Testament. An open-minded reading of up-to-date, sound scholarship could restore their confidence.

WHY READ THE OLD TESTAMENT?

Those who overcome these obstacles and read the Old Testament are abundantly rewarded. Who couldn't benefit from reading one of the finest pieces of literature ever produced? Even in translation, the artistry of the Old Testament is complex and incisive. Its poetry is among the most eloquent ever written. Thousands of years after it was written, its stories continue to confront and comfort us at our deepest levels. The teachings of the Old Testament represent some of the most profound human insights in all of literature.

Timeless Literature, Timeless Truths

This remarkable literature also allows us to better understand Western civilization. In his book *The Gifts of the Jews*, Thomas Cahill describes how the Jews and their sacred Scripture have enriched us. Their way of looking at the world, he says, made it possible to see how the universe operates under observable laws of cause and effect. Such laws allow people to think historically and scientifically.

The Old Testament reinforces humanity's value and dignity. "Democracy," Cahill writes, "grows directly out of the Israelite vision of *individuals*, subjects of value because they are images of God, each with a unique and personal destiny. There is no way that it could ever have been 'self-evident that all men are created equal' without the intervention of the Jews."[8]

Cross-Cultural Relevance

Although it is the basis for much of Western civilization, we have seen that the Old Testament arose from a very different world. By reading it, we are exposed to another time, another place, another way of thinking about life. This sort of cross-cultural education is one of the hallmarks of a well-educated person.

Familiarity with the Old Testament also allows us to better understand the three major world religions, all of which claim this book as sacred Scripture. Jews consider it their Bible, while Christians see it as Part One of their two-part Bible. Muslims also revere the Old Testament, regarding it as one of the holy predecessors to the Koran. A glance at the headlines today reinforces an obvious reality: The more the adherents of these three religions can understand each other, the better we can get along on this shrinking globe.

The Old Testament also helps us to understand ourselves better. Although separated from us by miles and millennia, the people of the Old Testament were human. They were motivated by the same things that motivate us: fear, pride, hope, anger, compassion. When we read the Psalms, for example, we hear the echo of our own voices crying out to God for relief, rejoicing at what God has done, calling on God to help us. Reading about Moses' anger in Exodus 32 helps us understand our own. Our frustration at God's silence finds expression in Job's complaints (read Job 31).

Jesus Read It

The Christian has several more reasons to read and understand the Old Testament. This is the Bible Jesus read, quoted, and believed. He asserted, "Do not think that I have come to abolish the Law or the Prophets;[9] I have not come to abolish them but to fulfill them" (Matthew 5:17).[10] Another time He announced, "Heaven and earth will disappear before the smallest letter of the Law does" (Luke 16:17 CEV).

When challenged, Jesus almost always turned to the Old Testament for His defense. As He was tempted by the Devil, Jesus quoted from the Old Testament.[11] When criticized for spending too much time with society's undesirables, Jesus sent His critics to study the Old Testament prophet, Hosea (Hosea 6:6).[12] Another time He told a group of Bible scholars, "You are in error because you do not know the Scriptures [that is, the Old Testament] or the power of God" (read Matthew 22:23–29). When He saw some religious leaders acting hypocritically, He blasted them for their "fine way of setting aside the commands of God [found in the Old Testament] in order to observe your own traditions!" (Mark 7:9; read 7:1–13).

Foundational to the Early Church

The early Christians shared Jesus' commitment to the Old Testament. The apostle Paul said, "All Scripture [by which he meant the Old Testament] is God-breathed and is useful for teaching, rebuking, correcting and training in righteousness" (2 Timothy 3:16). For the apostle Peter, "the word of the Lord stands forever" (1 Peter 1:25). The writer of Hebrews continually referred to the Old Testament as the words of God (read Hebrews 1 for several such examples).

The Old Testament was so important to the early church that the believers turned to it when they worshiped. Like the Jews before them, they sang the Psalms and read the Old Testament stories to learn about God. Using the Old Testament, the apostle James settled a very thorny debate that threatened to divide the young church (read about this in Acts 15, especially verses 15–18).

The Old Testament is the best commentary on the New Testament ever written. There we learn why Jesus had to come, why He taught what He did, and why He worked miracles. From the Old Testament we learn that Jesus had to die on the cross and rise from the dead (read 1 Corinthians 15:3–4). The Old Testament explains why the early church preached what it preached (read Peter's sermon in Acts 2 or Paul's explanation in Romans 15:4). Many New Testament terms that sound strange to us—for example, Son of Man, sanctification, Law, and circumcision—are words found frequently in the Old Testament. Two of the most puzzling books in the New Testament, Hebrews and Revelation, rely heavily on the Old Testament. Some Christians ignore the Old Testament and focus on the New, but only those who read the New in light of the Old really can learn what God is saying in His Word.

It Reveals God

Perhaps the most important reason to read the Old Testament is because of what it teaches us about God. What we learn there about God is just as important as what we learn from the New Testament. The Old Testament tells us a great deal about God's character and behavior! There we see His power, creating the universe, parting the Red Sea, and summoning water from the rocks. There we suffer His silence, as Job did. There we experience His anger and harshness.

Because some of these pictures of God seem unpleasant, many reject the Old Testament. Very early in the history of the church, a man named Marcion announced that the God of the Old Testament and the God of the New Testament were two different beings. The former was harsh and vindictive, while the latter was loving and forgiving. Although the early church decided Marcion was wrong, many modern Christians agree with him—if their neglect of the Old Testament tells us anything.

Marcion and his supporters have misunderstood the Old Testament. When reading how God acted in a harsh or angry manner, they assume they are seeing what God is really like. After all, that is how we make judgments about other people. We watch them in action and decide if they are gentle or mean, wise or foolish, good or bad. But even when evaluating people, we should always make room for the context. If you saw me grab my son by the arm and yank him toward me, you might conclude I was harsh and abusive. But if that incident occurred along a busy highway, you would call me quick thinking, crediting me with saving my son from being struck by a car. Before we determine character from behavior, we must consider the context.

We need to do the same when determining the character of God. We must consider what made it necessary for Him to act as He did. Don't just ask *what* He did, ask why. When you do, you will notice that God always works with people where they are, doing for them what they need most. When you see a young mother talking baby talk to her toddler, you don't assume the mother is mentally deficient. You assume she has stooped to her child's level of conversation because she loves her child and wants to communicate that love. There is always a good reason for what God does, even when we think a particular action is strange.

When God did not answer Job, it was because silence taught important lessons that words could never teach. When God killed Uzzah, who seemingly was trying to help, He did so because the help offered was actually harmful. When God behaved violently or asked His people to behave violently, it was not because He is violent. It was because the ancient Near East was a violent place. God had no choice if He wanted to be understood.

"Why didn't He teach them a better way?" He did. He showed them that violence is not the best response. Many laws of the ancient Near East commanded excessive and unfair punishments. You could be killed for insulting someone. An offense against an important official was punished more harshly than the same offense against a common person.[13]

Instead, God called His people to perfect equity: an eye for an eye and a tooth for a tooth. No more, no less, and no favoritism. It did not matter whose eye or tooth was damaged—noble or common person—the punishment was the same. Like a loving parent, God compassionately and gently taught His people a better way than violence. He told them to treat others the way they would like to be treated.[14]

A Radical Departure

A bird's-eye view of the Bible shows how God introduced a radically new and different ethical standard, one that placed great value on humanity. Then He gradually and carefully took His people from where they were to where He wanted them to be. When God called Abraham[15] in Genesis 12, every culture in the ancient Near East was polytheistic; that is, they believed in many gods, not just one.[16] Abraham himself grew up in a home where many gods were worshiped (read Joshua 24:2). Although there is only one God, and although this discovery would be an important cultural and religious step forward, God did not reveal this to His people all at once. At first He told them that they should worship and obey Him and no other gods (read Exodus 20:3–4). Later He made it clear there actually were no other gods, only Him.[17]

We can see God's gradual, patient strategy in ethical matters such as slavery. He began by allowing His people to own slaves but required them to be treated fairly, far more fairly than elsewhere in the ancient Near East. Further, slavery in Israel was limited to six years, like the indentured servant of America's colonial days. By New Testament times, the apostle Paul, though still allowing for slavery, planted the seeds for its abolition in such statements as "There is neither . . . slave nor free . . . for you are all one in Christ Jesus" (Galatians 3:28).

God commanded animal sacrifices, not because He likes to see animals sacrificed, but because this was how ancient people related to the gods. All ancient Near Eastern cultures offered animal sacrifices. God began where His people were, and taught them about himself through their culture. For example, through His instructions about sacrifices, He showed His people that forgiveness for sins was not mechanical, but personal and freely given. Eventually He replaced these sacrifices with the one sacrifice of His Son on the cross (read Hebrews 10).

When we see God's actions in the context of the ancient Near East and understand how patiently He taught His people, we see God not as a bloodthirsty barbarian, but as a loving heavenly Father. Not that we can understand everything about God, but what we do understand about Him reassures us that there is a good reason for what we do not understand.

What matters most is understanding God; this is the primary reason He gave us the Bible. He knew we could never be fully human and reach our potential unless we understood something about who made us and why. He knew that without revealing himself, we could not embrace the salvation He offers us in Christ. We can find many uses for the Bible, even many good uses like learning about history, but the most important reason is to learn about God. The Bible, including the Old Testament, tells us all we need to know about God so we can be all we need to be.

But the Old Testament is not just a biography of God. Instead, it is a description of God in action. Being able to see a bird's-eye view of God's panoramic, overarching design helps to clarify His individual actions as we see them throughout the Old Testament. We are off to this scenic overlook in chapter 2.

endnotes

1. Or the Tanakh. The Jews divide their Bible into three parts: Torah (the first five books), Nevi'im (the prophetic books), and Ketuvim (the Writings, which include books like Psalms and Proverbs). To come up with the title "Tanakh," they took the first letters of these three Hebrew words (T, N, and K) and added vowels.

2. A.D. abbreviates the Latin phrase *anno Domini*, meaning "in the year of the Lord." It has been used for centuries to describe the years since Jesus' birth, as in A.D. 2009. The years prior to the birth of Jesus are followed by the abbreviation B.C. ("before Christ"). This was determined by counting backward from what was thought at one time to be the year of Jesus' birth. Thus, 500 B.C. would be about five hundred years before Jesus was born.

3. As a matter of respect, I capitalize the pronouns for God and Jesus. I will also refer to God using male pronouns (He, Him, His), although I realize that God is neither male nor female.

4. Jews include the same material found in these thirty-nine books, but organize it differently. Roman Catholics and Orthodox Christians add several other books, called the Apocrypha. We will have more to say on this in a later chapter.

5. By 100 B.C. almost everyone, whether Jew or Christian, read the Bible in Greek, the common language of the day. The Greek version of the Old Testament was prepared about two hundred years before Christ was born. It is called the Septuagint, sometimes abbreviated LXX. We'll have more to say about this later.

6. There used to be more forests in ancient Palestine, but they were not the dense woods with tall oaks and pines familiar to most people in North America. Centuries of abuse have left Israel with relatively few trees, a problem modern Israelis are attempting to solve with massive reforestation projects.

7. Such as the biblical minimalists who, in the face of clear evidence, deny that David or Solomon ever existed.

8. Thomas Cahill, *The Gifts of the Jews: How a Tribe of Desert Nomads Changed the Way Everyone Thinks and Feels* (New York: Nan A. Talese-Doubleday, 1998), 249.

9. The Law is comprised of Genesis, Exodus, Leviticus, Numbers, and Deuteronomy. These five books are also called the Pentateuch. The Jews spoke of the Former Prophets (Joshua, Judges, 1 and 2 Samuel, and 1 and 2 Kings) and the Latter Prophets (Isaiah, Jeremiah, Ezekiel, and the twelve Minor Prophets).

10. Books of the Bible are divided into chapters and each chapter into verses. Matthew 5:17 means this passage is found in the seventeenth verse of the fifth chapter of Matthew.

11. Read Matthew 4:1–11, where three times Jesus quoted from Deuteronomy.

12. You can read about this confrontation in Matthew 9:9–13.

13. One ancient law code written about 1700 B.C. (about five hundred years before Moses lived) called for the blinding of a nobleman who blinded another nobleman. But if that nobleman blinded a commoner, he only had to pay a fine. ("The Code of Hammurabi," numbers 196, 198, in James B. Pritchard, ed., *Ancient Near Eastern Texts Relating to the Old Testament [ANET]* [Princeton, N.J.: Princeton University Press, 1969], 175).

14. We call this the Golden Rule and find it in Leviticus 19:18 and its more familiar form in Matthew 7:12 and Luke 6:31.

15. His name was originally Abram, but God changed it to symbolize Abraham's new role as ancestor of many nations.

16. In the 1500s B.C., Pharaoh Akhenaton tried to convince the Egyptians that there was only one god, not many, but his efforts failed to make a lasting impression in Egypt or elsewhere.

17. According to some scholars, this realization occurred within a generation of Israel's liberation from Egypt and before the Israelites entered Canaan. They cite passages such as Deuteronomy 32:39: "See now that I myself am He! There is no god besides me." They consider mention of other gods as referring only to objects made of metal, wood, and stone (as in Deuteronomy 4:28).

chapter two

A Panoramic View of God's Plan

In the last chapter we saw how it is so easy to get lost among the details that we miss the big picture of what the Old Testament is all about. In this chapter we want to survey God's plan, from the beginning of the Old Testament to the end of the New Testament. As in any bird's-eye view, we'll need to cover the material in a summary way. But don't worry—everything we cover in this chapter we'll develop in more detail in the rest of the book.

SLIPPING FROM PARADISE

Among the things we learn from the opening two chapters of the Old Testament is that God created everything and that originally everything was good. This was paradise: each human in harmony with nature, with other humans, and with God. But in Genesis 3, something went terribly wrong. The humans disobeyed God and His harmonious creation began to unravel.

From that point on, sin's effects spread like cancer. Nature, intended as an ally of humanity, began to work in opposition, sending weeds where crops should grow. The first human relationship soured. Designed as a partnership between equals, God had to make it a hierarchy. Someone had to be designated the leader and the other the follower, or sin would completely destroy any chance of happiness. Note too how sin turned humanity against itself. Prior to sin's entry, Adam and Eve knew inner contentment and peace. After sinning, inner contentment and peace were replaced by guilt and shame.

These effects of sin were all serious, but something even worse happened: Humanity became separated from God. Before sin, humans experienced pleasant, relaxing fellowship in relationship with God; after sin, they tried to hide from Him. Once this relationship was broken, humanity began a steep descent into near chaos.

Very soon, murder entered the picture, one brother killing another (Genesis 4). Then other sins followed, the disease spreading like cancer through creation. Before long, God looked at the creation He had once called good and determined to destroy it with a flood, leaving alive only one righteous man, Noah, to start again (Genesis 6).

This plan also was short-lived because Noah and his family carried the disease of sin within themselves. The puddles on the earth were not all dry before the disease began to spread again. God knew this plan would not solve the problem, but carried it through for two reasons: He wanted to demonstrate His concern for all humanity, and He wanted to show that sin was too serious to be solved by any plan that depended on sinful human beings.

Although they did not fully understand who God was or what He wanted, human beings knew they were out of fellowship with Him. They tried to solve this problem on their own by building a tower to the heavens (Genesis 11). God, knowing the futility of their efforts, shut down their building project. In only eleven chapters, God's creation had slipped from paradise to a world terminally ill and unable to help itself.

The Process of Restoration

How did God respond to this hopeless situation? He called Abraham (Genesis 12). With this seemingly insignificant action, God began the process that eventually would reverse the corruption caused by sin and completely destroy sin's power. The entire Bible—indeed, all of history—

swings on the hinge of this moment. God called Abraham to break with his past—to leave his family, his home, and his country—in order to begin something new. He would make Abraham's descendants into a great nation. This nation, Israel, would be a source of blessing to the whole world.

God confirmed this promise with a legal contract, what the Bible calls a covenant (Genesis 15, 17). In this covenant, God promised He would give Abraham many descendants and a land of their own in which to live. He also promised to protect and provide for Abraham and his family. All they had to do was remain committed to Him. The Old Testament often summarizes the terms of this legally binding agreement with the phrase "I will be your God; you will be my people." The covenant between God and Abraham was not the only covenant God made in the Old Testament, but it was the most important one. All the agreements that came before anticipated this one; those that came after built upon this covenant, further fleshing out details of how God would undo the damage caused by sin.

From Descendants to Nation

During the covenant ceremony described in Genesis 15, God told Abraham that his descendants would be prisoners in a foreign land. After many years they would be released and come to live in the land of Canaan.[1] That prediction came true and is described in the books of Exodus, Leviticus, Numbers, Deuteronomy, and Joshua. God chose an Israelite named Moses to lead Abraham's descendants out of slavery in Egypt. Through a series of devastating plagues and powerful miracles, God rescued the Israelites and brought them to a mountain in the wilderness between Egypt and Canaan. There, at Mount Sinai, God transformed a group of freed slaves into the nation of Israel.

To accomplish this transformation, God made another covenant with His people. It did not replace the agreement with Abraham; it further clarified it. In the Sinai covenant, God told the Israelites how they were to live. He gave them the Ten Commandments. He also gave about six hundred additional laws to clarify how to keep the Ten Commandments. Every single law reinforced the two most important tasks of a citizen of Israel: Love God with your whole heart and love your neighbor as much as you love yourself.[2] If they could maintain this love for God and neighbor, they could minimize the effects of sin among themselves.

God knew transforming the Israelites from a group of slaves into a nation that could bless the world would take more than laws. God would need to remind them often that He was present among them. He did so by miraculously providing food, sometimes raining bread from the sky and making water gush out of rocks. He sent a giant cloud that looked like smoke during the day and glowed like fire at night. This cloud was to guide the Israelites on their journey, but also to remind them that God was with them. He had them build a Tabernacle where they could worship Him. It was to be portable so they could take it wherever they traveled. God wanted them to realize that they were special; no less than the Almighty God himself had chosen to live among them.[3] He also wanted them to experience, at least partially, the blessing of fellowship with God that human beings had lost because of sin.

Having begun this process of transformation, the next step was to bring them into the land of Canaan. On the way, God taught them important lessons about trust and faithfulness. Although painful, God knew these lessons were necessary if Israel was to fulfill her mission as a source of blessing to the rest of the world. Finally, just before Israel entered Canaan, God had Moses repeat the Law so everyone would know what God required.[4]

Under the leadership of Joshua, Moses' successor, the Israelites conquered Canaan, the land God had promised them. Canaanite resistance was no obstacle as long as Israel kept trusting in God. He had promised that obedience would bring God's blessing but that disobedience would bring disaster.

Cycle of Sin

If God could have placed His people anywhere, why did He choose Canaan as the Promised Land? This small patch of real estate is not rich in natural resources. It has no abundant water supply and depends heavily on rainfall. God placed His people there so they would have to depend on Him to provide the rain for crops. He wanted to teach them about faith. God also placed them there to increase their influence in the ancient Near East. A bridge of land bordered on the west by the Mediterranean Sea and on the east by the desert, Canaan connected the continents of Asia to the north and Africa to the south. Whoever controlled this bridge exerted tremendous influence on the empires to the north and south. God put Israel at this strategic location so she could bless the nations as God had promised.

Once settled in the Promised Land, sin caused Israel to drift from her commitment to God. To bring the Israelites back, He allowed them to be oppressed by the surrounding nations. After the Israelites had suffered for a while, they cried out to God, who then sent a leader to rescue them. Freedom was followed by compromise, compromise by oppression, oppression by appeal, appeal by divine rescue, and so the cycle continued for several hundred years.

A new day dawned in the crowning of a young man named David. Although David was not perfect, God chose him to rule His people, ushering Israel into a golden age of obedience and blessing. Expanding on His original promise to Abraham, God made a covenant with David: He and his descendants would always sit on Israel's throne, so long as they obeyed God (read about this in 2 Samuel 7).

The golden age continued through David's reign and that of his son Solomon, but began to disintegrate at the end of Solomon's life. The alienating effects of sin turned Israelite against Israelite. One nation split into two. Israel, larger and more prosperous, was located in the northern three-fourths of the original country. Almost immediately, the Northern Kingdom turned from God and remained disobedient for the next two centuries. After repeatedly warning them through His prophets, God reluctantly allowed them to be destroyed.

The Southern Kingdom, Judah, continued for another century and a half, ruled by descendants of David. Although more righteous and stable than

Israel, Judah eventually lost sight of her mission and reaped the disaster that follows disobedience. Her cities and the Temple were destroyed, thousands were killed, and many of the survivors were taken into exile.

Starting Over

But God was not finished with His people or His plan for them. After about fifty years of captivity, He brought them back to their homeland to start over. Although no longer a sovereign nation but only a weak territory in the vast Persian Empire, the Jews rebuilt their cities and Temple, and devoted themselves more seriously to obeying God. The Old Testament closes with a picture of the Jews struggling to rebuild what they had lost.

Over the next four centuries, the Jews passed from the hands of one great empire to another. Briefly they regained their freedom but soon lost it again. Some Jews rejected God and embraced the prevailing culture. Others hung tenaciously to the hope that God would continue His plan through them.

GOD'S NEW PLAN

Their hopes finally came true! This time, God did not symbolize His presence in a building or cloud. This time He actually came in a human body as a Jewish man named Jesus. The four Gospels (Matthew, Mark, Luke, and John) describe Jesus' ministry. They explain how He preached to His fellow Jews about how much God loved them. They tell how He performed miracles to show God's power and how He invited everyone to become part of God's kingdom. This Kingdom was not a nation or territory, but a collection of people ruled by God. In this Kingdom, human beings would be reunited with their heavenly Father, the goal God had intended for humanity ever since the beginning.

Breaking Sin's Power

Jesus' death on the cross and His resurrection to life on Easter Sunday represent the most significant moments in God's plan. In one weekend, God broke sin's power over humans and made it possible for the effects of sin to begin to be reversed. When the Allied forces invaded France on June 6, 1944—what we call D-Day—World War II began to come to an end. It took almost a year for the German army to surrender, and still longer to defeat the Japanese military, but from D-Day on, the war began to end. Jesus' death and resurrection was D-Day in God's battle against sin. It marked the turning point in the struggle that had been going on since Adam and Eve.

After Jesus rose from the dead, the message of God's kingdom spread exclusively among the Jews. Eventually it jumped the fence and also began to spread among those who were not Jews—the Gentiles. This, said the apostle Paul, was just what God had planned: "The Scripture foresaw that God would justify the Gentiles by faith, and announced the gospel in advance to Abraham: 'All nations will be blessed through you.'"[5] God had kept His promise to Abraham that his descendants would bless all nations.

A New People

In the Old Testament, God had worked primarily with Jews to prepare them to be a light to the rest of the world, the Gentiles. Now in the New Testament, God joined Jews and Gentiles into a new people called the church. His purpose was to create a model of reconciliation in which people could experience what it meant to be reunited with God and with one another. The church has not always done well in living up to its calling, but it remains the best example on earth of the kingdom of God.

Was this all God had in mind? Was His plan only to create a model of reconciliation, and a flawed model at that? The Bible makes it clear that God is not finished. As long as sin's effects continue to scar this world, as long as sickness, suffering, war, evil, and death are still among us, God is not finished. He seeks to overcome these effects of sin using human beings. When two people or two nations are reconciled, God's work is being accomplished. When a medical or scientific discovery eradicates a disease or alleviates suffering, God's plan is being carried out. Even a simple kindness causes sin's effects to recede and the harmony of God's design to be seen more clearly. But the best efforts of human beings are not enough to overcome sin.

21

When Jesus Returns

God will complete His plan once for all. At some point in the future, God will interrupt human history by sending His Son Jesus back to earth. At that time, God will restore harmony to the universe. Never again will it be lost. Although not everything about the last book of the Bible, the book of Revelation, is easy to understand, this much is crystal clear: Someday God will finish His plan.

> And I heard a loud voice from the throne saying, "Now the dwelling of God is with men, and he will live with them. They will be his people, and God himself will be with them and be their God. He will wipe every tear from their eyes. There will be no more death or mourning or crying or pain, for the old order of things has passed away."
>
> Revelation 21:3–4

The "old order of things," the disharmony produced by sin, will have passed away, finally and forever!

This is the story of the Bible. The fellowship God originally intended was lost due to human disobedience. God began the process of restoring that fellowship using Abraham and his descendants, the nation of Israel. From that nation, God brought one Man, Jesus, who was and is God. Jesus' first coming began to undo sin's effects; His second coming will complete the job.

Keeping this panoramic view in mind will help you understand what you read in the Old Testament. Also key to understanding will be an awareness of the cultural differences between the Old Testament world and our own. Having gone up for a "bird's-eye" view, we now come down and turn back for a look into another world.

endnotes

1. Canaan and Palestine are two terms for the same territory where Abraham, his son, and grandson wandered as nomads. You can read about God's promise in Genesis 15:13–14.

2. You can find these two commands in Deuteronomy 6:5 and Leviticus 19:18.

3. The second half of Exodus and the book of Leviticus provide details of the Law and the Tabernacle.

4. You can read about the painful lessons in Numbers and the repeating of the Law in Deuteronomy.

5. Galatians 3:8; Paul is quoting God's words to Abraham in Genesis 12:3.

chapter three

The Culture of the
Old Testament World

While traveling overseas, I often see people behave in ways hard for me to understand. The portable typewriters set up on the street across from government offices, or the men who want a tip because they hand you a paper towel in the public restrooms—it is easy to be puzzled by such things, but far better to ask for an explanation. A knowledgeable guide can make perfect sense of the unusual.[1]

Reading the Old Testament can be like this. Animal sacrifices, male-dominated family units, and absolute monarchies leave us feeling like we are in another world. This chapter is written to serve as a guide, helping make sense of the major differences between ancient Near Eastern culture and our own.[2] Later, we'll look at how ancient Israel differed from her neighbors. For now, we will confine ourselves to a quick overview of the culture of the Old Testament world, focusing on the two most important differences between that world and ours.

FOCUS ON THE GROUP, NOT THE INDIVIDUAL

Western culture strongly encourages individualism. I decide whom I will marry, what my profession will be, what company to work for, where I will live, what kind of car I will drive, and what my reputation will be. While I certainly don't want to embarrass my family by what I do, family reputation is not the most important factor in my decisions. Our society dislikes people who "tell me how to live my life."

The Old Testament world was about as far from this individual orientation as you could get. What really mattered in that world was the group, whether that group was the family, a cluster of related families called a clan, or a cluster of clans called a tribe. Every individual decision was made for the good of the group. Honoring the group's reputation was one of the most sacred obligations. If someone in your group was killed, the rest of your group was responsible to avenge the group member's blood. The desire to avoid shaming the family kept many people from misbehaving.

Males Mattered Most

If you lived in the ancient Near East, you might have some choice regarding whom to marry, but the approval of your family was essential. Your mate would probably be related to you. We cringe when we learn that Abraham married his half-sister and Isaac married his cousin, but such arrangements were commonplace. That was one way to maintain group identity. After you married, you were expected to settle down near your family and clan.

The most important people in the group were the men. The father ruled his wife and children, and the oldest males held positions of authority. Men were responsible for the family livelihood, usually some form of agriculture. Sons meant more workers in the field and, more important, the preservation of the family name.

Women were valued, but not as equals. The wife's most important job was to bear children, preferably sons. She performed the household chores such as cleaning, making clothes, washing, preparing food, and drawing water. She also trained her daughters to do the same when they reached puberty and became ready for marriage. In spite of the hierarchical structure—man as primary, woman as secondary—family life seems to have been generally warm and nurturing.

Because of the importance of being able to carry on the family line, a woman's ability to bear sons was very important. When she couldn't, alternative plans had to be made. This could mean adding another wife to the family, often with the first wife's approval. Although God never encouraged polygamy, He did allow it because of the family's desire for sons.

Steeped in the Past

Modern cultures like our own are oriented to the future. Tradition is a dirty word; we would much rather speak of innovation and change. Knowing what *has* happened is much less important than knowing what *will* happen next. We worship youthfulness, going to great expense to maintain ours.

The traditional culture of the ancient Near East looked backward, not forward. While the people were interested in some aspects of the immediate future, like the upcoming harvest, they were much more concerned about the past. Stories of the group's history and ancient wisdom were passed down from generation to generation. Life was structured around the time-honored practices of the group, such as rites of passage and funeral customs. A traditional, group-oriented culture preserved its identity by being able to trace the family line. Some Arab nomads even today can accurately recite their family genealogy for ten generations or more.[3] Because it originated in this

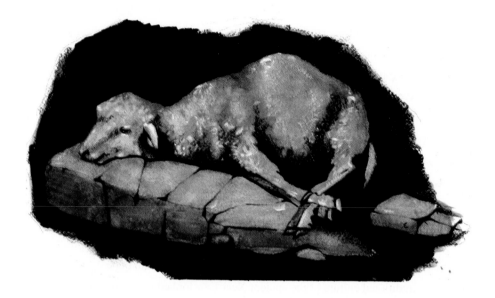

past-oriented culture, the Bible contains several genealogies. They may make dull reading for us, but for the ancient Israelites genealogies provided crucial information that connected them to their past.

Focus on the Elderly

Honor and authority were given to the elderly rather than to youth, in part because old people were experts in what mattered most, history. In some cultures, though not Israel's, worshiping dead ancestors was a way to honor the past. Israel chose instead to honor the past by esteeming the living, to "rise in the presence of the aged" and "show respect for the elderly" (Leviticus 19:32).

As you read the Old Testament, remember that this culture valued the group more than the individual, the past more than the present, the old more than the young. Men mattered more than women, and preserving what had been was more important than starting over with something new. That will help you avoid one big stumbling block when passing through this "foreign land."

GOD CENTERED, NOT HUMAN CENTERED

Another major obstacle to understanding the Old Testament involves the importance ancient people put on the supernatural world. There were no atheists in the ancient Near East. Everyone believed in at least one god and most believed in many. Not just the ancient Israelites but all their Near Eastern neighbors were devoutly religious. The supernatural world was as real to them as the physical world, and every result had a supernatural cause.

This isn't true in modern Western culture. We have left very little room for the supernatural. Even devout Christians and Jews are more likely to watch the Weather Channel than pray for rain. When natural disasters strike, we look for answers from meteorologists, not God. Every year scientists take over more of the territory that, for centuries, has belonged exclusively to God—whether mapping the genetic code, eliminating deadly diseases with vaccines, or creating disease-resistant crops. I, for one, welcome the triumphs of the scientific world, but with those triumphs comes the danger of excluding God from everyday life. For many, God has become only Honorary Chairman of the universe.

One Eye on the Heavens

This kind of practical atheism was unknown in the ancient Near East. Everyone believed in the existence of the divine and considered the supernatural world the most important part of everyday life. God or the gods were responsible for almost everything. What we call natural disasters were, to them, supernatural disasters, even if natural causes had something to do with the cataclysm. For example, every year in ancient Egypt, the Nile River flooded its banks and brought fertile soil from upstream to enrich the fields below. An ancient account tells of a time when the floods did not come for a period of seven years. The resulting famine prompted the pharaoh (what the Egyptians called their king) to take action. He consulted not his engineers, but his priests. He wanted them to discover what the gods were doing. As the story goes, a god appeared to the pharaoh in a dream and promised to correct the problem. In response, the overjoyed king offered a sizable gift to this god.[4]

Even if a man or woman could take some credit for what occurred, the gods were seen as ultimately responsible. Cyrus, king of the Persians, defeated the Babylonians in 539 B.C., but credited his victory to the gods. He believed they had become angry with the king of Babylon. The chief god, Marduk, looked for someone to remove this "weakling." "He scanned and looked through all the countries, searching for a righteous ruler willing to lead him in the annual procession. Then he pronounced the name of Cyrus, king of Anshan, [and] declared him to become the ruler of all the world."[5]

Decisions were always made with one eye on the heavens, because no one wanted to offend the gods. After all, they could make life very uncomfortable. One of the most famous pieces of ancient literature, the *Epic of Gilgamesh*, describes how a goddess tried to kill the story's hero because he had insulted her.[6]

Appeasing the Gods

In this world where gods were so important, people believed the needs of the gods were satisfied by sacrifices. The ancients saw this bloody work that so offends our modern sensibilities as absolutely essential. How else, they would argue, can we keep the gods happy?

Because the ancient world considered natural and human events to be the gods' doing, they did not think scientifically. True, their mathematical and technological skills continue to amaze us. They practiced medicine and were adept at such sciences as astronomy. However, while they could describe and employ the natural world, they relied on religion, not science, to understand that world.[7]

Israel versus Her Neighbors

The ancient Israelites and their Near Eastern neighbors disagreed on several things. First and foremost, they disagreed on the number of gods. Israel insisted there was just one, whom they called Yahweh. The other nations believed there were many. The belief in one god is called monotheism; belief in many gods is called polytheism. Another important difference was the relationship of the deity to the natural world. In ancient Near East polytheism, the gods could be manipulated through magic. However, Yahweh had created nature, which put Him above all supernatural powers. In spite of these differences, Israel, like her neighbors, viewed the world and herself as being in the hands of the supernatural.

Our culture has moved far from this view of the world—perhaps too far. In any case, if a modern reader is going to make sense of the Old Testament, he or she must keep in mind this preference for the supernatural.

ACCOMMODATING CULTURE

The culture of the ancient Near East differed significantly from Western culture today, especially in how it viewed the individual in relation to the group and how it viewed people in relation to the supernatural. What difference does this make for modern readers of the Old Testament?

Just because we meet God in the Old Testament world does not mean He is limited to that world. Since the Bible reflects a pre-scientific world, some people have a hard time accepting that God understands particle physics and black holes. More common is the assumption that God must be barbaric because He commanded animal sacrifices and allowed violence. God doesn't prefer the ancient Near Eastern culture to other cultures, nor did He create the world to operate in that way. He created men and women to live as equals, not in a patriarchal, male-dominated society. There was no violence or slavery in paradise. Although He chose to work with people in a particular culture, He transcends all cultures, ancient or modern.

No Favorites

When it comes to cultures, God has no favorites. He loves people. In order to show that love, however, He must work within the framework of that people's culture—just as He finds them. This means He must accommodate himself to that particular culture. Accommodation means that God tolerates the limitations of that culture. If you fell in love with and married someone from a foreign culture and went to live with your spouse in his or her country, you would have to accommodate yourself to that culture. That might mean giving up certain luxuries, a sacrifice you would gladly make for the sake of your beloved.

Because God wanted to show His love to people who lived in the ancient Near East, He had to work with people steeped in patriarchalism and violence. For God to work in our present culture, He must accommodate himself to our extreme individualism and human-centeredness. But He loves people, so He works with them wherever He finds them.

However, God loves people too much to leave any culture as He finds it. He works to remove anything that devalues or harms the humans He loves. In the world of the ancient Near East, God moved people from polytheism to monotheism, from patriarchalism toward equality, and from group identity toward greater recognition of the value and responsibilities of the individual.

Defending the Message

Since God is not partial to the culture of the ancient Near East, we need not be either. If you accept the Old Testament as God's Word, as I do, you are not required to accept or even appreciate the culture you find there. Those offended by that culture don't need to reject God's message. Those who want to defend God's message need not defend that culture.

We should treat Old Testament culture as we treat Old Testament language. God did not inspire these books to be written in the Hebrew language because He speaks Hebrew in heaven. He accommodated himself to that language because He was passionate to communicate to the Israelites and that was the language they spoke. Hebrew is a difficult language to learn, but I don't condemn the Old

Testament for that reason. As I use Hebrew to better understand the Old Testament, so I must use ancient Near Eastern culture to better understand this sacred literature.

That culture is the setting where God first revealed himself to human beings. Learn what you can from it, but don't be distracted by it. Pay attention to the scenery, but only so you can better understand the drama. Keep your eyes on God, listen to what He says, and watch Him work. Watch how He accommodates himself to that culture and then makes it a better place for the people He created and loves.

Many misunderstandings of the Old Testament occur because people fail to properly consider the cultural differences between that day and our own. Others come about when readers fail to give proper attention to the different kinds of literature they meet in this library of thirty-nine books. The next chapter describes these types of literature and suggests how to properly read them.

endnotes

1. The guide could explain that the typewriters and their operators are there to help people fill out government documents, like visas. The people handing you the paper towels prefer this type of work to begging.

2. The ancient Near East describes the region extending from Egypt in the south to Turkey in the north, and from the Mediterranean in the west to Iraq in the east, as this territory existed during the Old Testament period.

3. Cyrus H. Gordon and Gary A. Rendsburg, *The Bible and the Ancient Near East*, 4th ed. (New York: W. W. Norton, 1997), 113.

4. J. A. Pritchard; ed., "The Tradition of Seven Lean Years in Egypt," in *Ancient Near Eastern Texts Relating to the Old Testament* (ANET), 3rd ed. (Princeton, N.J.: Princeton University Press, 1969), 31–32.

5. ANET, 315.

6. ANET, 84.

7. *The New Encyclopaedia Britannica*, 15th ed., s.v. "The History of Science."

chapter four
A Walk Through the Library

On the shelves of your neighborhood public library you can find all kinds of literature: novels, biographies, poetry, children's books, histories, and more. Go to the "library" called the Old Testament and you can find five major types of literature: stories, laws, poems, "wisdom" books, and prophecies.[1]

FOLLOW THE RULES

Whether found in the public library or the Old Testament library, we should read each type of literature according to the "rules" or guidelines the author used when writing that literature. For example, poems make heavy use of symbolism. When Emily Dickinson wrote these lines—

> *Safe in their Alabaster Chambers—*
> *Untouched by Morning—*
> *And untouched by Noon—*
> *Lie the meek members of the Resurrection—*
> *Rafter of Satin—and Roof of Stone!*[2]

—she was symbolically describing dead people lying in their coffins. She didn't call them "dead people"; she described them more poetically as "meek members of the Resurrection." Instead of "coffin," she spoke of a "Rafter of Satin—and Roof of Stone." Poets use symbolic language and readers must keep this in mind when interpreting. Imagine the reader who ignored this and understood these lines literally, picturing meek people living in homes with satin rafters and stone roofs!

When you read a history book, you do not expect much symbolism. You expect facts and the interpretation of those facts by someone who has carefully examined the data. The author can have his or her point of view and can even promote that viewpoint, but not by avoiding or deliberately misinterpreting the facts. That would violate the "rules" of historical writing. Every type of literature has certain guidelines that the author had in mind and that the reader must follow to understand what the author wrote. The same is true for the literature found in the library of the Old Testament, including narrative, legal material, poetry, wisdom, and prophecy.

Narratives

Perhaps as much as 40 percent of the Old Testament consists of stories or narratives.[3] Narratives contain a point of view, setting, characters, and a plot. Most of the biblical stories are told from the narrator's point of view, although a few are told in the first person.[4] Every story happens somewhere. The setting can be as luxurious as Pharaoh's throne room or as primitive as a campsite in the open air, but it is an important element to keep in mind.

When it comes to characters, biblical stories are pretty simple. We rarely learn as much about a character's nature, motives, thoughts, or intentions as we would like to know. Instead, the narrator tells us just enough to communicate the story's main point. Sometimes the narrator tells us whether the actions performed were good or bad; other times we must decide for ourselves. We may learn about a character by seeing how he or she contrasts with another character. For example, Joshua 6 describes the faith of Rahab, a foreign woman who willingly became part of God's people. The next chapter (Joshua 7) describes Achan, an Israelite man who deliberately disobeyed God and was punished for it. By placing these two stories next to each other, the narrator allows us to compare and contrast them.[5] In every biblical story, the main character is always God. Even when He doesn't appear, the narrator wants us to picture Him witnessing what is said and done. Sometimes He approves, sometimes He disapproves; His opinion always matters most in what happens next.

Like all good stories, biblical narratives have a plot or story line. After a brief introduction, those involved face some kind of difficulty. An enemy may attack, a natural disaster may strike, one character may harm another, or someone may face a perplexing ethical dilemma. The crisis reaches a climax, then resolves either happily, as when the Israelites were delivered from the Egyptian army at the Red Sea (read Exodus 14), or sadly, as when God punished the Israelites for their rebellion in the wilderness (read Numbers 14).

Understand the Historical Context

What guidelines should you use to properly read narratives? First, be sure you know the historical context for the passage, the time and place when the story occurs. That way you can better understand why a character acts a certain way and whether that action is good or bad. By realizing that the story of Abraham and Sarah took place in ancient Canaan, I understand why Sarah told Abraham to sleep with Hagar, her maid (Genesis 16:2). In that place at that time, a barren wife could give her maid to her husband as a second wife and any children would be legally considered children of the maid's owner—in this case, Sarah. A good study Bible with explanatory notes in the margins will provide helpful insights on such questions.

Understand the Literary Context

Second, you must also keep in mind the literary context of the passage. The literary context is the "neighborhood" of the story, the adjoining stories of which your passage is one part. Ask any real estate agent: The value of a house depends largely on its neighborhood. A large, beautiful home in a rundown neighborhood is probably worth less than a smaller home in an upscale neighborhood. In this same way, the neighborhood or location of a passage tells us much about what that passage means. Genesis 22 describes God's command to sacrifice Isaac, but only by reading the earlier stories do we understand the great significance of that command. From those earlier stories we learn that Isaac was the son God had promised and for whom Abraham had waited a quarter of a century. Knowing the literary context helps us better appreciate the shock Abraham must have felt when he heard God's command.

Examine the Big Picture

Third, read each individual story in light of the big picture. The Old Testament is not a collection of short stories. Instead, each story is part of a bigger story, which is part of a still bigger story. Beyond the individual story is the literary context, the adjoining stories. Then comes the story of Israel, God's work that began with Abraham. Then there is the biggest story, the story of God's ultimate plan to reconcile humanity to himself (as we described in chapter 2). Genesis 22, a powerful story by itself, grows richer from what we learn about Isaac from the literary context that describes how long Abraham and Sarah had waited for him. Read in light of Israel's history, we can appreciate Genesis 22 still more, since without Isaac there would be no nation of Israel. Understood in light of God's overarching plan to reconcile humanity to himself, Genesis 22 grows still deeper in significance. We realize that God asked this sacrifice to demonstrate the importance of faithful obedience in the ultimate fulfillment of God's plan.

Understand the Purpose

When reading Old Testament narratives, also keep in mind their purpose, why they were given to us. Although they record history, they were not written just to tell us historical facts. Don't assume you are reading a newspaper. Newspaper articles tell the facts impartially in chronological order, with abundant and precise details.[6] A newspaper story that jumped around from present to future to past would confuse us. If it gave only approximate facts or avoided facts altogether, it would annoy us. If the author's bias were blatantly evident in the article, we would complain to the editor.

Writers of Old Testament narratives (and other ancient historians) did not write history by these rules. Authors could step out of chronological order without confusing their readers. They could approximate or adjust details and still satisfy their ancient readers' demand for the truth. For example, biblical authors used numbers to give a general impression rather than communicate precise details. As for being impartial, biblical writers would resist this label. They were all believers who told their stories to emphasize certain points about God and His plan.

Of course, there are many similarities between an Old Testament historian and a modern historian. Both write from a particular point of view and hope to persuade the reader. Both are selective in what they include and both interpret the data. Both ancient and modern historians want you to see what they meant to say; they don't want you to read into their work something that isn't there. Finally, both ancient and modern historians write according to accepted literary characteristics, such as those discussed in this chapter.

Old Testament narratives were not included to provide examples of right and wrong behavior. We see many examples of good and bad behavior in these stories and would be wise to follow the good and avoid the bad. But limiting them to morality lessons trivializes the stories. What's more, this approach may lead to confusion, since we aren't always told if an action is right or wrong. Abraham lied about his wife, not once but twice (Genesis 12, 20). Am I supposed to do the same?

Some think the Old Testament stories were primarily given to predict Jesus' coming. The Old Testament does describe God's plan to reconcile humanity and this plan eventually did include Jesus, but the Old Testament stories were not told primarily to predict Jesus. When the narrator described how the Jews were freed from Egyptian slavery, he was not thinking about how Jesus' death on the cross freed us from our sins. To use these stories only to predict Jesus is to miss so much of what God is trying to say through them.

Just what is God trying to say through them? Although each biblical author had his own agenda and purposes, all these stories were included to tell us about God and His overarching plan of reconciliation. When we read them, our chief questions should be (1) What do I learn about God's nature from this story? and (2) How does this story fit into God's plan?

Law

New Year's resolutions to read the Old Testament usually sail happily through Genesis and early Exodus, only to run aground in early spring on the legal passages in Exodus, Leviticus, Numbers, and Deuteronomy. The Jewish rabbis counted 613 commands in the Law, but when reading through these passages, it seems like 613,000! In spite of how it seems to us, the Israelites didn't dread the Law—they loved it. All 176 verses of the longest chapter in the Bible, Psalm 119, celebrate this Law.

Stick to the Main Lesson

One reason they became excited and not exhausted by the Law was that they kept its main lesson in mind. They knew all the laws could be reduced to two: "Love the LORD your God with all your heart and with all your soul and with all your strength" (Deuteronomy 6:5) and "Love your neighbor as yourself" (Leviticus 19:18). God was not commanding 613 different things. He was asking them to do two things and providing 613 specific ways for them to do so. You will appreciate this legal material more if you keep in mind this guideline: All the laws are about how to love God and your neighbor.

The Jews also appreciated the Law because they realized it was parental direction from their heavenly Father, not a set of arbitrary demands from a slave owner. They realized God had given the laws for their benefit, not His own. He did not need their obedience to make Him happy; they needed to obey these laws for their own happiness. Following their example, read this material as good news from a loving heavenly Father.

What about Today's Christian and the Law?

Must Christians still obey these laws? Some think we should—at least the laws we can still obey. They would say that since we have no temple in which to offer sacrifices, we can overlook the laws dealing with sacrifices. However, since we can avoid eating pork, we should continue to obey this law. This approach seems too arbitrary, allowing us to pick and choose.

Others think we are only responsible to obey the Ten Commandments (Exodus 20:1–17) and none of the other laws. These are definitely the ten most important laws, the laws on which all the others are based. The problem with this view is that even the Ten Commandments would be pretty hard to obey today without some adjustment. Should we worship on Saturdays, given the command in Exodus 20:8: "Remember the Sabbath day by keeping it holy"? If we change the worship day to Sunday, haven't we changed the commandment? If so, by whose authority did we make this change? Those who claim to obey the Ten Commandments actually obey a modern version of these commandments, a stance that seems bold and inconsistent.

A Better Way

A better way is to recognize that Christians are only obligated to obey the essence of the Law—love for God and love for neighbor—and none of the specific laws given to the Israelites. Jesus considered the whole Law to be summed up by these two (Matthew 22:37–40). The early church no longer required Christians to live by the 613 laws, insisting instead that they must obey these two in ways that were appropriate to that culture.[7] God gave all the other laws, including the Ten Commandments, to explain how the ancient Israelites were to love God and neighbor in their culture. God wants us to love Him and our neighbors in ways that make sense in our own day.

Here is where the Ten Commandments come in. While I am not bound to obey them, they provide clear ways to love God and neighbor in any culture.

How can I love God with all my heart if I worship anything besides Him? How can I love God and abuse His name?

How can I love God without setting aside a day to worship Him? It does not need to be the Sabbath day, but if I cannot find a day to honor Him, how can I claim to love Him?

How can I claim to love my neighbor when I dishonor my parents?

How can I love my neighbor if I murder him, commit adultery with his wife, steal from him, lie about him, or even want what he has?

While not legally bound to the Ten Commandments, I find I cannot ignore them and still love God and my neighbor. So I obey them as principles rather than laws.

Although we are not obligated to obey the 613 commands, they are still God's Word. They show us what He cares about; from that we can learn what God is like. The God who told people not to lie values truth. When He commanded that a dangerous ox be destroyed, He demonstrated how much He values life. Read this material asking what you can learn about the Lawgiver from the Law.

Put It in Context

Finally, knowing the historical context makes this material much easier to understand. The more we know about the culture of Israel and the ancient Near East, the easier it will be to make sense of these laws. When I learn that Israel's neighbors had laws that called for harsh and extreme punishments, I can appreciate the equity and fairness of God's requirement of an "eye for eye, tooth for tooth" (Exodus 21:24).

Poetry

The Hebrew people loved poetry and music. They turned to it whenever they wanted to express some heartfelt sentiment, whether joy or sadness. Someone has estimated that one-third of the Old Testament is poetry. Nearly every book contains poetic passages; some books are written entirely in poetry.

Poetic Elements

Most modern translations of the Bible print poetry differently from its counterpart, prose. Often they center each line or they indent each line a certain number of spaces, making it easy for us to recognize a poem. Since no such distinctions marked poetry in the original Hebrew, modern translators must first decide whether something was poetry based on other factors. They look for passages that make heavy use of symbolism, since this is characteristic of poetry. Just as you would not try to build a house with satin rafters and a stone roof, do not treat a symbol as anything but a symbol when you interpret. When the poet compares himself to an olive tree in Psalm 52:8, he doesn't mean he has sprouted leaves. Psalm 68:4 describes God as riding on the clouds, but don't look for Him to blow by on the next stormy day.

The translators also decided whether a passage was poetry based on something called "parallelism." As you might guess from the term, parallelism describes how the poet said one thing, then immediately said something very similar using different words. The two "lines" are parallel, like a railroad track. Here is an example of parallelism from Psalm 19:1:

The heavens declare the glory of God;
the skies proclaim the work of his hands.

The second line uses synonyms for the terms in the first line: "skies" is a synonym for "heavens," "proclaim" for "declare," and "the work of his hands" for "the glory of God." This type of parallelism is called synonymous.

Synonymous parallelism is the standard variety of Hebrew poetry, but there are many variations. Sometimes the second line will state the opposite of the first. This is called antithetic parallelism and can be illustrated from Proverbs 10:1:

A wise son brings joy to his father,
but a foolish son grief to his mother.

43

Incomplete parallelism, as the name suggests, leaves something out of one line that is found in the other:

> LORD, who may dwell in your sanctuary?
> Who may live on your holy hill?

In this example from Psalm 15:1, "LORD" is missing from the second line.

The Hebrew poets made heavy use of parallelism, whether synonymous, antithetic, incomplete, or another variation. By remembering this when you read, an obscure term can often be clarified by its synonym. The parallelism in Psalm 78:51 helps me discover that "tents of Ham" refers to Egypt. Keep parallelism in mind and you will avoid the mistake of thinking the poet had two things in mind when he really was referring to only one thing using two terms. When we read in Psalm 8:4 of "man" and "son of man," we know the poet is using two terms to describe humanity, not talking about a father and son team.

Often the poet will strengthen or clarify the first term with the second. For example,

> He will make your righteousness shine like the dawn,
> the justice of your cause like the noonday sun.
>
> Psalm 37:6

Notice how "dawn" has brightened to the "noonday sun." Stay alert to this feature of Hebrew poetry and you will appreciate it even more.

Context and Character

Two other guidelines will help in your reading of Hebrew poetry. First, pay attention to the context. We can only understand the symbols and ultimately the poem if we know what those symbols meant to the poet. When I read about the ocean roaring and foaming in Psalm 46:3, I must not think of the lovely seaside vacations of my childhood. Instead, I must remember that most people in the ancient Near East feared the ocean.

Second, read these poems to learn what you can about God and His plan. You will gain wonderful insights into His character from hearing Him praised in the Psalms. You will appreciate His wisdom by reading Job, Proverbs, and Ecclesiastes. You can even learn about God from the love poetry of Song of Songs.

Wisdom Literature

Even those unfamiliar with the Old Testament have heard a few of its proverbs:

A gentle answer turns away wrath,
but a harsh word stirs up anger.

Proverbs 15:1

Pride goes before destruction,
a haughty spirit before a fall.

Proverbs 16:18

A friend loves at all times,
and a brother is born for adversity.

Proverbs 17:17

Principles, Not Promises

A proverb is a short saying, often just two lines, packed full of a time-honored truth about life. Someone has compared the proverb to a bumper sticker—light on explanation but long on impact. Proverbs were written to teach true principles: With your words you can bring calm or anger; be humble or risk being destroyed; be loyal.

Proverbs were not meant as promises from God, but as statements of what is generally true. Gentle words usually bring peace, but not always. Pride doesn't always precede destruction. For example,

Train a child in the way he should go,

and when he is old he will not turn from it.

Proverbs 22:6

This proverb does not promise that proper child-rearing techniques will automatically guarantee godly children. That would contradict common sense and other passages that speak of the child's freedom to choose his or her own destiny. The proverb states the principle that our best hope for raising godly children comes through careful, godly parenting. Proverbs were meant to be used as principles, not promises.

Weighty Matters

Proverbs represent only one kind of wisdom literature in the Old Testament. A more philosophical variety can be found in Job and Ecclesiastes. These books wrestle honestly with deep, age-old issues such as the reason for suffering and the meaning of life. As with any discussion of such weighty matters, it is especially important to "hear" all that is being said. Some passages of Ecclesiastes can be pretty depressing if you miss the larger point the book is trying to make. Some of the characters in the book of Job make statements that sound true but are proven false as the book ends.

Emphasized in all Old Testament wisdom literature is the importance of reverence for God. True wisdom is not a matter of IQ, experience, "street smarts," or education. The wise person has a healthy respect for God that shows itself in the choices he or she makes. Read this material as a student in God's classroom of life, looking for what He wants to teach you about yourself, and especially about himself.

Prophecy

Most people find the prophetic books very difficult to understand. Since they make up about 40 percent of the Old Testament, that can be discouraging. These books contain relatively few narrative passages, and those that occur are not always in chronological order. Instead, we find a large number of messages from God, called oracles. Since these don't usually provide much historical background, they can be hard to understand, somewhat like walking into the middle of a conversation.

Why So Difficult to Understand?

Most of the prophets wrote in poetry, which is harder to understand than prose. They were also very fond of hyperbole—a deliberate exaggeration as a figure of speech. When we complain that "this book weighs a ton," those listening know what we mean and don't interpret our words literally. So when Isaiah described a world where the "wolf will live with the lamb, the leopard will lie down with the goat, the calf and the lion and the yearling together; and a little child will lead them" (Isaiah 11:6), he was speaking figuratively, not literally. Figurative language, while more beautiful and expressive, is also harder to understand than literal language. Many of the oracles are optimistic and hopeful, but many are pessimistic, critical, and hopeless, making them harder to hear.

The "End Times" Connection

Another reason people find the prophetic books difficult to understand has little to do with the books themselves. Having heard preachers use the Old Testament prophets to predict the events of the "end times," some people assume this to be the purpose for these books. Many avoid the prophetic books because "that end-times stuff is too confusing." Those who look in these books to find such predictions usually come away more confused, tending to avoid the books after that.

The prophetic books were not written to predict the end of the world. They were written to communicate God's message to His people, Israel. He put that message in the mouths of His messengers, the prophets. Many of these messages are critical and pessimistic because they came during three very dark centuries. From the mid-700s B.C. until the mid-400s B.C., Judah and Israel were morally, socially, and spiritually decadent and had abandoned their commitment to God. He knew the disaster that would follow their disobedience and what this would mean for His plan, so He sent His prophets to try to turn Judah and Israel back to Him.

Sometimes these oracles announced what would happen if God's people did not repent. Sometimes they looked beyond the judgment and promised to rescue the Israelites. In other words, these oracles did predict the future, but predicting the future was not the primary reason God voiced the oracles. They were given to produce a change in the Israelites.

When I tell my son to do his chores, I sometimes add a threat: "If it isn't finished by supper, you won't get your allowance for this week." If he gets busy with other things and forgets to finish his chores, he loses his allowance. My primary purpose in the command was not to predict his punishment but to prompt his obedience. In a similar way, though prophetic oracles contain some predictions, their primary purpose was to produce an obedient response.

To properly understand the predictions, keep in mind that more than 90 percent of these predictions were fulfilled in the lifetimes of the prophets or shortly after. Many speak of the punishment that came on God's people at the hands of the Assyrians and Babylonians. Those oracles that describe the rebuilding of Jerusalem were fulfilled when God resettled His people after their return from exile in Babylon. If someone objects that the oracles were not fulfilled literally, remember that the prophets often used hyperbole.

Of the remaining 10 percent of prophecies, many were fulfilled through the life and ministry of Jesus and the early church. These include predictions of Jesus' virgin birth in Bethlehem (Isaiah 7:14; Micah 5:2) and the Holy Spirit's coming at Pentecost (Joel 2:28–32). Others were meant to be fulfilled symbolically in the lives of Christians and in heaven. This is the best way to interpret the passages that predict a future glorious kingdom of Israel, one that follows the lead of early Christian integration. These early Christians—Jews and Gentiles—believed the Old Testament referred to them (Romans 15:4). The apostle Paul considered all Christians, even Gentiles, as children of Abraham (Galatians 3:26–29). Elsewhere he described the church, composed of both Jews and Gentiles, as God's new people (Ephesians 2:11–22; 3:7–13). He even called the church the "Israel of God" (Galatians 6:16). The apostle Peter agreed, describing his Gentile Christian readers as "a chosen people, a royal priesthood, a holy nation, a people belonging to God" (1 Peter 2:9; read verses 4–10), terms used in the Old Testament to refer to the nation of Israel.[8] As the new Israel, the church inherited all the unfulfilled promises of the Jews and believed these promises were symbolically fulfilled in their own experience.

That leaves only 1 percent of all Old Testament prophecy as predictions that have yet to be fulfilled. This small amount refers to the end of the world, an event most agree has yet to occur.[9] Reading Old Testament prophecies to predict the future is a futile exercise.

Not every Christian agrees with this approach. Many will want to give future prediction a more prominent role. One reason for the disagreement lies in how the prophets presented their predictions. They predicted events that were imminent; then, in the next breath, predicted events that would not occur for many years, even centuries. For example, Isaiah 7 predicts events that would occur in the immediate future, alongside predictions that would be fulfilled in the birth of Christ seven hundred years in the future.

To properly understand how the prophet was thinking, envision two mountain peaks from a distance. Far away, they look about the same height and seem to be standing next to each other. However, as you come closer, you realize that one mountain is much smaller and much nearer to you, miles away from the larger peak. The prophet had the distant view and thus described both events as if they were to happen at the same time. Now that more time has passed, we can tell how and when the predictions were actually fulfilled, realizing how much time has elapsed between them.

A Figure of Speech and Other Guidelines

Another reason why prophetic predictions are difficult to interpret has to do with the prophets' preference for hyperbole and other uses of highly figurative language. Rather than say that the Jews would prosper in the days following their return from Babylonian exile, Isaiah predicted that those who lived to be a hundred would be thought to have died prematurely. Natural enemies like the wolf and the lamb would live together in harmony and no one would be hurt or sad anymore (Isaiah 65:17–25). Joel pictured a day when "the mountains will drip new wine, and the hills will flow with milk; all the ravines of Judah will run with water" (Joel 3:18). Though some interpreters look for these promises to be fulfilled literally, the prophetic style suggests we should look for a symbolic meaning instead.

Prophetic predictions can be hard to interpret for still another reason. Some seem to have been fulfilled more than once. For example, Isaiah 7:14 predicts that the wife of the prophet will have a son, which she presumably did in the 700s B.C. But the early church also considered this prediction to have been fulfilled when Mary gave birth to Jesus seven hundred years later (read Matthew 1:22–23). Daniel spoke of a terrible figure who would come to persecute the Jews. An early Jewish interpreter believed this was fulfilled in the Greek king Antiochus IV (175–164 B.C.), and also by the Romans two hundred years later. While we cannot deny the possibility of double fulfillment, such things are more clearly seen in hindsight than beforehand.

Prophetic oracles are much easier to understand if the historical context is kept in mind. The three hundred years during which these prophecies were spoken saw significant military and political changes in the ancient Near East. God's people were right in the middle of things. Each of these oracles addresses these circumstances in some way, so knowing when the prophecy was delivered and what was happening at the time makes understanding much easier.

One final guideline for prophetic passages: Read to learn what you can about God and His plan. Although these passages are primarily concerned with events long past and addressed to an audience long gone, the God who spoke through the prophets is the same God today. We can learn much about His character by listening in. For example, He repeatedly rebuked His people because He is a holy God who expects obedience. He promised future victory because He is a God who controls the destiny of nations.

Stories, laws, poems, wise sayings, and prophetic oracles—this is what you will find on the shelves of the Old Testament library. Recognizing what kind of literature you are reading and applying the appropriate guidelines will help you unlock this life-changing collection. Unlike your public library, however, this one revolves around a single important theme: the character and work of God, the subject of our next chapter.

endnotes

1. A sixth type of literature, apocalyptic, is more like a subcategory of prophecy. We will deal with apocalyptic literature when we come to the book of Daniel.

2. George McMichael, ed., stanza one from poem number 216 in *Anthology of American Literature: Realism to the Present* (New York: Macmillan, 1974).

3. Gordon Fee and Douglas Stuart, *How to Read the Bible for All Its Worth: A Guide to Understanding the Bible,* 2nd ed. (Grand Rapids, Mich.: Zondervan, 1993), 78.

4. Such as in the book of Nehemiah or parts of the book of Daniel.

5. This and other helpful insights can be found in "Narrative" by Walter C. Kaiser in D. Brent Sandy and Ronald L. Giese, Jr., *Cracking Old Testament Codes: A Guide to Interpreting the Literary Genres of the Old Testament* (Nashville: Broadman and Holman, 1995), 74.

6. Actually, no writer writes with complete impartiality. We all want to make a point, correct a misconception, or demonstrate a new perspective. This is true for the biblical writers as well.

7. Read what the apostle Paul had to say about this in Galatians 5:13–14.

8. Deuteronomy 10:15; Exodus 19:6; 6:7; Jeremiah 7:23; 11:4; 30:22; Ezekiel 36:28.

9. In these statistics I follow Fee and Stuart, *How to Read the Bible for All Its Worth,* 2nd ed., 165–186.

chapter five
Keep Your Eye on the Goal

The 23,214 verses of the Old Testament teem with so many details one can easily lose sight of the big picture.[1] Readers can stay on track by always returning to this single theme: the character and actions of God. More specifically, readers of the Old Testament should continually be asking two questions: (1) What can I learn about God's plan? and (2) What can I learn about God?

IMPORTANT QUESTIONS

God's plan, described in chapter 2, was to undo the effects of sin and bring the world back into relationship with Him. Every chapter and every verse fit into this plan, either directly or indirectly. It is fairly easy to follow the big story through the narrative material. After the entry of sin, God's plan took shape with the calling of Abraham, the liberation of the Israelites from Egypt, the giving of the Law on Mount Sinai, and the conquest of Canaan under Joshua. Early struggles gave way to brighter days under David and Solomon. The period of the kings who followed revealed Israel's disobedience until, finally, God punished them with exile.

The plan can be seen in the rest of the Old Testament as well. When reading the prophetic oracles, remember that God—sometimes scolding, sometimes encouraging—was calling His people back to himself and to their part in His great plan. Don't lose sight of the plan in the beautiful poetry of the Psalms, where Israel praised God for choosing and living among them. Remember the plan when wading through the "bumper sticker" wisdom of Proverbs, the philosophical reflections of Job and Ecclesiastes, and the love poetry of Song of Songs. Each of these books allows us a look into the hearts and minds of God and His covenant people. Any passage in the Old Testament will make more sense if you ask what it can teach you about God's plan.

As important as this question might be, you must ask a still more important question of every passage: What does this tell me about God? After all, God's plan came about because of God's character, not the other way around. Because God is loving, He seeks to restore all to a loving relationship with Him.

Of all we can learn from the Bible, nothing is more valuable to us than insight into the character of God. His nature is the only fixed reality in the universe. Everything else will change, but God does not (read Malachi 3:6). If we discover something to be true of God's character, it will always be true. At a time when nothing remains the same, how reassuring it is to find Someone you can count on!

It is also important to learn about the character of God because of who we are as people. Every one of us was created to know God. That is our ultimate purpose for living. Because God knew this, He kept showing himself to His people. He appeared in a burning bush, in the fire on Mount Sinai, in the wilderness Tabernacle, in Jerusalem's Temple, and in many other ways. Finally, He revealed himself in Jesus of Nazareth. He showed himself to us so He could accomplish His purpose and we could accomplish ours.

By learning about Him, we realize He loves us. We discover that He has a plan to remove the effects of sin; this plan is what the Bible calls salvation. We learn that this plan required God first to lovingly work with rebellious, disobedient people and then to show up as Jesus and die on the cross. When we accept His gift of salvation, we enter a relationship with God that allows us to know Him better. Both the Old and New Testaments describe salvation as knowing God (read Hosea 6:3; John 8:31–32). Just as marriage helps a husband and wife to become better acquainted, salvation allows us to know God better than we did before. The more you know God, the more you understand how He wants you to live and the easier it becomes for you to obey. Such obedience brings contentment and freedom. When you come to the end of your life, you can look back without regret and look ahead without fear. As a believer, death brings you even closer to God.

"What does this passage tell me about God?" is a question anyone can ask, whether you are a novice or an expert. You don't need special training, only the belief that God has spoken to us through the Bible and close attention to what is written there. Watch what He does. Watch what He doesn't do. Hear what He says or doesn't say. Listen to what inspired witnesses say about Him.

FOUR SAFEGUARDS

This question "What does this passage tell me about God?" is not without its dangers. To avoid misunderstanding, remember these four safeguards.

First, look for an attribute of God, not just an action. God may do something only once; we know of only one time that God parted the Red Sea (Exodus 14). We can't assume He will do the same thing twice. But every one of His actions reveals some aspect of His character. Because He parted the Red Sea, we know He is powerful. He may act differently in different situations, but He will always be powerful.

Second, what you learn about God's character in one passage should be compared with what you know of Him from other passages. The Bible presents a composite sketch from many witnesses with varied perspectives over a long period of time. Sometimes God seems to be cruel, like when He refused to allow Moses to enter Canaan (Numbers 20:12). At many other times He shows himself to be loving. You would not want your character judged by a single action; give God the same break.

Third, keep in mind that everything we learn about God is by analogy. That is, we can only know something about God because He compared himself to something we are familiar with. He is like a father, like a king, and like a shepherd. God is as different from us as we are from insects. He is eternal; we are boxed in by time. He is infinite; we are limited. Because of our limitations, He must use analogies when describing himself.

How would you describe the ocean to people who had known only the desert? You would show them the biggest body of water you could find—even if only a bucketful—and explain that the ocean is like this but much, much larger, and with a salty taste. A bucket of water and the ocean are very different things, but you must find some way to draw the analogy using what is at hand. God described himself by comparisons we can understand: He loves us like a father, He rules as a king, He cares for us like a shepherd. Sometimes the word *like* is included; when missing, it must be assumed. Even descriptions of God's eye or hand are analogies. They cannot describe actual reality because God does not have a physical body.[2]

Describing God by comparisons may not tell us "scientifically" what God is like, but "a picture is worth a thousand words." What we lose in precision, we gain in impact. Which makes your jaw drop in amazement: reading the definition of "sunset" in the dictionary or watching the sun sink below the horizon in a marvelous burst of color? Although "pictures" of God don't allow us to know Him with dictionary precision, they do let us experience more of what God is really like.

An experience with God is ultimately what He wants for us. The fourth and final safeguard is to remember the goal is not just to know about God. He wants us to experience a relationship with Him. He is not an object to learn about, like your car or house. He is personal and wants to know us and be known by us on a personal level. Would your best friend be content just knowing facts about you? The Jewish teachers who killed Jesus knew more about God than Jesus' disciples. But those disciples had a relationship with God that emboldened them later to die for that relationship. Learning about God from the Bible should do more than give us information. It should produce and strengthen our relationship with God.

Reading and understanding the Old Testament does not come easily. It helps, though, to keep in mind God's plan and the significant cultural differences between that day and our own. Recognizing the different kinds of literature and applying the appropriate guidelines will add further clarity. Finally, by asking two simple questions (What can I learn about God's plan? What can I learn about God?), we reach the heart of what the Bible was meant to give us. We are now ready to turn our attention to the individual books of the Old Testament, starting "in the beginning" with Genesis.

endnotes

1. H. L. Wilmington, *Book of Bible Lists* (Wheaton, Ill.: Tyndale, 1987), 34.

2. Read John 4:24.

chapter six

A Good Beginning Spoiled
Genesis 1–11

SUGGESTIONS FOR READING GENESIS 1–11

Since these chapters are mostly narrative, keep in mind the following guidelines as you read. First, know the historical and literary context. Remember that this material takes place long ago and far away. You will read an account of creation that sounds more like a poem than a scientific report. Remember that a pre-scientific culture like Israel was more interested in the "why" questions than the "how" questions. You will also meet two genealogies—long lists of names. These were very important in the traditional culture of the Old Testament. We'll say more about them later.

Second, read each individual story as part of bigger stories. Creation, the Flood, and the Tower of Babel are fascinating tales, but can only be understood when read in light of the history of Israel and God's plan to undo the effects of sin. Third, read to learn about God's plan and His character. A few summary paragraphs address these two areas toward the end of this chapter. Careful attention to who God is and what He is doing will show you much more.

INTRODUCTION

The opening chapters of Genesis are as relevant to our lives as this morning's paper. These chapters answer many fundamental questions, the kind that keep us awake at night: What is my purpose in life? How did the world come to be? How can we know happiness? Why is there evil and suffering in the world?

OVERVIEW

The opening words of Genesis—"In the beginning"—describe its theme, particularly the theme of the first eleven chapters. Genesis is a book of beginnings. Chapters 1 and 2 describe the beginning of the world, created in six "days." Many modern readers struggle with this description of creation. They cannot reconcile these verses with what they learned in science class. What about evolution? Why no mention of dinosaurs? Where are the millions of years that are supposed to have elapsed? Faced with this apparent contradiction, some reject the biblical account. Others reject the scientific account and cling to a literal interpretation of the Bible.

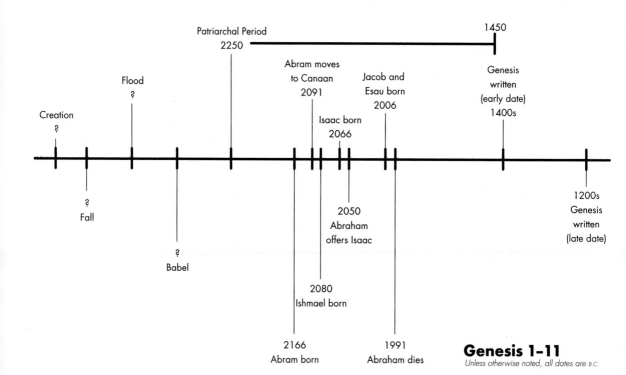

Genesis 1-11
Unless otherwise noted, all dates are B.C.

Still others try to reconcile the Bible with the scientific account. They observe that the Hebrew word for "day" can also describe an indefinite period of time. Notice how "day" is used in Genesis 2:4 (RSV): "In the day that the LORD God made the earth and the heavens."[1] Therefore, the six "days" of creation may have been six long ages, perhaps each millions of years in length. Others locate science's millions of years in what they see as a long gap of time between Genesis 1:1 and 1:2.

Although reconciling the Bible and science is a worthy goal, it probably won't be entirely successful.[2] The Bible is not trying to answer the questions science is asking. Science wants to know *when* things came into existence; the Bible says only it was "in the beginning." Science wants to know exactly *how* something came to be; what was the chain of events that produced it? The Bible is more concerned about identifying the ultimate cause for everything:

Why all these names?

Genesis 4, 5, and 10 contain lists of names, called genealogies. These are "linear"; that is, they trace the line of descent from an ancestor forward. For example, Genesis 5 begins with Adam (verse 3) and ends with Noah (verse 32). These genealogies are included to show how the original humans spread to the various parts of the ancient Near East. They don't claim to document each and every generation, but to make clear the lines of ancestry. In traditional cultures, ancestry is one of the most important things about a person.

Elsewhere in the Bible we find "vertical" genealogies, which present the development of a single family, more like our "family trees" (see Genesis 36:1–5 for an example). This type was meant to show who belonged in the group and who did not.

(John H. Walton, Victor H. Matthews, and Mark W. Chavalas, *The IVP Bible Background Commentary: Old Testament* [Downers Grove, Ill.: InterVarsity Press, 2000], 35.)

God. Not *how* but *who* is the question that really matters to the biblical author.

Genesis 1 and 2 give us not a scientific but a theological account of creation. They tell us that God alone created the heavens, the earth, and everything in them. From the chaos of 1:2, God brought the order of 1:3–31. God made this creation—from plants to humans—so that it could reproduce itself. Everything God made was very good. These chapters were written to show that Israel's God was superior to the gods worshiped by Israel's neighbors. By knowing this, the Israelites were reassured that God was worthy of their trust and obedience.

Creation Stories: Significant Differences

Israel was not the only nation with a creation story. A comparison of this account with those of other nations reveals several similarities and differences. All the stories trace the universe back to its ultimate cause, divine action. That is, all accounts focus more on the *who* than the *how* and all agree that the gods or God were the *who*. The accounts also agree that creation represents the victory of order over chaos or disorder. They even share a common picture of chaos, namely the sea. According to Genesis, God brought order out of what was "formless and empty" (Genesis 1:2), a biblical description of chaos.

But Israel's story is very different than those of her neighbors. First, Israel's God created the universe from nothing, while the gods of neighboring nations organized material that was already existing.[3] Second, Israel's God made this world to reproduce itself and, in doing this, put a distance between himself and creation. God was not to be found in a flower or sunset. He created these but was not limited to them. Other gods, however, were perceived as more intimately involved in the ongoing cycle of life. Some suggest that Israel's neighbors considered rain as a god's semen dropped down from the heavens to fertilize the earth. The writer of Genesis 1 and 2 was interested not only in the beginning of the universe, but especially in the beginning of human beings. The creation of humanity is introduced in

What is happening with the "sons of God" and daughters of men (Genesis 6:1–4)?

This is one of the most puzzling passages in the whole Bible, particularly what the writer meant by "sons of God." This term could refer to angels. If this is what the writer meant, he was condemning the intermarriage of angels and humans ("the daughters of men"). Sin had made it impossible for humans to associate with God's world. Others believe these verses criticize marriages between the righteous descendants of Seth (Genesis 4:25–26:5) and the unrighteous offspring of Cain (Genesis 4:17–24). Still others believe "sons of God" refers to human rulers. In that culture, these rulers had the right to sleep with any man's bride on her wedding night. God condemned this depraved ritual and the fertility it was supposed to accomplish.

(John H. Walton, Victor H. Matthews, Mark W. Chavalas, *The IVP Bible Background Commentary: Old Testament* [Downers Grove, Ill.: InterVarsity Press, 2000], 36.)

1:26–30 and described more fully in 2:4–25. We see, first, that human beings were created in the image of God (Genesis 1:26–27). This doesn't mean we were made to look like God; He is a spirit and does not have a physical body. Being made in God's image says something about our own creativity and our role as rulers of creation (1:28).

Second, we see that humanity was created as the climax of creation. God made us to be His special representatives on earth. Humanity was assigned the job of ruling the whole world, but was also given the Garden of Eden, an especially beautiful and well-watered piece of real estate (Genesis 2:8–15) where human beings could enjoy fellowship with their Creator.

Israel's neighbors did not see humanity as the high point of creation, but as an afterthought. In the Babylonian account, the gods had finished creating the important things when they realized they would need servants. So, from the blood of an evil god, they created humans and assigned them the task of feeding and worshiping the gods, who could then relax and take it easy.[4]

A Mortal Wound

According to Genesis 3, which describes the beginning of sin and evil in the world, the "very good" world God created (Genesis 1:31) suffered a mortal wound. No one in the ancient world needed to be convinced of the presence of evil. They did wonder where it came from, however. The Babylonians believed humans were created evil because they were made from the blood of a rebellious god.

The Bible tells a different story. Humans were created "good" but chose to disobey God. Once again, we get a theological rather than a scientific account. The writer did not pause to explain what the Tree of the Knowledge of Good and Evil looked like or what kind of fruit it bore, nor did he describe how the first sin could affect the rest of the world. He explained that the reason for sin was pride and that the result of sin extends to every human being.

Did the Flood really happen?

Israel is not the only ancient Near Eastern culture to speak of a widespread flood. Several details are similar among these accounts: The flood is sent to destroy humanity for displeasing the gods; certain humans are rescued; the boat comes to rest on a mountain; birds are used to detect the extent of the flood; and rescue is followed by sacrifices. Since these other accounts were written before Genesis, some argue that the author of Genesis modified them to suit his purposes.

More likely, all accounts reflect an actual catastrophe in which all or part of the earth was submerged for a long time, but the accounts differ in details. The scientific evidence is mixed, neither proving nor disproving the existence of such a flood. Once again, the Bible is more concerned with why this happened than how.

That first sin set in motion a terrible catastrophe. God had created the world to operate in wonderful harmony, like a healthy human body, but sin destroyed that harmony. Now humans were forced to fight nature, wrestling "thorns and thistles" (Genesis 3:18) for control of the ground. The harmonious relationship that existed between the man and woman was lost, replaced by patriarchalism, where man rules over woman (3:16). Sin made Adam and Eve feel guilty about being naked (3:7), showing they were no longer at peace with themselves. Worst of all, sin broke their relationship with God. They hid from Him because they feared Him (3:8).

This once good world was now a world in pain. The man was punished with the pain of hard work (3:17–19), while the woman felt the pain of childbearing (3:16). Even nature felt pain (3:15). The biblical writer made it clear that the world's painful realities were not of God's doing, but evidence of human rebellion against God.

Genesis 4 through 11 describes how sin spread through the human family like terminal cancer through a human body. This was the beginning of the end. Sin made one brother kill another out of jealousy (Genesis 4). The malignancy grew until, by Genesis 6, God decided to remove the tumor by radical surgery and begin again—this time with a righteous man and his family to repopulate the earth. This plan did not prevent the continued spread of the cancer of sin. In fact, it soon became clear that the tumor remained. Inside the ark, inside the human heart, sin remained alive and began to spread at the first opportunity.

Genesis 11 represents the human race at its most arrogant and most needy. Grasping for significance, these people built a tower to the heavens to make a name for themselves. The solidity and durability of the bricks were also meant to help the people overcome their inner fears. Pride—the chief cause of sin—joined with alienation—the chief result of sin—in a doomed attempt to overcome the effects of sin. God frustrated their efforts, knowing they would not succeed but would only make their spiritual failure more permanent.

GOD'S GREAT PLAN IN GENESIS 1–11

God's goal in creation was for humanity to experience the joy of knowing and serving Him. Everything was arranged so that it would be easy for human beings to obey. Their minds were clear, their relationships affirming, their environment wholesome, their circumstances pleasant, their potential limitless, their God near at hand. Because God did not want robots, He did not remove their freedom to choose but did everything to help them choose wisely.

They failed. Their disobedience set off a chain reaction of catastrophes that turned paradise into pain. Genesis 1–11 describes how sin robbed humanity of the joy of being human. Instead of knowing God, they forgot Him. Instead of serving God, they served themselves. Even their technological successes were vain attempts to overcome the emptiness of human failure. It seemed that the only outcome for humanity was to let the cancer of sin run its terminal course.

WHAT WE LEARN ABOUT GOD FROM GENESIS 1–11

Among the many insights into God's character evident in these chapters, three stand out: God as Creator, God as lover of humanity, and God as holy.

God as Creator

The opening chapters of Genesis present God as a powerful Creator. Unlike the gods of the ancient Near East who created out of material already on hand, God started from scratch. Unlike these gods, He did not need the help of any goddess to "father" the world through celestial sex. Like an ancient king who needed only to speak and his will was accomplished, God spoke the "heavens and the earth" (Genesis 1:1) into existence. He created the stars and planets, whose presence and movements have fascinated ancients and moderns alike. Israel's neighbors looked to these heavens as the home for their gods, but Israel knew the One who created those heavens. The more we know of the vast extent of the heavens, the more our respect for God's power should grow.

Through His powerful word, God created the earth and called it very good. Even now, suffering from the effects of sin, this world continues to be a beautiful place. Here humans can find satisfying happiness, contentment, and pleasure, though not to the same degree God originally intended. Just as the ruins of ancient Athens reveal the greatness of Greek civilization, the devastating effects of sin cannot hide the beautiful place God created for us.

God Loves Humanity

Having worked by His powerful word to bring the world and humanity into existence, God then changed His method. He did not force humans to do His will, but sought to persuade them. That "God works by persuasion and not by force" demonstrates a second aspect of God's nature, His love.[5]

God did not need to create people for His benefit. He wasn't lonely for fellowship or bored with nothing to do. God created people for their benefit, not His. It was out of love that He made Adam and Eve and put them in a beautiful place to live. Their assignment—to know and serve God—was not because God needed their love or service. He knew that a person's greatest joy would come from knowing and serving Him. Everything God does, He does from love.

He even loved humanity when He was punishing them for their disobedience. Without this punishment, there would have been no hope of ultimate restoration. Like the surgeon who must remove diseased tissue for the sake of the whole body, God had to perform a painful operation for the greater good. God loved humanity too much to leave it sick and dying.

God Is Holy

These chapters also demonstrate God's holiness. Because God is holy, He cannot tolerate disobedience. We usually consider intolerance to be a bad quality, but for God to tolerate sin would mean He would have to stop loving. When we sin, we aren't just disobeying God; we are choosing a path that, ultimately, will destroy us. Since we were created to serve God, disobeying Him violates our purpose for living. God loves this world too much to let it destroy itself. The next chapter reveals the beginning of His unusual plan to undo the effects of sin and bring the world back into fellowship with Him.

Genesis 1–11 at a Glance

Authorship: Traditionally understood as Moses

Date of writing: Probably written in the 1200s B.C., although many would argue for the 1400s B.C. In either case, the author used much older written or oral material

Date of events: From the very beginning of time until about 2000 B.C.

Purposes for writing:

1. To describe how God created everything
2. To describe how sin corrupted God's original creation

Form: Primarily narrative with some poetry

Part of God's plan: To show how God's original plan for humanity was destroyed by sin

Key elements of God's character: Creator, Lover, holiness

---

application questions

1. How are we to care for God's world since He created it?
2. What difference does it make that you were created in the image of God?
3. If God created the world by His word, what problems are you facing that would be too difficult for Him to handle?
4. What are some ways that God has recently demonstrated His love to you?
5. What difference does it make to you that God is too holy to tolerate sin?

questions for study and discussion

1. What can we learn about human beings from Genesis 1–2? Why does the author include two accounts?
2. What can we learn about sin from Genesis 3? What additional truths about sin can we learn from Genesis 4–11?
3. How do we see the pain and alienation caused by sin operating in our culture?
4. Are science and the Bible incompatible? Why or why not?
5. What would it be like to live in the world of Genesis 1–2?
6. What else can we learn from these chapters about God?
7. What else can we learn from these chapters about God's plan?

endnotes

1. As in Psalm 110:5 and Isaiah 2:11–12, for example.

2. The biblical and scientific accounts, while different, share several common beliefs. Both agree that the world had a beginning, was created to reproduce itself, betrays a measure of orderliness, and was created in roughly the order described in the Bible.

3. Alexander Heidel, *The Babylonian Genesis* (Chicago: University of Chicago Press, 1951), 89.

4. "Enuma Elish," ANET, 68.

5. Wolfhart Pannenberg, *Systematic Theology*, vol. 2 (Grand Rapids, Mich.: Eerdmans, 1994), 16.

chapter seven

The Beginning of a New Beginning
Genesis 12-50

SUGGESTIONS FOR READING GENESIS 12–50

Like the first eleven chapters, Genesis 12–50 is primarily narrative, so keep in mind the historical and literary contexts. You will read about people doing odd things like cutting animals in half and marrying more than one wife. Things like this were normal in the ancient Near East.

Remember to read each story in light of the bigger stories of Israel's history and God's plan to solve the "sin" problem. Also, keep your eye on God. He is, after all, the hero of every story.

INTRODUCTION

After what human beings did to God's perfect world in only eleven chapters, we might have expected God to destroy it all and start again. Instead, He set in motion a plan that would lead, nearly two thousand years later, to a manger in Bethlehem and a cross outside Jerusalem. From there the plan has developed and will continue until God restores paradise once again.

Genesis 12–50 describes the earliest days of this plan that was meant to change our lives.

OVERVIEW

The closing verses of Genesis 11 introduce Abraham, a resident of the city of Ur, son of Terah, and husband of Sarah.[1] As we learn from Genesis 12, God chose this man to begin His plan to undo the effects of sin. Childless and in his mid-seventies, Abraham hardly seemed qualified to be the ancestor of many nations. He had been raised to worship many gods, like the rest of the people in the ancient Near East. Like all of us, Abraham was infected by sin. The only explanation for why God chose Abraham is grace, God's free, merciful favor shown to someone undeserving. God called Abraham for the same reason He calls anyone—not because of what Abraham had done or would do, but because God loved him.

God's love was not just for Abraham but for the whole human race. He would express this love for all humanity through His work with Abraham and his family. God planned to give Abraham and Sarah a son and from that

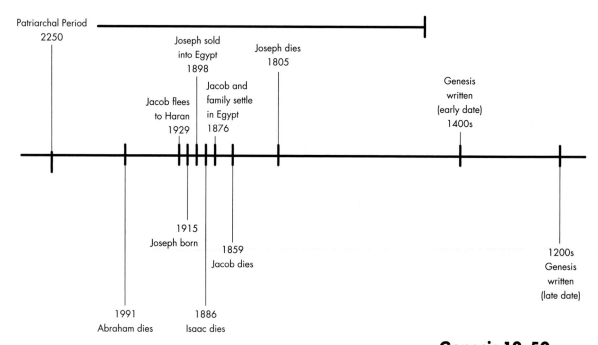

Patriarchal Period
2250

Joseph sold
into Egypt
1898

Joseph dies
1805

Genesis
written
(early date)
1400s

Jacob and
family settle
in Egypt
1876

Jacob flees
to Haran
1929

1915
Joseph born

1859
Jacob dies

1200s
Genesis
written
(late date)

1991
Abraham dies

1886
Isaac dies

Genesis 12–50

Unless otherwise noted, all dates are B.C.

Why all the name changes?

In the culture of the ancient Near East and in the Bible, names had great significance. People were given names to reflect something about them. Isaac's name means "he laughs" to remind his parents how they responded to God's announcement of his birth (read Genesis 17:17–19; 18:12). Ishmael means "God hears," recalling how God heard of Hagar's difficulties (read Genesis 16:11). At times a person's name was changed to reflect a new role or identity. In Genesis 17, God changed Abram's name to Abraham and Sarai's name to Sarah to acknowledge their roles as father and mother of a great nation. Later, God would change Jacob's name to Israel (Genesis 32:28) to signify a major change in his life.

son to create the nation of Israel (the Jews) to whom He would give the land of Canaan. Through this nation, God would bless all nations. Over the centuries, the Jewish people have enriched the world in many ways, but especially by producing Jesus, who solved the sin problem forever on the cross. The rest of the book of Genesis fleshes out the beginning of God's plan and how He preserved that plan in the face of numerous obstacles.

From Ur to Canaan

Ironically, most obstacles came from the very people God had chosen—Abraham, his son, grandson, and great-grandsons. Shortly after Abraham arrived in Canaan, a famine struck that country. Abraham headed south to Egypt, where he lied about his wife, saying she was his sister. Deceived, the king of Egypt married Sarah, throwing God's plan into jeopardy. How could God produce a nation through Abraham if Sarah was married to someone else? How could this nation receive the land of Canaan if Abraham and Sarah remained in Egypt? Thankfully, God intervened, but it would not be the last time He had to step in because of human disobedience.

MAP 2 The Ancient World at the Time of the Patriarchs

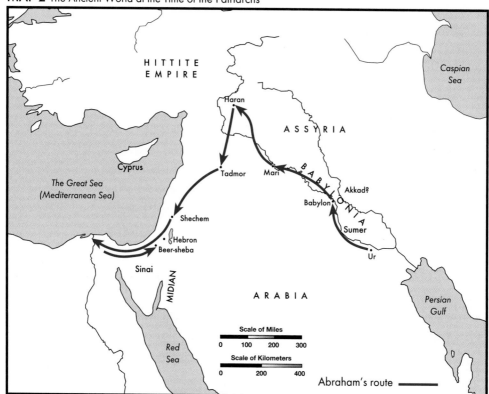

The Meaning of Covenant

Genesis 15 tells how God appeared to Abraham, in part to bolster his faith and make it easier for him to obey. God not only appeared to Abraham, He also entered into a covenant with him. Today, when two parties enter into a legal arrangement, they sign a contract. In the ancient Near East, the parties would make a covenant. Sometimes the covenant was between two partners, like a business deal or marriage. At other times the covenant was an agreement between a stronger and a weaker party, such as when a powerful nation agreed to protect a weaker nation in return for loyalty. God made this second kind of covenant with Abraham in Genesis 17.

In a third type of covenant, the stronger party made an unconditional promise, one not dependent on the weaker party's response. A king might make a covenant with one of his subjects, promising to give him a piece of land. The promise was unconditional, given as a reward for past faithfulness. This was the kind of covenant God made with Abraham in Genesis 15. He promised to give him a son from his (Abraham's) own body and to give his descendants the land of Canaan. Then God confirmed this covenant with a legal ceremony commonly practiced in the ancient Near East. It involved cutting animals in half and laying their carcasses on the ground. The stronger party would walk between the pieces as a guarantee that he would keep his promise. By walking between the pieces, God solemnly promised to keep His word to Abraham.

MAP 3 Abraham and Isaac in the Land of Canaan

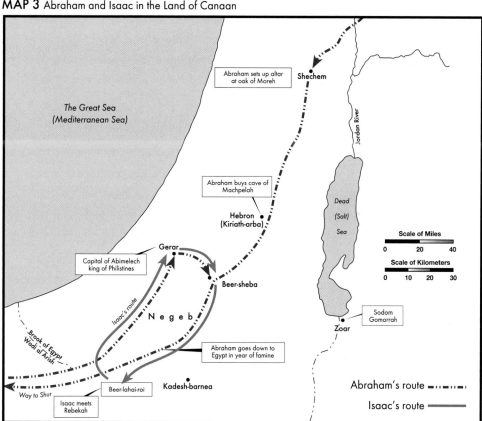

Why did God choose circumcision as the sign of the covenant?

Circumcision, the removal of the foreskin from the penis, was practiced by other nations in the ancient Near East. Only Israel was commanded to perform this surgery on every male infant at eight days of age (Genesis 17:12–13). God chose this way to teach His people about the nature of the covenant. First, God wanted them to understand that serving Him would sometimes be painful. As the surgery was performed in a private part of the body, God also wanted to remind them that His covenant was to be personal and individual. Since the penis was the instrument of procreation, God also wanted to illustrate the connection between their fruitfulness as a nation and their faithfulness to God. Finally, God chose this to remind them continually that they were distinctive, unique, and holy—God's chosen people. In Egypt, only priests were circumcised. By requiring this of all Israelite males, God declared the entire nation holy, a kingdom of priests (Exodus 19:6).

Human error was not the only obstacle to God's plan. God himself seemed to oppose it when He asked Abraham to kill Isaac, the promised heir. In Genesis 22:1 we are told that God meant this only as a test, but Abraham was never informed beforehand. This request must have bewildered him. Why would God make him wait twenty-five years for a child, and then tell him to kill that child? Was God like the other gods of the ancient Near East who approved of child sacrifice? Most perplexing of all, how would God keep His solemn promises if Isaac were killed?

In spite of his questions, Abraham obeyed, even to the point of tying his son with ropes and raising a knife to strike the deathblow. At the last moment, God intervened and stopped Abraham, sparing Isaac's life. In response to this demonstration of great faith, God enthusiastically made another promise of numerous descendants who would bless the whole earth.

God's plan faced another obstacle, finding a wife for Isaac (Genesis 24). If Isaac married one of the women from Canaan, his offspring gradually would be absorbed into the general population and be unable to complete God's plan. To prevent this, Abraham sent his servant back to his homeland to find a wife among his relatives. Once again, God protected His plan and provided Rebekah as a wife for Isaac.

Isaac and Rebekah had twin sons, Esau and Jacob. As God had decided to create the chosen people from Isaac rather than from Isaac's older brother, Ishmael, He chose to continue that line through Jacob rather than his older brother, Esau. Jacob was not more righteous than Esau. In fact, he was a schemer (that is what his name means) who tricked his brother and father and ended up running away to save his life (Genesis 27–28). He returned to his mother's homeland, went to work for his uncle Laban, and married two of his cousins (Genesis 29).

Why did Sarah offer her slave girl to Abraham?

Knowing that God had promised to produce a nation through Abraham must have put great pressure on Sarah. She already felt humiliated because she was barren; now she felt responsible to fulfill God's promise. If she lived in our day, Sarah might have gone to a fertility clinic or an adoption agency. In that culture, a barren woman was allowed to produce a child through her slave girl. The slave would be given to the woman's husband as his concubine, a baby-making machine without full legal rights as a wife. The child of such a union would not belong to its birth mother, but to the concubine's mistress—in this case, Sarah. After Sarah permitted her slave, Hagar, to become Abraham's concubine, Hagar produced Ishmael. But this was not God's way to produce the nation of Israel. Sarah's attempt to "help" God only led to disappointment for everyone involved.

Why did God command Abraham to sacrifice his son?

Even though God never intended for Abraham to kill Isaac, it seems like an unreasonable request and a cruel joke on Abraham, Sarah, and Isaac. There were, however, factors present in that culture that made the test more understandable. While God's command would be devastating, it would not be surprising. Abraham knew about child sacrifice from his travels. He knew that other gods required it, especially of the firstborn son. Since he had only known this God for a few decades, he was probably unsure about all that God would ask of him.

Because our culture does not practice child sacrifice and because we know so much more about God, He would never make such a request today. He required this of Abraham to show him and his descendants that they must reject such a barbaric practice. God also wanted to show the importance of faith. At the very beginning of His plan, God wanted to make clear that faith was essential to its success. Abraham's example would show all his descendants that God's people must live by faith.

By prospering at his uncle's expense, Jacob became so unpopular with his in-laws that he had to run away (Genesis 29–31). He returned to Canaan, reconciled with his brother, and settled once again in the land God had promised to Abraham's descendants (Genesis 32–35). Here Jacob, renamed Israel, lived with his four wives and twelve sons.

From Canaan to Egypt, Genesis now turns its focus to one of Israel's twelve sons, Joseph. This young man so angered his brothers that they sold him into slavery and then lied to their father about what they had done. Eventually, Joseph arrived in Egypt, where he was sold to an important Egyptian official. There he was falsely accused, thrown into prison, and forgotten by everyone. Everyone, that is, except God, who used all these difficulties to prepare Joseph for an important part in His plan. Through a series of remarkable circumstances, God elevated Joseph to become the "prime minister" of Egypt (Genesis 37–41).

Meanwhile, a great famine was threatening to starve God's chosen people. Israel (Jacob) sent his sons to buy grain in Egypt, where food was abundant, thanks to Joseph's planning. Once there, Joseph and his brothers were reunited. Joseph brought Jacob and all his brothers and their families to live in the land of Egypt, where they prospered. Long before this famine, God was working to preserve His people and His plan (Genesis 42–50).

GOD'S GREAT PLAN IN GENESIS 12–50

Genesis 11 describes the Tower of Babel, humanity's failed attempt to reverse the effects of sin. How interesting that the very next chapter describes the beginning of God's plan to do the same thing! Actually, building a tower to the heavens seems more logical than the plan that emerges in Genesis: Call a man to wander without even telling him where he is going . . . call him to be the father of many nations when he and his wife are old and childless . . . promise them a land already inhabited . . . wait

Who did Jacob wrestle and why?

The night before he was to meet his brother, Jacob wrestled all night, probably with an angel who looked like a man (Genesis 32:24). As we see in the next verse, the angel could easily have handled Jacob. God prolonged the wrestling match because He wanted to teach Jacob a lesson. Up to this time, Jacob had been living up to his name, "trickster." Now God gave him a new identity, one more suitable to his role in God's plan. He renamed him Israel, which means, "he struggles with God." Now he and his descendants were to live by faith in God.

twenty-five years to fulfill the promise of a son . . . marry that son to a woman who can't bear children . . . marry the grandson to another woman who can't bear children . . . then send the chosen people away from the Promised Land because of a famine and into a land where they will eventually be held as slaves.

It may seem strange, but this is exactly how God wanted His plan to develop. Slowly but surely, God was preparing His people to become a source of blessing for the whole world. Not a step was wasted. Every obstacle was overcome. God even turned human mistakes into something good. His plan was off to the perfect start.

WHAT WE LEARN ABOUT GOD FROM GENESIS 12–50

More than anything, these chapters reveal God as a gracious promise maker. We usually think of grace as a New Testament word, but it has always been the hallmark of God's relationship with humanity, the best description of the way He works with people. Why else would God create humanity? Why would He bother to set about undoing the effects of sin, except for grace? There was nothing in it for Him; every benefit belonged to humanity.

By Grace

God chose Abraham because of His grace, not because of who Abraham was or what he could do. God persisted with His plan, in spite of obstacles and imperfect participants, only because of grace. Throughout the Old Testament, everything God said and did was motivated by this free, undeserved love. Even His punishments were tempered by mercy and patience. He always has been a "compassionate and gracious God, slow to anger, abounding in love and faithfulness, maintaining love to thousands, and forgiving wickedness, rebellion and sin" (Exodus 34:6–7).

God revealed His grace in these chapters by making promises, particularly to Abraham. This suggests, first, that He loves people enough to commit himself to them. Making a promise is like assuming a debt. We commit ourselves to keep that promise, no matter what the cost. That is why we usually reserve our promises for those we care about, our family and friends. God voluntarily entered into a relationship with Abraham. No one forced Him; He did it out of love. He demonstrated how much He loved him by promising offspring and territory to Abraham. He obligated himself to keep those promises.

By Faith

By definition, a promise means that the thing promised is not yet here. The promise of spring means it is still winter; the promise to marry means the wedding is still to come. A promise-making God puts a high premium on faith. He knows that faith is the only way to relate to an invisible God. How else can we trust a God whose actions surprise us? How else can we continue to obey God when the rewards for obedience and punishment for disobedience are so far off? This is why the writer of the New Testament book of Hebrews said, "Without faith it is impossible to please God" (Hebrews 11:6).

God's plan to solve the problem of sin can only succeed by faith. No one can prove God exists; it must be claimed by faith. Nor can we prove God loves humanity, except by faith. Only by faith can we accept that God is working out a plan to reverse the effects of sin. We read about God bringing forth a nation from Abraham and about Jesus dying on the cross; however, without faith, these are just historical details. Only by faith can we accept these details as part of God's great plan.

Only by faith can we personally become part of this plan. God offers to forgive our sins, but we can only be forgiven by faith. We can't do anything to earn it; we can only take God at His word and receive His gift. This is what the apostle Paul meant when he wrote, "For it is by grace you have been saved, through faith" (Ephesians 2:8). With faith so crucial to the success of God's plan, no wonder He makes it such a high priority. No wonder He makes so many promises.

Only faith in God's promises could sustain the Israelites during the dark centuries to follow. They went down to Egypt as the family of the prime minister, but eventually became slaves. Only by trusting in God's promises could they find the courage to escape and follow an invisible God into the wilderness, as described in the book of Exodus, where we turn next.

Genesis 12–50 at a Glance

Authorship: Traditionally understood as Moses

Date of writing: Probably written in the 1200s B.C., although many would argue for the 1400s B.C. In either case, the author used much older written or oral material

Date of events: About 2000 to 1500 B.C.

Purposes:

1. To describe the beginning and preservation of God's plan to reverse the effects of sin

2. To describe the historical beginnings of the Jewish nation

Form: Primarily narrative with some poetry

Part of God's plan: To show how God began His plan by calling Abraham and continued to develop that plan in spite of obstacles

Key elements of God's character: Graciousness, Promise Maker

---

application questions

1. What specific evidence for God's grace can you find in these chapters?

2. In what ways has God shown His grace to you?

3. What more can we say about God, based on His nature as promise maker?

4. In what ways can you do better at living by faith?

questions for study and discussion

1. Read Genesis 12:1–9.

    a. What did God call Abraham to do in Genesis 12:1?

    b. What did God promise Abraham in Genesis 12:1–9?

2. Read Genesis 15.

    a. What does it mean that Abraham's faith was credited to him as righteousness (Genesis 15:6)?

    b. Did Abraham's responses in Genesis 15:2–3, 8 show doubt or faith? What is the difference between a question asked in doubt and one asked in faith?

3. Read Genesis 17. Are Christians required to circumcise their children? Why or why not?

4. Read Genesis 21.

    a. What did Sarah see, as recorded in Genesis 21:9?

    b. Identify several reasons why this chapter may be included in the Bible.

5. Read Genesis 22.

    a. Why did God test Abraham this way?

    b. Describe Abraham's response in Genesis 22:3–5.

    c. Do you agree that God would not ask someone today to do this? Why or why not?

6. Read Genesis 25:19–34. Why do you think God made Isaac wait twenty years for the birth of his sons (Genesis 25:20, 26)?

7. Read Genesis 27–35.

    a. Why did God use Jacob if he was so deceitful?

    b. Identify the twelve sons of Jacob and the mother of each one.

8. Read Genesis 37 and 39:1 — 46:7.

    a. Why does the story focus on Joseph?

    b. What does Joseph mean in Genesis 45:8?

    c. Why did God reassure Jacob with the words of Genesis 46:3–4?

9. What else can we learn from these chapters about God?

10. What else can we learn from these chapters about God's plan?

endnote

1. Actually, his name was Abram and hers Sarai until God changed their names (Genesis 17).

chapter eight

Free at Last
Exodus

SUGGESTIONS FOR READING EXODUS

Since much of Exodus is narrative, keep the historical and literary contexts in mind. Like Genesis, the world of Exodus is strange to most of us; by referring to your study Bible, you'll find that world becoming more familiar. Second, read each story in light of the bigger stories. The liberation of Israel from Egypt is an important part of God's plan to free all of us from the problem of sin. Although Moses occupies center stage for most of the book, God remains the main character of the story. Keep your eye on Him.

The second half of this book contains the Law, including the best known legal passage, the Ten Commandments (Exodus 20:1–17). Remember, these laws were given for Israel's good. They were intended to show the Israelites how to love God and love one another. While they are not our laws, we can appreciate what God was trying to teach the Israelites about himself and about how they were to live together.

INTRODUCTION

Freedom. Every human longs for it but, sadly, not all experience it. This book describes how God freed the Israelites from slavery in Egypt so they could help free humanity from slavery to sin.

OVERVIEW

Exodus tells the story of how God liberated His people. First, He freed them in dramatic fashion from slavery to the Egyptians (Exodus 1–18). But a deeper work of liberation was needed. The generation of Israelites who left Egypt had known only slavery. Before God could use them to further His plan, He had to liberate them from their self-identity as slaves. He had to help them see themselves not as a group of slaves, but as a chosen nation. One way He accomplished this inner liberation was by giving them the Law (Exodus 19–40).

Liberating the Slaves (Exodus 1–18)

The book opens on a dark note. During Joseph's lifetime and for years following, Egypt had been Israel's haven. However, over time Egypt became

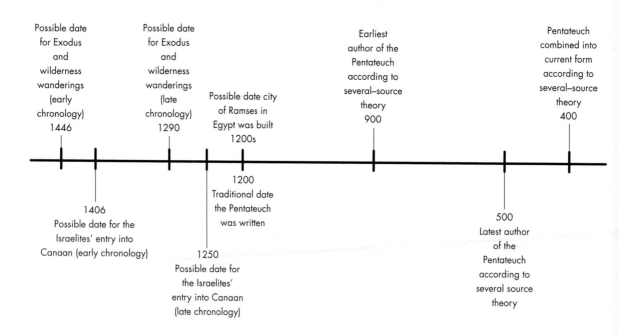

Possible date for Exodus and wilderness wanderings (early chronology) 1446

Possible date for Exodus and wilderness wanderings (late chronology) 1290

Possible date city of Ramses in Egypt was built 1200s

Earliest author of the Pentateuch according to several–source theory 900

Pentateuch combined into current form according to several–source theory 400

1406 Possible date for the Israelites' entry into Canaan (early chronology)

1200 Traditional date the Pentateuch was written

1250 Possible date for the Israelites' entry into Canaan (late chronology)

500 Latest author of the Pentateuch according to several source theory

Exodus
Unless otherwise noted, all dates are B.C.

What is God's name?

God has many names in the Bible, but at the burning bush He called himself "I AM" (Exodus 3:14). By using this name, God emphasized His nature as eternal—He always is. To the Israelites in Egyptian slavery, God was assuring them that He would keep the promises He had made to Abraham many years earlier.

"I AM" in Hebrew is Yahweh. Because early scholars misunderstood the language, this name is sometimes mispronounced Jehovah. Most English versions of the Old Testament will translate Yahweh as LORD (note the use of small capital letters). Yahweh was the name by which God revealed himself to the Israelites. When they addressed Him as Yahweh (rather than as God or Lord), they were emphasizing their unique covenant relationship with Him.

Israel's prison. In a few centuries, the Israelites went from being Pharaoh's welcomed guests to Pharaoh's chain gang, building his cities and working in his fields. He even ordered the death of every Israelite boy as a form of population control (Exodus 1).

One Hebrew mother, desperate to save her infant son, hid him among the reeds along the Nile River, only to have him discovered by the daughter of Pharaoh. The princess felt sorry for the boy and instead of having him killed, adopted the boy as her son. She named him Moses, which means "drawn out," because of his rescue from the water (Exodus 2). God would later use this Moses to rescue His people from slavery.

The Call

Forty more years of suffering went by. Moses, now a grown man, tried to take Israel's well-being into his own hands. His plan backfired and he had to run away from Egypt, a fugitive wanted for murder. While wandering in the

Who wrote the Pentateuch?

For centuries, Jews and Christians agreed that Moses wrote the first five books of the Old Testament (the Pentateuch). The Old Testament writers assumed this, as did the New Testament writers and the authors of other ancient Jewish books. This view began to come under heavy criticism several hundred years ago. Scholars questioned how one author could permit so much repetition, such as two different accounts of creation (Genesis 1 and 2). They denied the Pentateuch was written by one author in the 1200s B.C., instead proposing it was written by several different people—the earliest writing about 900 B.C. and the latest about 500 B.C. These several sources were eventually combined about 400 B.C. into what we know as the first five books of the Old Testament.

Although this theory has been widely held, it offers no compelling reason to abandon the traditional view that the Pentateuch is the carefully crafted composition of Moses. He no doubt relied on earlier sources (for example, read Numbers 21:14–15) and his work was probably edited after his death, but the material most likely came from his pen around 1200 B.C.

desert of the Sinai Peninsula, he joined up with a tribe of nomads, married a woman from that tribe, and became a shepherd. One day while tending the flock near Mount Sinai, he saw a remarkable sight. A bush was on fire but the fire wasn't burning up the bush. The leaves remained green, even in the middle of the flames.

As Moses moved closer to investigate, God spoke to him from the flames. Like this bush, God's people were surviving in the midst of oppression. But the time had come for them to be freed, and Moses was God's man for the job. Needless to say, Moses was reluctant to take on the assignment. After all, he was wanted for murder in Egypt. How could he possibly return and convince Pharaoh to release the Israelites? God heard Moses' hesitation but was insistent: God was going to free Israel, and He would use Moses to do it (Exodus 3–4).

Moses' first attempts at liberation were disastrous. He went to Pharaoh and demanded the king release the Israelites. Pharaoh, angered by this demand, made their lives even more miserable. The Israelites were now doubly discouraged and less willing to listen to Moses. All this was exactly what God intended. He was setting up a showdown that would both demonstrate His power to Israel and punish Egypt for oppressing His people (Exodus 5–6).

The Showdown

The showdown came in the form of ten plagues or judgments, each designed to prove that Israel's God was stronger than the Egyptian gods.

When did the Exodus happen?

Some scholars propose an early date for the Exodus, around 1450 B.C. First Kings 6:1 says that Solomon began to build the Temple 480 years after the Israelites left Egypt. Counting back 480 years from the start of Solomon's Temple (around 970 B.C.) brings us to 1450 B.C. This date also fits the evidence of Judges 11:26, which says that Israel ruled Moab for three hundred years.

Others argue for a late date, sometime in the 1200s B.C., based primarily on evidence from archaeology. The city of Ramses mentioned in Exodus 1:11 was not built until the 1200s B.C., and there is some evidence of Canaanite cities being destroyed around this time, as described in the book of Joshua. These scholars believe that the 480 years of 1 Kings 6:1 and the three hundred years of Judges 11:26 are only approximate dates.

MAP 4 The Exodus: From Egypt to Mt. Sinai

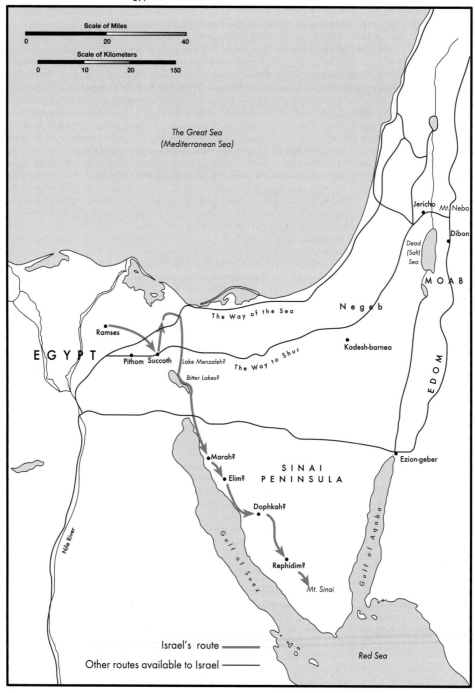

Some of the plagues directly challenged particular Egyptian gods. The Egyptians worshiped the Nile River in the form of the god Hopi. When Yahweh turned its waters to blood, He showed that He was greater than Hopi (Exodus 7:14–24). The frog goddess, Heqt, was mocked in the second plague when frogs overran the country (Exodus 8:1–15), as were the bull gods (Apis and Mnevis), the cow god (Hathor), and the ram god (Khnum) with the plague on livestock (Exodus 9:1–7). When God brought darkness in the daytime (Exodus 10:21–29), He demonstrated He was greater than the Egyptian sun god, Ra.

Other plagues ridiculed the Egyptian deities indirectly. The earth god, Geb, could not stop gnats from rising from the ground. Nor could the sky goddess or the air goddess keep the hail, flies, and locusts from passing through the air to harm the Egyptians. None of the Egyptian deities could prevent the plague of boils (Exodus 9:8–12) or the death of the firstborn son (Exodus 11). By showing himself as greater than these gods and goddesses, Yahweh gave Israel solid reasons to trust Him.

Had Pharaoh given in and released the Israelites, his country would have been spared. But each plague only made him more resolved to say no. By the time the ten plagues were finished, Egypt was in ruins. Israel not only was permitted to leave; the Egyptians paid them to go. Liberation had begun.

The Journey

The trip from Egypt to Canaan, their destination, could ordinarily be done on foot in less than one month. Instead of taking them north out of Egypt along the Mediterranean Sea, God led them southeast into the desert of Sinai. He took them that way to teach them some important lessons. Blocking this escape route was a large body of water called the Red Sea (or Reed Sea). The Red Sea, in its present location, is too far south to have blocked the path of the escaping Israelites. In those days, however, it probably extended as far north as the Bitter Lakes, or even beyond to Lake Menzaleh, making it a barrier to freedom. But God miraculously parted the waters of the Red Sea and destroyed the Egyptian army to show that He would protect the Israelites.

91

He sent food and water in unusual ways to show that He would provide for their needs. By appearing as a huge column of fire and cloud, He showed that He would be with them and would guide them (Exodus 12–19). Only by taking them on this longer, more difficult, more frightening route, could God prepare them for their new role. By the time they reached the barren, rocky wilderness of Mount Sinai, they were ready to learn what it would mean to be God's chosen nation.

A Deeper Work of Liberation (19–40)

Israel was now free from Egyptian bondage but not from the centuries-old effects of that bondage. God continued His liberating work in the second part of Exodus (chapters 19–40) by freeing His people from their self-identity as slaves. One way He reshaped their identity was by entering into an agreement with them through the Law He gave on Mount Sinai.

To speak of a law that liberates sounds contradictory. How could limiting freedom by laws actually produce freedom? These laws were not just a list of rules; they were part of an agreement between God and the Israelites. Building on the covenant He had made earlier with Abraham (Genesis 12), God entered into a formal relationship with these former slaves. Just as we saw with the covenant between God and Abraham in Genesis 17, this was a two-part agreement. God would do His part—caring for them, accompanying them, and protecting them—and they must do their part. Israel's part in this agreement is found in the Law.

Living by the Rules

This agreement brought freedom by changing how the Israelites understood themselves. They were no longer a group of slaves, but God's "treasured possession," a "kingdom of priests and a holy nation" (Exodus 19:5–6). God not only freed them from slavery, but He also freed them from their identity as slaves.

Imagine that you have adopted a poor, orphaned girl from another country. When she is able to understand, you explain to her the rules by which she will live. You do so not to restrict her freedom, but because she is your daughter.

She has been freed from her old identity as an orphan; the rules of your household prove to her that she is a member of your family.

Living among Them

God found a second way to change the identity of His people from slaves to children. He demonstrated again and again that He was actually present among them as a loving Father. If a famous person moves to your town, it elevates the status of the town. It becomes "the town where so-and-so lives." As the status of your town rises, you and your fellow citizens see yourselves as more respectable. You realize there must be something special about your town if "so-and-so" chooses to live there.

Israel needed to see herself for what she really was: God's chosen people. What better way for God to bring about this transformation in self-understanding than by showing that He was present among them? This was why He created the pillar of cloud and the pillar of fire (Exodus 13:21–22). God wanted the people to be able to look up at any moment, day or night, and see that He was with them.

This is why He had them build the Tabernacle, a portable temple representing God's house. This is why He had them set it up in the middle of the camp (Exodus 25–40). The Tabernacle was to serve as another physical reminder that God was with them. As He said in Exodus 25:8, "Have them make a sanctuary for me, and I will dwell among them." They built the sanctuary, and God kept His promise by visibly moving in (Exodus 40:34).

GOD'S GREAT PLAN IN EXODUS

In order for God to accomplish His plan to redeem the world through the nation of Israel, He first had to create this nation. He began this process in Genesis, choosing Abraham and shepherding Abraham's son, grandson, and great-grandsons in Canaan and into Egypt, where they became a large group of people. He continued this process of nation making by liberating the Israelites from Egyptian slavery and making a covenant with them at Mount

Sinai. Once they were free and could better understand their role as God's people, He could proceed with His plan to reunite the world to himself.

God's liberation not only prepared Israel to carry out His plan of reconciliation, it also showed them what reconciliation with God meant. As the Israelites were slaves to the Egyptians, unable to free themselves, so humanity was enslaved to sin and its effects because of the first human sin. As God rescued the Israelites through His great grace, so He would mercifully rescue all humanity. God's ultimate goal has always been to restore people to fellowship with Him; in Exodus we see Him coming to live among the Israelites. In so doing, God not only furthered the process of reconciliation, He also illustrated what reconciliation means. Little wonder that Jews and later Christians would look back to the events of this book as symbolizing God's plan.

WHAT WE LEARN ABOUT GOD FROM EXODUS

Repeatedly in Exodus, God revealed His concern for the Israelites. He heard their cries for help, chose Moses, called him at the burning bush, and granted him success in liberating the Israelites. Over and over, as they traveled toward Mount Sinai, God supplied their needs for protection, food, and water, like a shepherd for his sheep. Often He would work miraculously: parting the Red Sea so the Israelites could escape, drowning the Egyptian army to prevent them from following, sending bread from heaven, providing huge flocks of quail on the wind, and furnishing water from rocks.

By giving the Law, God demonstrated His compassion. He gave these commands for Israel's benefit so their society would be just and fair. They were told to avoid what would harm them and pursue what would benefit them. Giving the Law also mercifully altered Israel's self-understanding from that of slave to "treasured possession" (Exodus 19:5). He patiently put up with all their complaints. Even when He judged them, God was compassionate and merciful. Like a father, He punished only as much as necessary to preserve Israel's faithful obedience.

God Is Compassionate

When God wanted to describe himself to Moses and the Israelites, He emphasized His compassion: "The LORD, the LORD, the compassionate and gracious God, slow to anger, abounding in love and faithfulness, maintaining love to thousands, and forgiving wickedness, rebellion and sin (Exodus 34:6–7a). After suffering in slavery for all those years, the Israelites needed this reminder of God's compassion. For centuries to come, they would look back to the Exodus from Egypt as God's most merciful moment.

God Is Powerful

Exodus also emphasizes God's power. The ten plagues revealed how much stronger He was than Pharaoh and all the gods of Egypt. By parting the Red Sea and providing food and water in unusual ways, God displayed His power over the natural world. On Mount Sinai, God's power—evident in the thunder, lightning, fire, cloud, smoke, and trumpet blast—so terrified the people that they trembled with fear.

Why does God flex His mighty muscle so often in this book? The obvious answer is that He needed to. Egypt would not allow the Israelites to leave without a fight. The Hebrews could not walk on water; the sea had to part if they were to escape. The Sinai wilderness was no breadbasket; finding food for the Israelites required a miracle.

Perhaps less obvious is that God often deliberately backed himself into a corner in order to demonstrate His power. He could have led Israel out years earlier, before Pharaoh began to oppress them. He could have led the Israelites out by another route and bypassed the Red Sea. He could have taken them through more hospitable territory, where food and water were easier to find.

God created situations in which to show His power because Israel needed to see His power. They needed to see that He was trustworthy. Just as Abraham had to learn to walk by faith, so did the Israelites. Only by depending on God in faith could they accomplish their mission. So God put them in situations where they had to trust Him, and then He came through for them. The Exodus was not just about liberation from Egypt. It was also about liberation from doubt. God continued to build their faith all the time they were in the wilderness. The next chapter explores this faith-building process as described in Leviticus, Numbers, and Deuteronomy.

The Sinai Wilderness

Exodus at a Glance

Authorship: Traditionally understood as Moses

Date of writing: Middle 1400s B.C. or late 1200s B.C.

Date of events: Middle 1400s B.C. or late 1200s B.C.

Purpose: To describe God's liberation of the Israelites from captivity in Egypt and their establishment as His chosen nation

Form: Primarily narrative and law

Part of God's plan: To show how God continues to prepare His people to be a source of blessing for all by liberating them and illustrating what redemption means

Key elements of God's character: Compassion, power

application questions

1. Have you ever sensed God leading you in ways that didn't make sense?
2. In what other ways, beside those mentioned in the chapter, did God reveal His compassion to the Israelites?
3. List several ways God has shown His compassion to you.
4. Are there situations in your life God may be using to demonstrate His power to you?

questions for study and discussion

1. Read Exodus 1:1—6:12.
   a. Why did God wait so long to rescue the Israelites?
   b. God names himself "I AM" in Exodus 3:14. Why is this significant for the book of Exodus?
2. Read Exodus 7–12.
   a. Why did God harden Pharaoh's heart but then punish Pharaoh?
   b. How might God show His power if the Exodus took place today?
   c. Why did God institute the feast of Passover?
3. Read Exodus 14–17.
   a. Did the use of a strong wind to part the Red Sea make this any less a miracle? Why or why not?
   b. List how the description of the parting of the sea in chapter 14 differs from the description in chapter 15.
4. Read Exodus 19:1—20:21.
   a. Why was God so concerned that Israel not touch the mountain?
   b. Categorize each of the Ten Commandments into those concerned with how to love God and those concerned with how to love one's neighbor.
5. Read Exodus 40.
   a. Why does Exodus have so much to say about the Tabernacle?
   b. Why are the last five verses so significant for the overall message of Exodus?

6. What else can we learn about God from this book?

7. What else can we learn about God's plan from this book?

chapter nine

Constitution for a Holy Nation
Leviticus, Numbers, Deuteronomy

SUGGESTIONS FOR READING LEVITICUS, NUMBERS, DEUTERONOMY

Much of the material in these books is Law. Remember, these laws were given to show Israel how to love God and love one another. We are not obligated to obey the laws, but we are required to ask what they tell us about God's character.

Read the narrative passages with an eye on the historical context. That is, understand each passage in light of the cultural and historical setting of the ancient Near East. What God asked from Israel and how He responded to them was entirely appropriate to that setting. These things seem strange to us because our setting is so different. Also keep the literary context in mind. In other words, understand any given passage in light of the passages before and following. Read these stories as part of bigger stories and understand that God, the hero of the story, is working out His eternal plan in and through Israel and her laws.

INTRODUCTION

Welcome to the three most neglected books in the Old Testament: Leviticus, Numbers, and Deuteronomy. It is hard to see what all these sacrifices and laws have to do with us. And why does God have to be so harsh? As we will learn in every book of the Old Testament, God works with people where they are to accomplish His plan. If we remember this, what seems strange to us will reveal interesting and relevant insights into who God is and what He was doing.

OVERVIEW

The books of Leviticus, Numbers, and Deuteronomy describe forty years of Israel's history. They begin where Exodus left off, at Mount Sinai, where God made a covenant with Israel. As they end, Israel is prepared to cross the Jordan River and enter the Promised Land of Canaan. While at Mount Sinai, God had more to say about how they should live; these laws are found in Leviticus. Numbers describes how the Israelites were organized for their journey to Canaan. This book also describes the trip and explains why it took

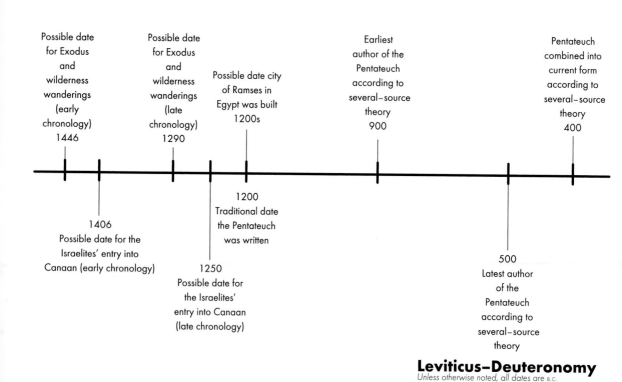

Possible date for Exodus and wilderness wanderings (early chronology) 1446

Possible date for Exodus and wilderness wanderings (late chronology) 1290

Possible date city of Ramses in Egypt was built 1200s

Earliest author of the Pentateuch according to several-source theory 900

Pentateuch combined into current form according to several-source theory 400

1406
Possible date for the Israelites' entry into Canaan (early chronology)

1200
Traditional date the Pentateuch was written

1250
Possible date for the Israelites' entry into Canaan (late chronology)

500
Latest author of the Pentateuch according to several-source theory

Leviticus–Deuteronomy
Unless otherwise noted, all dates are B.C.

MAP 5 The Exodus: From Mt. Sinai to the Promised Land

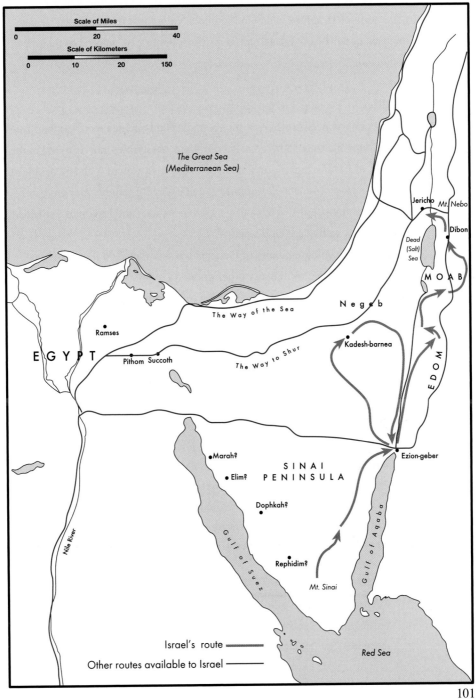

Scale of Miles
0   20   40

Scale of Kilometers
0   10   20   150

The Great Sea
(Mediterranean Sea)

Jericho   *Mt. Nebo*

Dibon

Dead
(Salt)
Sea

M O A B

The Way of the Sea

N e g e b

Ramses

•Kadesh-barnea

E G Y P T

Pithom Succoth

The Way to Shur

E D O M

•Marah?

S I N A I
P E N I N S U L A

•Elim?

Ezion-geber

Dophkah?

Nile River

Gulf of Suez

Gulf of Aqaba

•Rephidim?

Mt. Sinai

Israel's route ━━━━━

Other routes available to Israel ━━━━━

Red Sea

much longer than necessary. In Deuteronomy, Moses reminds a new generation of Israelites what God requires, calls them to recommit themselves to His covenant, and helps them prepare to succeed in their new homeland.

Leviticus: Laying Down the Law

Every nation needs rules by which to live. The Israelites received their rules from God while they gathered at Mount Sinai; these rules can be found in the last half of Exodus and in Leviticus. God made a covenant with His people at Mount Sinai, a covenant He summarized this way: "I will be your God, and you will be my people." The laws we find in Exodus and Leviticus explained to Israel how to live as "God's people."

From the opening chapters of Genesis we saw that God is holy. He is special and unique, unlike any other gods. As a holy God, He required His people to be special and unique too. He told them, "You are to be holy to me because I, the LORD, am holy, and I have set you apart from the nations to be my own" (Leviticus 20:26). How they were to be special and unique

What did it mean to be "clean"?

Leviticus 11–15 talks a lot about what it means to be clean and unclean. Uncleanness is not the same thing as sin. Sin required a choice, and many of the things that made a person unclean did not come by choice. Certain bodily functions—like a woman's period or a man's nocturnal emission—made a person unclean. Some animals were clean and could be eaten by the Israelites, while others were unclean and off limits.

By requiring that only clean animals be eaten and by limiting participation in society to only those people who were ritually clean, these laws taught the Israelites how to be holy.

is the theme of Leviticus, in which the word *holy* occurs more than eighty times.

Holy through Sacrifice

Leviticus begins where Exodus left off, describing the worship of the Israelites. The opening ten chapters describe the sacrifices God required. God commanded His people to offer five basic types of sacrifices. By these they could express their holiness or reclaim it when it had been lost because of disobedience. In the burnt offering, an animal was killed, then completely burned on the altar as a gift to God. Wealthy people were to offer an expensive animal, while the poor could offer a less expensive one. All the animals were to be free of any defect that would reduce their value. This was a voluntary offering the worshiper gave to show his or her complete dedication to God. The nation was also required to offer two burnt offerings every day, a small token of tribute to their heavenly King.

Two other voluntary offerings expressed gratitude. Grain mixed with oil, incense, and salt was given to the priest, who kept a portion as his payment and burned the rest on the altar. A second type of voluntary sacrifice, the fellowship offering, could be any animal. After the fat and some of the organs were burned and a portion given to the priest, the rest was returned to the worshiper. This person, together with his guests, was to enjoy the meat as the main course in a communal meal.

The person who accidentally sinned was to bring a sin offering to the Tabernacle. The type and value of the sacrifice depended on that person's wealth and level of responsibility in Israelite society. Those with more wealth and responsibility had to present a more valuable animal. The very poor needed only to bring a small quantity of flour. With some intentional sins, such as theft or cheating, restitution was possible. In this case, the guilty person would also bring a ram as a guilt offering along with the money to make restitution, plus 20 percent more. The money was returned to the offended party, a portion of the sin and guilt offering was burned, and the rest of the animal went to the priest.[1]

From this quick overview of the sacrificial system, we can draw several conclusions.

First, the sacrifices themselves did not automatically remove sin. If they did, everyone would have to offer a sacrifice of the same value. Instead, we see God create a sliding scale for the sin offering, which implies that it was not the sacrifice itself that God desired but costly repentance on the part of the sinner. God forgave sins then just as He does now, by grace through faith.

Second, we see that sin was to have no place among God's covenant people. As soon as a person became aware of having sinned, he or she was to immediately offer the needed sacrifice. God's people must be holy, set apart from deliberate wrongdoing.

Third, these sacrifices required the assistance of a priest. An entire tribe, the Levites (for whom Leviticus was named), was set aside for this purpose. Members of one clan from within this tribe, the descendants of Aaron (Moses' brother), were to serve as priests. Priests performed the sacrifices on behalf of the people, while the Levites assisted and maintained the Tabernacle.

Fourth, most of the sacrifices were voluntary and had nothing to do with forgiveness from sin. They were intended to give the Israelites a chance to celebrate the blessed experience of being part of God's covenant people. God gave the Israelites plenty of ways to say thank you. Finally, forgiveness came when an animal died as a substitute for the sinner. Sometimes, the person bringing the sacrifice actually put his hands on the head of the animal as a way of symbolizing this substitution. God wanted to show the Israelites that forgiveness had a price, but that the price would be paid by a substitute. In this way He prepared them to anticipate the sacrificial death of Jesus for the sins of the world.

Holy through Cleanliness

We find lots of laws in these books, laws dictating how to be clean, what clothes to wear, what seeds to plant, how to build houses, and hundreds of others. Why did God require all these of the Israelites? Some laws were given to protect them from physical harm. Isolating the carrier of a

How many Israelites were there in the wilderness?

If we take the number of men counted in the first census and add the corresponding number of women and children, two to three million Israelites left Egypt. This seems unlikely. That many people could easily overwhelm the Egyptian army, estimated at only twenty thousand. Stretched out in a line of march, the last Israelites would still have been crossing the Red Sea when those first in line were approaching Mount Sinai. Feeding that many people in the barren wilderness would have been next to impossible. About three million people were living in Canaan at that time, but Deuteronomy 7:1, 7, and 22 indicate considerably fewer numbers of Israelites.

Those who take the numbers literally point out that the Egyptians and Canaanites feared the Israelites, and also that God provided for the needs of the Israelites in the wilderness. Some contend that the numbers were exaggerated, not to deceive, but to emphasize how Israel was strengthened by God. Others argue that the term translated "thousand" may not mean one thousand, but a clan or fighting unit of undetermined size. One hundred thousand would then refer to one hundred units of soldiers. This approach, though not without its problems, reduces the total number of Israelites to less than four hundred thousand.

communicable skin disease helped prevent its spread. Avoiding sexual relations outside of marriage helped to prevent the spread of sexually transmitted diseases. Other laws protected the Israelites from a more serious disease: idolatry, the worship of other gods. Yahweh would not let them practice sorcery (Leviticus 19:26) because this was one of the religious practices of Israel's neighbors. By avoiding such things, the Israelites would be less likely to slip into false religions.

When obeyed, these laws made Israelite society a fair and orderly place to live. Marriages and families would be free of the damage caused by infidelity and immorality. By requiring all meat to be drained of blood, God reinforced the importance of life. God wanted to create a healthy society, one ruled by honesty, faithfulness, and justice. Such a society would make it easier for Israel to fulfill her appointed role.

Holy through Identity

Many laws were given to remind the Israelites of who they were and what God had commanded them to do. They were to wear tassels on their clothing (Numbers 15:37–40) and avoid mixing types of cloth in a garment, not because there was anything virtuous about tassels or bad about blended fabrics. Rather, such things would mark them as different. This is the primary reason for circumcision, the removal of the foreskin from the penis. It would be a constant reminder to every Israelite man—at his most mundane moment when relieving himself, and at his most intimate moment when having sexual intercourse—that he belonged to God. If the Israelites were to experience God's blessing and accomplish God's purpose, they had to remember they were a holy people.

Holy through Holy Days

Leviticus also describes special days the Israelites were to observe. Chief among these was the seventh day of the week, the Sabbath. The Israelites took this day off to recognize how God rested after creation and to remember their liberation from slavery in Egypt. By resting on the Sabbath, they also demonstrated their belief that God was in charge.

In their first month, corresponding to our early spring, they celebrated several holidays. On the fourteenth day of that month they observed Passover, and for the following week they celebrated the Festival of Unleavened Bread to recall their deliverance from Egypt (Leviticus 23:5–8). During this month they gave thanks for the beginning of the barley harvest at the Festival of First Fruits (23:9–14). Two months later they thanked God for the wheat harvest in the Feast of Weeks, later called Pentecost (23:15–21).

In their seventh month (our early fall), they observed the Feast of Trumpets with sacrifices and a holiday from work (Leviticus 23:23–25). A few days later, they observed the holiest day in the Jewish year, the Day of Atonement or Yom Kippur (23:27–32). On this day they confessed their sins, refrained from eating, and offered sacrifices for forgiveness from sin. Only on this one day each year would the high priest enter the Holy of Holies in the Tabernacle and sprinkle blood on the ark of the covenant. On this day, Israel experienced a clean slate before God, who responded to their repentance and faith with forgiveness.

Later that same month, the Israelites would celebrate the Feast of Tabernacles (Leviticus 23:39–43). This had the double purpose of expressing gratitude to God for that year's harvest and remembering how God had provided for them as they wandered in the wilderness after leaving Egypt. During this seven-day festival, the Jews would live in booths or huts to remind them of their travels through the wilderness.

God provided these occasions to remind them of what He had done and was doing on their behalf. The Israelites could then respond to God's faithfulness with gratitude and recommitment. On these holy days, God wanted them to experience both the joy and the responsibility of being His holy people.

Every seven years they were to plant no crops, but were to live on what had been grown the year before. The poor were allowed to eat what grew on its own. People who had sold themselves into slavery to pay a debt were to be freed. After seven such periods (forty-nine years), the Israelites were to observe the Jubilee year. Again the fields were left unplanted, Israelite slaves were to be freed, and all property was to be returned to the family to whom it originally belonged. The sabbatical and Jubilee years were meant to refresh the land so that it would remain fruitful, what modern farmers accomplish with fertilizer and crop rotation. Always concerned about fairness, God also wanted these years to restore equality to Israelite society.

107

Numbers: On the Way

Having been told what God expected of His holy people, the Israelites were almost ready to begin their journey to the Promised Land. First, however, God had to get them organized (Numbers 1:1—10:10). This process began with the counting of all the men, women, and children. Although everyone

Why was God so brutal to the Canaanites?

God's treatment of the Canaanites is one of the hardest things for modern readers to understand about the Bible. It may be helpful to think of God's command to totally destroy the Canaanites (sometimes called the "ban") as something like radical surgery on a cancerous tumor. Canaanite society was a contagious malignancy. Their worship included bestiality, widespread prostitution, homosexuality, and incest (read Leviticus 18). Still worse, they practiced child sacrifice (Leviticus 18:21). Allowed to continue, the Canaanites would have completely destroyed Israelite society as Moses warned in Deuteronomy 20:16–18. Given the important role Israel would play in reconciling the world to God, her spiritual health was very important!

God had tried to treat this disease in less radical ways. He had sent His witnesses among the Canaanites, men like Abraham, Isaac, and Jacob. He had given these idol worshippers hundreds of years to repent (read Genesis 15:16). They chose instead to reject His gracious offers and deny His rightful ownership of the land He had created. The cancer grew worse. Unless removed entirely, it would spread until it destroyed God's plan. Israel was only the scalpel, executing the will of the Divine Surgeon. If there had been some other way to preserve the Canaanites whom God had created and whom He loved, the surgery would never have taken place.

was counted, emphasis was placed on the men twenty years and older, probably because they would serve as soldiers in the army when fighting became necessary (Numbers 1:2–3). Next, God organized the Tabernacle. The process of counting the Levites, those who carried out the work of the Tabernacle, is described in great detail (Numbers 3–4). A description of the offerings given at the Tabernacle's dedication takes a whole chapter (Numbers 7). As a way of emphasizing His central role among the Israelites, God tells them to erect the Tabernacle right in the middle of their camp.

A Costly Detour

More than two years after leaving Egypt, on a signal from God, the Israelites left Sinai on their way to Canaan. Their trip, described in Numbers 10:11—25:18, got off to a rocky start and went downhill from there. Complaints about the menu and squabbles over leadership hinted at the dark days to follow. As the Israelites approached the border with Canaan, God instructed Moses to secretly send out twelve men to investigate the Promised Land and bring back a report (Numbers 13). The spies returned with a mixed message: The land was wonderful but the people living there were too powerful to defeat. This report threw the Israelites into a panic. They ignored the minority report of Caleb and Joshua, who reminded them that God was stronger than any enemy. Instead, they considered returning to Egypt. God angrily announced that because of their lack of faith, none of the Israelite adults would live to enter Canaan. The whole nation was condemned to wander in the wilderness until all these adults had died. Then their children and grandchildren would be allowed to enter, along with Caleb and Joshua.

Perhaps all the grumbling and dissension in the wilderness got the best of Moses. A few chapters later, even he disobeyed God (Numbers 20). Although his sin seems minor compared to all the great things he did, it was serious enough to keep him out of Canaan.

"Do Only What I Tell You"

After forty years of wandering in the wilderness, the new generation of

Israelites once again approached the border of Canaan and camped in the land of Moab. The king of Moab, fearful of these unwelcome guests, sought a way to dispose of them. He knew his army was powerless against them and that their strength came from their God. He also believed, like everyone in the ancient Near East, that words had the power to bring blessing or harm. If he could hire someone to curse the Israelites, they would be destroyed. So he sent messengers to Balaam, a well-known professional curser—like an ancient Near East "hit man"—to finish off the Israelites.

At first, Balaam refused to accept the job. Knowing something of Israel's God, he knew he could not succeed. Finally, after repeated and insistent requests from the king of Moab, and after receiving permission from Yahweh, Balaam went. "But do only what I tell you," God warned him (Numbers 22:20). As God so often does in the Bible, He worked with what the people understood. He used this view about the power of words to accomplish His purposes.

On the way to Moab, God again reminded Balaam to do only what He told him. When he arrived and looked over the Israelite camp from atop a nearby mountain, Balaam spoke, but instead of cursing the Israelites, he blessed them. The king of Moab was horrified and furious. This was the worst-case scenario, a complete disaster. Instead of destroying the Israelites, Balaam had made them more powerful. The king angrily dismissed this professional curser without paying him a nickel. God had taken what was meant to harm Israel, and turned it into blessing.

Finally, the time for wandering was over and the Israelites were ready to cross the Jordan (Numbers 26–36). Another census was taken, revealing that all the adults in the original census had died in the wilderness. Only Moses, Caleb, and Joshua remained from this older generation. At God's instructions, Moses appointed Joshua to succeed him, then provided final instructions about various matters pertaining to life in the new country.

Numbers is about failure: Israel's and Moses'. How much better if they had obeyed. They could have entered Canaan years earlier and avoided the trail of tears in the wilderness. But this sobering tale also demonstrates how God patiently transformed them into a holy people. It also provides an important warning about the dangers of disobedience and unbelief.

Deuteronomy: Pause to Remember and Recommit

If the material in Deuteronomy sounds familiar to you, there is a reason. You have read much of it before in Exodus, Leviticus, and Numbers, although in slightly different form.[2] God knew the Israelites needed to hear this message again. The adults who had stood at Mount Sinai had died in the wilderness; their children must hear it for themselves if they were to obey. Moses did not simply repeat what he had said before; he rearranged the material according to the six parts of an ancient treaty.

Reiterating the Covenant

The book opens by introducing the speaker (Deuteronomy 1:1–5), then briefly describes the relationship between the two parties (1:6—3:29). The biggest chunk of Deuteronomy tells the obligations of the covenant (chapters 4–26). The three other parts of an ancient treaty are also found in

10 Commandments	Main Concept	Passage in Deuteronomy
No gods before God	God as final authority	6–11
No idols	Proper worship	12
Respect God's name	Commitment to God	13:1—14:21
Observe the Sabbath	Honor God	14:22—16:17
Honor father and mother	Honor human authorities	16:18—18:22
Don't murder	Respect for human life	19:1—21:23
Don't commit adultery	Maintain purity	22:1—23:14
Don't steal	Value personal property	23:15—24:7
No false testimony	Maintain trust	24:8–16
Don't covet	Maintain individual rights	24:17—26:15[3]

Deuteronomy: a statement explaining where the treaty was to be stored and when it was to be read (27:2–3; 31:9–13, 24–26), a list of witnesses to the treaty (chapters 31–32), and the curses and blessings that would follow disobedience or obedience (chapter 28). Moses arranged the book this way to help the Israelites understand that they were in a covenant relationship with Yahweh, a relationship just as binding as one between two nations who sign a treaty.

Reiterating the Theme

Very possibly, the central part of Deuteronomy was meant to explain the Ten Commandments. Introduced in chapter 4, the commandments are restated in chapter 5, and the main concept of each is explained in chapters 6—26, as seen in the preceding chart.

Moses wanted the Israelites to understand that if they would love God with all their heart (Deuteronomy 6:4–5), they would prosper in the land God had promised to their forefathers, to Abraham, Isaac, and Jacob. But if they disobeyed, God would punish them severely and they would lose possession of that land. This theme—obedience brings blessing but disobedience brings disaster—echoes throughout the Historical Books that follow.

GOD'S GREAT PLAN IN LEVITICUS, NUMBERS, AND DEUTERONOMY

These three neglected books reveal much about God's ultimate plan for reconciliation. In them we see God working among His covenant people, preparing them for their part in the plan. In particular, He shows them the need for holiness expressed in love for God and love for one's neighbor. In the sacrificial system, God hints at the process by which He will ultimately remove the problem of human sin through the sacrifice of His Son on the cross.

These books also give a clue as to what life will be like when God's plan is finally accomplished. What was the highlight of human experience in the garden before sin entered? Fellowship with God. What was the worst thing about sin's effects? Loss of fellowship with God. The emphasis in these books about God's presence among His people—in the pillars of cloud and fire, the Tabernacle, and other ways—was meant to remind Israel and us that fellowship between God and humanity is at the heart of God's ultimate plan.

WHAT WE LEARN ABOUT GOD FROM LEVITICUS, NUMBERS, AND DEUTERONOMY

Over and over in the pages of these books, we are confronted with a holy God. As noted above, holy essentially means different, designated for a special purpose. Holy objects, like the table or lampstand in the Tabernacle, were set aside from other tables and lampstands. A holy nation, like the Israelites, had a purpose different than all other nations. Holy people, such as the priests and Levites, were chosen from the people to help them relate to a holy God.

God Is Set Apart

To say that God is holy means He is set apart from everything else. Although He made the universe, He is greater than the universe. Although He made us in His image, He is greater, more powerful, and more majestic than we can imagine. All the places where the Bible describes God in human terms are only figures of speech. He is not just a person, only larger; He is something quite different. He is too different, in fact, for us to completely understand.

God Is Perfect

God's holiness also implies that He is without sin. As Moses described Him in Deuteronomy 32:4, "He is the Rock, his works are perfect, and all his ways are just. A faithful God who does no wrong, upright and just is he." God's perfection is not only the absence of sin, but also something quite positive. Everything about Him is perfect. He loves perfectly, never with too much sentimentality and never for the wrong reasons. When He judges, He does so perfectly. He never disciplines selfishly or carelessly, but only for the good of the one being disciplined. All His characteristics are perfect and perfectly balanced. When God called Israel to be holy as He is holy, He had this sense in mind. They were to avoid sin and live balanced, whole lives.

God Hates Sin

One other aspect of God's holiness merits our attention. Not only does God's holiness mean that He refuses to tolerate sin, it also means that He will not tolerate the effects of sin. In other words, He both hates sin and what sin has done to His perfect creation. He hates sin so intensely, He can't stand its existence. His holy hatred has set in motion a plan to reverse sin's effects; He will not be content until His plan is accomplished.

Leviticus, Numbers, Deuteronomy at a Glance

Authorship: Traditionally, Moses
Date of writing: Mid 1400s or late 1200s B.C.
Date of events: Mid 1400s or late 1200s B.C.
Purposes:
1. To describe the history of Israel from Mount Sinai to the edge of the Promised Land
2. To describe the terms of the covenant between God and Israel
3. To demonstrate the importance of holy living

Form: Law and narrative
Part of God's plan:
1. To reveal more details of God's covenant with His people
2. To remind us of God's desire for fellowship with His people

Key element of God's character: Holiness

---

application questions

1. If God is totally unlike humanity, how can we possibly come to know Him?
2. What practical steps can you take to live as God's holy person, avoiding sin and seeking to live a balanced, wholesome life?
3. Why is living a holy life so difficult?

questions for study and discussion

1. Read Leviticus 1–7, 23, 25.
   a. What do the sacrifices reveal about God?
   b. What insights do chapters 1–7 provide into Israel's understanding of sin?
   c. What did God want to teach the Israelites through the holidays He designated?
2. Read Numbers 13–14, 20.
   a. Why did the Israelites refuse to listen to Caleb and Joshua?
   b. Why didn't God give these Israelites a second chance?
   c. Why was God so hard on Moses in Numbers 20?
3. Read Deuteronomy 4–6, 31–32.
   a. What evidence do you find in Deuteronomy 4–6 that God wanted the Israelites to obey from love, not duty?
   b. Why is Deuteronomy 6:4–5 one of the most important passages in the Bible?
   c. What do we learn about God from Deuteronomy 31–32?
4. What else can we learn about God's plan from these books?
5. What other characteristics of God do you see in these books?

endnotes

1. Some scholars suggest that these offerings were not for *any* unintended sin, but only for those sins that concerned the Tabernacle. That is, I would only be responsible if I accidentally broke the Tabernacle rules, like entering the Tabernacle when I was unclean. If this is the correct view, the average Israelite may never have been obligated to offer the sin or guilt offering.

2. In Greek, Deuteronomy means "Second Law."

3. Based in part on a chart found in Bill T. Arnold and Bryan E. Beyer, *Encountering the Old Testament: A Christian Survey* (Grand Rapids, Mich.: Baker, 1999), 147.

chapter ten

Obedience Brings Blessing
Joshua

SUGGESTIONS FOR READING JOSHUA

Since the book of Joshua is almost entirely narrative, read this material against the backdrop of its cultural and historical context. The abundant bloodshed might trouble the modern reader but would not have offended a person living in the ancient Near East. War, bloodshed, and violence in the name of the gods was an accepted part of life. For God to communicate His truth in a way the ancient world could understand, He used not only their language, but their culture as well.

The book of Joshua continues the story we find in the Pentateuch, the story of the Israelites. Read the events of this book in light of the bigger story of Israel's history and God's ultimate plan for redemption. Joshua plays a central role in the book that bears his name, but he is not the central character. Although Joshua illustrates good lessons on leadership and faithfulness, the real hero of this book is God.

INTRODUCTION

After trudging through the legal passages in Exodus, Leviticus, Numbers, and Deuteronomy, the thrilling narratives of Joshua make us feel as if we're entering our own Promised Land. The book of Joshua continues the history of the Israelites by describing how they conquered and settled in the land of Canaan. Through these narratives, we see God at work accomplishing His plan.

OVERVIEW

With the book of Joshua we enter the category of the Old Testament known as Historical Books. This category in our English Bibles includes Joshua, Judges, Ruth, 1 and 2 Samuel, 1 and 2 Kings, 1 and 2 Chronicles, Ezra, Nehemiah, and Esther. These books relate about eight hundred years of Israel's history, from their entry into Canaan until after their return from exile in Babylon.

Although historical, these books do not tell history the way we are used to hearing it. While we expect history to be impartial, the authors who wrote

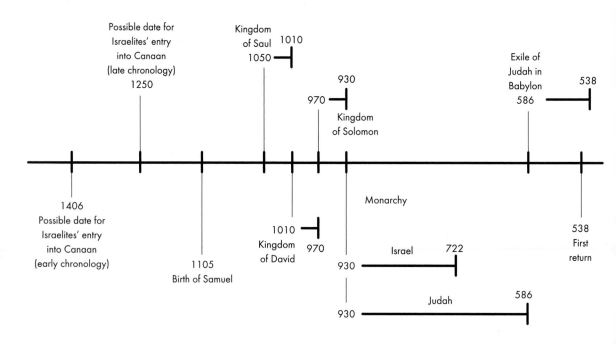

Joshua
Unless otherwise noted, all dates are B.C.

MAP 6 Early Israelite Settlement in Canaan

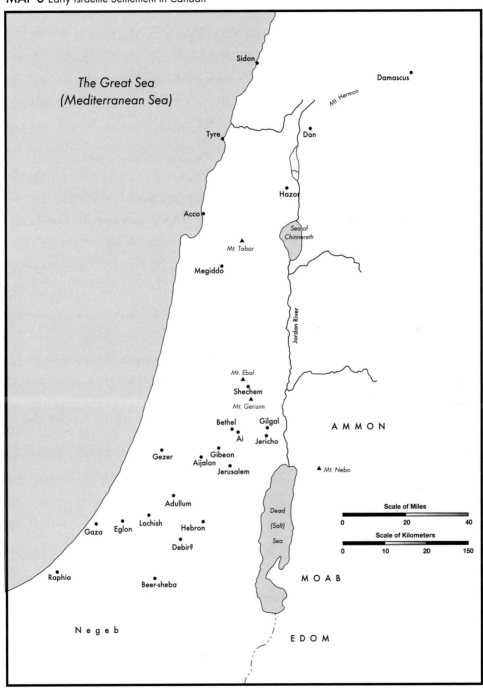

*The Great Sea
(Mediterranean Sea)*

Sidon

Damascus

Mt. Hermon

Tyre

Dan

Hazor

Acco

Sea of
Chinnereth

Mt. Tabor

Megiddo

Jordan River

Mt. Ebal

Shechem

Mt. Gerizim

Bethel

Gilgal

Ai

Jericho

AMMON

Gezer

Gibeon

Aijalon

Jerusalem

Mt. Nebo

Adullum

Dead
(Salt)
Sea

Gaza

Eglon

Lachish

Hebron

Debir?

Raphia

Beer-sheba

MOAB

Negeb

EDOM

Scale of Miles

0   20   40

Scale of Kilometers

0   10   20   150

Why was Achan's whole family killed?

Many find it hard to understand why Achan's family would have to die along with him. According to one early version of this story found in a very early translation of the Old Testament known as the Septuagint, they didn't; only Achan died for his sins.

If Achan's whole family was killed, it may have been for their own guilt, since it would have been hard for him to hide the loot under his tent floor without the family knowing about it. Another reason why they may have died concerns the group culture of the ancient Near East. Unlike the individual orientation of Western culture, group cultures see a person primarily as a member of some collection of people. Every action on the part of that person is seen to affect everyone in that group; an action this serious would mean dire consequences for everyone involved.

When Achan stole the objects, he did so aware that his guilt, if discovered, would be shared by all in his family—even his children. Every Israelite who heard of this sin would have expected the whole family to be punished and would have been relieved that all the Israelites had been spared further punishment.

these books were very partial. They were wholeheartedly committed to God and wrote for theological reasons. These books are more like sermons than newspaper reports: They tell what happened, but for the purpose of teaching about God and His plan. In fact, the Jewish people do not refer to these books as historical, but as the Former Prophets.[1] They understood that these books had a message from God, just as much as Isaiah, Jeremiah, Ezekiel, Daniel, and the Minor Prophets, which they called the Latter Prophets.

The Obedience Connection

One of the central lessons of all the Historical Books can be expressed this way: Obedience brings blessing; disobedience brings disaster. This was one of the major themes of Deuteronomy, Moses' farewell sermon to the Israelites. Having heard this sermon, the Historical Books provide the illustrations. We see the positive results of obedience in Joshua as the Israelites experience one victory after another. We see the negative side in Judges as the disobedient Israelites spiral downward from one catastrophe to another.

The strong connection between obedience and success resonates throughout the book of Joshua. Joshua was told he would triumph if he carefully obeyed God's Law (Joshua 1:7–8). Only after the Israelites were circumcised, symbolizing their commitment to God, could they begin the battle (5:1–12). Victory over Jericho came because they obeyed; defeat to Ai resulted from disobedience (chapters 6–7). Initial victories were followed by a ceremony in which the Israelites renewed their covenant with God (8:30–35). Because the Israelites understood the connection between obedience and blessing, they reacted quickly when they saw what they thought was disobedience (chapter 22).

Although this moral provides an important theme in the book of Joshua, the book's purpose goes beyond just illustrating the point. More than anything, the book was written to show how God kept His promise to bring Israel to the land of Canaan. Joshua possessed great skills as a general and the Israelites were obedient, but these were only tools in God's hands. Israel defeated the Canaanites and took possession of their land because God gave the land to them, as He had promised. God always keeps His promises.

Moses' successor, Joshua, is probably responsible for much of the material in the book that bears his name. This would account for the book's vivid detail and is supported by Joshua 24:26, which describes Joshua recording "these things" in a book. Joshua was probably not responsible for its final form. The phrase "until this day" occurs several times and implies a date later than Joshua. At one point, the author quotes Joshua as his words were recorded in the lost Book of Jashar (Joshua 10:13). If Joshua wrote the book, his words would not need to be quoted from another source. The final form of the book was probably completed prior to Solomon's day. By that time Jerusalem was no longer a Jebusite city (18:16) and the town of Gezer had become Israel's property, something not yet true in the book of Joshua (read Joshua 16:10; 1 Kings 9:16).

Victory through God Alone

Every portion of the book of Joshua reinforces the truth that obedience brings blessing but disobedience brings disaster. The theme of God's pep talk to Joshua (Joshua 1:1–9) and the substance of what the spies learned in Jericho (2:9–11, 24) was the same: God alone will bring the victory. When He brought the Israelites out of Egypt, Yahweh deliberately backed them up against the Red Sea so He could demonstrate His power. God led their children to the bank of the Jordan River at flood season when the waters were as much as a mile wide. He could have led them into Canaan from the south where there would have been no river to cross. He could have brought them to the Jordan at another time of the year when the river is more like a small creek. He chose instead to work another miracle so this generation could see the power of God for themselves.

Before the battle of Jericho, Joshua met the "commander of the army of the LORD," who reinforced that victory would come not because of Israel's power, but because God would fight on Israel's side (Joshua 5:13–15). God proposed the strange strategy of marching around Jericho and shouting because it would demonstrate that victory comes from God alone (Joshua 6:1–27).

So long as the Israelites obeyed, God continued to work miracles on their behalf. Disobedience, such as that described in Joshua 7, brought a halt to God's help. Achan had stolen what belonged to God and hid it under the floor of his tent. For that reason, the little town of Ai was able to defeat the much larger army of Israel. When the thief was caught and punished, God again brought victory.

Scattered throughout the book are clear indications that the victory belonged not to Israel, but to God. For example, after God sent large hailstones down on Israel's fleeing enemy, Joshua said that "more of them died from the hailstones than were killed by the swords of the Israelites" (Joshua 10:11). The defeat of the southern coalition is summarized this way: "All these kings and their lands Joshua conquered in one campaign, because the LORD, the God of Israel, fought for Israel" (10:42).

Since this book was written to show how God kept His promise to give Israel the land, several chapters are devoted to the distribution of the land among the tribes (Joshua 13–21). This emphasis resounds in the closing verses of this section:

> So the LORD gave Israel all the land he had sworn to give their forefathers, and they took possession of it and settled there. The LORD gave them rest on every side, just as he had sworn to their forefathers. Not one of their enemies withstood them; the LORD handed all their enemies over to them. Not one of all the LORD's good promises to the house of Israel failed; every one was fulfilled.
>
> Joshua 21:43–45

GOD'S GREAT PLAN IN JOSHUA

After calling Abraham, caring for his descendants in Canaan, rescuing them from Egypt, establishing them as a nation with a constitution at Mount Sinai, and guiding them through the wilderness, the next step in God's plan was to provide the Israelites with a land of their own. He had made this promise to Abraham several times and had reaffirmed this promise to his descendants. The book of Joshua describes the fulfillment of that promise.

Chosen to Model

Aside from the obvious reason that the Israelites needed a place to live, why was the land so important to God's plan? First, the land demonstrated that they were God's people like a wedding ring demonstrates that someone is married. Being given the land demonstrated that God favored them. Later, after many years of disobeying God, they were forced to leave the land and go into exile in Babylon. When restored to the land in the post-exilic period, the Israelites were like "men who dreamed" (Psalm 126:1). The land symbolized their having been chosen to carry out God's plan.

The land was important to God's plan for a second reason. It was to be the stage on which God would display His model community. Here the covenant people were to exhibit the joys of being in a relationship with God, the relationship God intended for all people. Here Israel was to illustrate the peace, justice, and rest that would prevail when God was present. The light of Israel's example was to draw the darkened nations into fellowship with God.[2] Unfortunately, Israel's light glimmered only faintly and briefly before the stage grew dark.

The fulfillment of this promise furthered God's plan in at least two more ways. First, the treatment of the Canaanites demonstrated to Israel and to everyone watching that God would not tolerate sin. His plan called for sin's removal, both from within individuals and from within society. Because the Canaanites persisted in their terrible depravity, God removed them as an act of mercy toward the rest of humanity. Second, having seen God keep His promise to give them the land, the Israelites were given greater confidence that God would accomplish His planned reconciliation of the world. He had proven himself to be not only a promise-making but a promise-keeping God.

WHAT WE LEARN ABOUT GOD FROM JOSHUA

From Abraham's life we learned of God, the promise maker. The experiences of his offspring as recorded in the book of Joshua show us God, the promise keeper. As Abraham wandered over this land, God repeatedly assured him that one day all this would belong to his descendants. Many obstacles intervened to prevent this from happening. Famine drove his offspring from the land, and slavery in Egypt kept them away. Once freed from Egypt, the Israelites' fear and disobedience blocked their entrance and

forced them to wander for forty years. The stronger inhabitants of the land—
the Canaanites, Jebusites, and all the other "ites"—were not going to
surrender their homes and fields without a fight to the death. In spite of all
these obstacles, God kept His word. He preserved the Israelites in distress,
rescued them from slavery, and provided for them in the wilderness. When
they finally crossed the Jordan, their enemies disappeared like fallen leaves in
a gust of wind. God had kept His promise.

Motivated by Love

What does this mean for us? First, it demonstrates God's tremendous
power. If He was able to accomplish His will against all odds, what can't He
do? What situations do we face that are too big for God to handle? A promise-
keeping God gives us reason for confidence and hope. Sometimes we keep a
promise only from a sense of obligation, not out of love. We show up for
work not because we love our boss, but because we feel a sense of duty.
When God kept His promise, He was fulfilling the obligation He had
voluntarily assumed. But what really motivated God to keep His word was
not grudging duty, but love for Abraham, his descendants, and all the world.
As Moses told the Israelites, "It was because the LORD loved you and kept the
oath he swore to your forefathers that he brought you out with a mighty hand
and redeemed you from the land of slavery" (Deuteronomy 7:8).

Committed to Reconciliation

Earlier we saw that a promise-making God puts a strong premium on faith.
If so, then a promise-keeping God rewards faith. Sometimes following God
means believing in the face of suffering, disappointment, and unanswered
prayer. This example of promise keeping reminds us that such suffering does
not go unnoticed by God. He honors faith. We must continue to depend on
Him when faith is hard to come by, knowing that as God came through for the
Israelites, He will keep the promises He has made to us.

Even more, He will accomplish His plan. Because He kept His promise to
Israel, we can be assured He will keep His promise to undo the effects of sin.

As the land symbolized God's favor to Israel, it also represents a guarantee that one day God will reconcile the world to himself.

Joshua at a Glance

Authorship: Anonymous, although accepting Joshua as the author would explain much about the book, including the vivid details

Date of writing: Although much of the book comes from eyewitness accounts, the finished version may not have been completed until two hundred years later.

Date of events: Either the end of the 1400s and beginning of the 1300s or the end of the 1200s B.C.

Purpose: To show that God kept His promise to bring the Israelites into the land of Canaan

Form: Primarily narrative

Part of God's plan:
1. To symbolize God's selection of Israel as His covenant people by giving them the Promised Land
2. To provide a stage on which God could demonstrate the joys of covenant relationship
3. To further guarantee the fulfillment of God's ultimate plan

Key element of God's character: Promise keeper

application questions

1. What problems are you facing that make it difficult to exercise your faith? How does knowing God as promise keeper encourage you?
2. What other promises has God given us?
3. Contemplate God's motives in making and keeping His promises. What do they teach us about God?

questions for study and discussion

1. Read Joshua 1–11.

   a. What does it say about God that He rescued Rahab, included her in His people, and even allowed her to be part of Jesus' family line (Matthew 1:5)?

   b. Aside from the death of Achan's family, what other examples of group identity can you see operating in this book?

   c. Why did God command the Israelites to be circumcised after they crossed the Jordan River and entered enemy territory, rather than before?

   d. Find the location of Gibeon on a map. Why did the Israelites allow themselves to be tricked into making a covenant with the Gibeonites (Joshua 9)? What does it say about that culture and the Israelites that they kept their word to the Gibeonites (Joshua 10)?

2. Read Joshua 23–24.

   a. In our previous discussion of Deuteronomy, we saw the six parts of an ancient covenant. Can you find these six parts in Joshua 24?

   b. Find specific passages in these two chapters that demonstrate how

      1. Obedience brings blessing but disobedience brings disaster.

      2. Victory came because God kept His promise.

3. What else can we learn about God's plan from this book?

4. What other characteristics of God do you see in this book?

endnotes

1. The Former Prophets include the books of Joshua, 1 and 2 Samuel, and 1 and 2 Kings. The other Historical Books are located in the third section of the Hebrew Bible, the Writings.

2. "Listen to me, my people; hear me, my nation. The law will go out from me; my justice will become a light to the nations" (Isaiah 51:4).

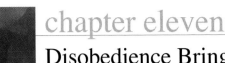

chapter eleven

Disobedience Brings Disaster—Part 1
Judges and Ruth

SUGGESTIONS FOR READING JUDGES AND RUTH

As with earlier narrative passages, keep the literary and historical contexts in mind. People do strange things in these books, like cut off the big toes of their enemies. God even acts in unusual ways, allowing ungodly behavior to go unpunished. By reading these stories against their cultural and historical background, you can avoid many misunderstandings.

These stories were not provided to show us how to live. Although Gideon discovered God's will by putting out a wool fleece, this was an example of doubt that God tolerated, not an example of faith to be copied. Instead, read these stories in light of Israel's history and God's ultimate plan of reconciliation. Judges has a few heroes, such as Deborah, but the real hero of these books is God. The truly helpful lessons are to be learned from examining His character.

INTRODUCTION

The book of Joshua illustrates the first part of the motto: obedience brings blessing. The book of Judges illustrates the second, for Israel's disobedience brought one disaster after another. Hope for God's plan was not completely extinguished, however, but continued to glow in the hearts of godly individuals such as Ruth and Boaz.

OVERVIEW OF JUDGES

We are not told who wrote this book, although many have assumed it to be the prophet Samuel. If not written by him, it was probably written during his lifetime due to the repeated phrase "in those days Israel had no king" and the fact that the Jebusites still controlled Jerusalem (Judges 1:21), which they ceased to do under King David. Whoever wrote the book of Judges wanted to make it clear that the disastrous decades following Joshua's death were not God's fault, but the fault of the Israelites. God had proven His ability to handle any enemy. The blame for the Israelites' repeated failures and increasing chaos rested solely in their laps.

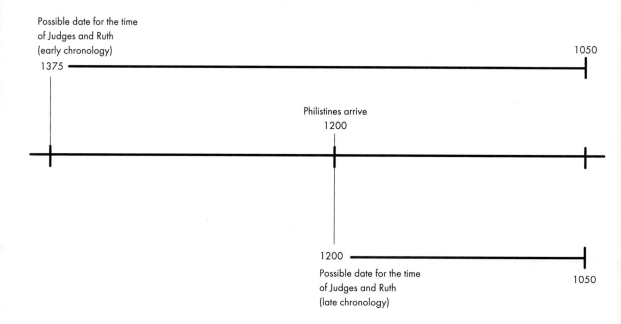

Possible date for the time
of Judges and Ruth
(early chronology)

1375 ———————————————————————————— 1050

Philistines arrive
1200

1200 ———————————— 1050

Possible date for the time
of Judges and Ruth
(late chronology)

Judges and Ruth
Unless otherwise noted, all dates are B.C.

Who were all these nations and why were they fighting Israel?

The Canaanites battled by Deborah (Judges 4) were the original inhabitants of the Promised Land. Joshua fought them in his northern campaign (Joshua 11) but did not eliminate them. Those who remained tried to reassert themselves against the struggling Israelites during the early period of the judges.

The Canaanites were only one of several nationalities living in this land. The Philistines (Judges 13–16) arrived in the 1200s from the area around Greece. A sea-going people, they settled in cities on the Mediterranean Sea coast. Although the term "philistine" is used today to describe a smug, unenlightened ignoramus, the Philistines were much more cultured and sophisticated than the Israelites.

Israel also faced opposition from neighboring nations. Aram Naharaim (Judges 3:7–11) was located northeast of Canaan around Damascus. The Moabites (Judges 3:12–30) lived southeast of Canaan and were descendants of Abraham's nephew, Lot (Genesis 19). Gideon fought the Midianites (Judges 6–8), who were related to the Israelites through one of Abraham's wives (Genesis 25). The Ammonites, also descended from Lot (Genesis 19), lived east of Canaan, and were defeated by Jephthah (Judges 11:6–12:7).

Things started out well. The Israelites knew they must complete the conquest Joshua began. They even asked God how to do it and then faithfully obeyed His instructions with good success (Judges 1:1–18). Eventually, they met enemies too tough to dislodge. At this point we don't see them asking God why. Rather, they accepted these mediocre results and enslaved the enemies instead (1:19–36). In the opening verses of Judges 2,

131

we learn why they were growing increasingly weak. They had disobeyed God's instructions and were beginning to pay the consequences (2:1–5), consequences summarized in Judges 2:10–23. Their disobedience would bring disaster.

Judges: Good and Bad

As an act of compassion, God still helped them by sending "judges." When you hear this term, don't imagine a serious-looking figure wearing a black robe and sitting behind a tall desk in a courtroom. Some judges did settle disputes among the Israelites, but their main job was to deliver the Israelites from oppression by other nations. They enforced God's justice by rescuing His people from foreign persecution.

Six major judges are described in this book: Othniel (Judges 3:7–11), Ehud (Judges 3:12–30), Deborah (Judges 4–5), Gideon (Judges 6–8), Jephthah (Judges 10:6—12:7), and Samson (Judges 13–16). The book also mentions several minor judges. Unlike Joshua, probably none of the judges ruled all twelve tribes of Israel. Their authority was limited to just a portion of the country.

Judges 3:7–11 provides a good example of the cycle of events that made it necessary for God to send the judges. After stating that "the Israelites did evil in the eyes of the LORD" (Judges 3:7), the author then describes specific evils. As a result of their disobedience, God became angry and "sold them into the hands of" some enemy, in this case, "Cushan-Rishathaim king of Aram Naharaim, to whom the Israelites were subject for eight years" (3:8). When the Israelites "cried out to the LORD, he raised up for them a deliverer," in this case, Othniel, "who saved them" (3:9). With his success, "the land had peace for forty years" until that judge died. Then Israel turned from God and the pattern was repeated: sin, oppression, an appeal to God, rescue, peace, sin, oppression, and so forth.

Spiraling Downward

Not only do we see this repeated pattern, we also notice a deterioration in the quality of the judges. The author has only positive things to say about

Othniel, Ehud, and Deborah. Gideon began well, although somewhat fearfully. By the time we leave him, however, he has led the Israelites into sin. He took an offering from his followers and used the gold to make an ephod, a part of the priests' wardrobe. Eventually, his ephod was worshiped by the Israelites. At first an idol smasher (Judges 6:27), in the end, Gideon became an idol maker (8:27).

From this point on, the major judges grew increasingly worse. God called Jephthah to rescue His people from the Ammonites (Judges 11:29). But Jephthah made a foolish vow. He promised God he would sacrifice the first thing that came out of his house if he were successful in battle (11:30–31). He had to know this might be his only child, a daughter, but apparently he assumed Yahweh was like the neighboring gods who approved of human sacrifice. When his daughter stepped outdoors to welcome her victorious father, her doom was sealed. Rather than realizing the error of his vow and breaking it—which, in this case, would have been God's will—he sacrificed her (11:34–40).[1]

The last of the major judges was the worst. Although Samson's miraculous birth signaled a great future (Judges 13), his conceit and lack of self-control spoiled everything (14:1 — 16:23). He was successful in battle, but never rescued Israel from Philistine oppression. In the end, he died a tragic death at his own hands.

The author adds two more stories that picture the terrible state into which the Israelites had fallen. The first describes how the tribe of Dan, under the direction of Moses' own descendants, set up a shrine and worshiped idols instead of Yahweh. The second describes a civil war among the Israelites. Twice within this section, the author explains the reason for the internal chaos: "In those days Israel had no king; everyone did as he saw fit" (Judges 18:1; 21:25). God allowed Israel's disobedience—He never forces us to obey—but must have grieved over how far the Israelites had fallen.

OVERVIEW OF RUTH

While Israel was disobediently spiraling downward toward disaster, God was still at work in the lives of righteous individuals. The book of Ruth describes the family of Elimelech, forced by famine to leave its hometown of Bethlehem and travel to the neighboring country of Moab. While there, Elimelech's two sons married Moabite women. Shortly after, Elimelech and his two sons died, leaving behind three widows. Naomi, Elimelech's wife, encouraged her two young daughters-in-law to return to their families. There they could remarry and start again. One did, but the other insisted on returning to Israel with her mother-in-law. Whether out of love for Naomi, devotion to Yahweh, or both, Ruth turned her back on her homeland and gods, and accompanied Naomi to Bethlehem.

Kinsman-Redeemer

They arrived just as the barley harvest was beginning in mid-spring. The Law permitted the poor to find food by gleaning, following the workers who were harvesting the crop and gathering what they left behind.[2] Ruth went to glean in a field that, unknown to her, belonged to Boaz, one of Naomi's relatives. Boaz noticed her and learned that she was the woman from Moab whom everyone was talking about. He was so moved by her commitment to Naomi that he gave her special privileges among the gleaners. When she returned home that evening, she carried an enormous amount of barley, perhaps thirty to fifty pounds. No wonder Naomi wanted to know in whose field she had gleaned that day! When she learned that Ruth's bounty was because of Boaz, she recognized the hand of God at work. He was one of their kinsman-redeemers.

God had created the role of the kinsman-redeemer to look after the interests of clan members. If someone in the clan had been murdered, the kinsman-redeemer was to avenge the death. When the clan lost property, this person was to help reclaim it. Naomi had owned a field but probably had sold it before leaving for Moab. Israelite law permitted someone to repurchase the property, but Naomi could not afford to do so. If she could find a kinsman-redeemer to buy back her field for her, her financial problems would be solved. Even more important, the purchase of the field meant Boaz would get Ruth as his wife. The firstborn son from that marriage would legally continue Elimelech's family line, which would otherwise die out. Such a marriage was not without its costs to Boaz. Beyond the cost of the field, if Ruth's son became his only surviving heir, all of Boaz's property would transfer from his family to Elimelech's.

To discover if Boaz was willing to take these risks and marry Ruth, Naomi sent Ruth to where he was spending the night. There she was to offer herself to Boaz in marriage. She took a great risk in going to him at that place, at that time of night, and for that reason, but Boaz honored her boldness by accepting her offer. She could have sought a younger or richer husband, but instead obeyed Naomi.

Faithfulness Honored

One problem remained. There was another kinsman-redeemer who had first rights to the land. The next day in court, Boaz spoke to this man. He eagerly agreed to buy the field, since it belonged to two widows. Once they died, the field would become part of his permanent property. Then Boaz reminded him that along with the land came the obligation to marry Ruth and continue Elimelech's family line. That changed everything. The field would not belong to his family; it would belong to Elimelech's descendants. Under these terms, he wanted out of the deal.

The last obstacle removed, Boaz bought Naomi's property and married Ruth. Throughout this experience, Boaz and Ruth behaved honorably and righteously. Their son, Obed, grew up to become the father of Jesse, who became the father of King David. While the nation of Israel struggled with the consequences of disobedience, a poor foreign widow, because of her faithfulness to God and others, was given a tremendous honor. She became the great-grandmother of Israel's greatest king and an ancestor of Jesus, through whom God would accomplish His ultimate plan (Matthew 1:5).

GOD'S GREAT PLAN IN JUDGES AND RUTH

The book of Judges reminds us that sin is a huge problem. Up to this point we have seen many examples of sin's destructive power. From the Garden of Eden, Cain and Abel, the Tower of Babel, Joseph's brothers, the golden calf, and forty years of unnecessary wandering in the desert, we have seen plenty of sin. However, there is something horrible about sin as we meet it in Judges. Perhaps it is the loss of the success the Israelites enjoyed under Joshua, or the needless bloodshed, or the civil war among God's people, but this book brings home the horror of sin in graphic detail. If we wonder whether God really needed to solve the problem of sin, the book of Judges removes all doubt.

Judges and Ruth also help us better understand the nature of God's plan. From its absence in Judges and its presence in Ruth, we learn the importance of righteousness for God's covenant people. We also better understand God's promise to Abraham that all nations would be blessed through his descendants. By watching how God blessed a simple foreign woman, we begin to see the glorious future God has in store for the whole world.

WHAT WE LEARN ABOUT GOD FROM JUDGES AND RUTH

God Is Just

Through the tragedy of Judges and the simple beauty of Ruth, we see God's justice at work in several ways. As a righteous judge, He refused to tolerate the wickedness of His people; they had to be punished. That their punishment came as the consequence of their own disobedience is just another example of God's justice.

God's justice also means He insists that people treat each other fairly. He appointed judges whose role was primarily to deliver His people from oppression, even though the Israelites brought this oppression on themselves. God built this fairness into the Law by providing for the poor and creating the role of kinsman-redeemer.

God Is Patient

These books also demonstrate God's patience with His people. He had warned them many times that if they disobeyed, they would be thrown out of the land. But year after year, God disciplined them, gave them time to repent, and sent judges to rescue them, even though He knew their return would be only temporary. For what they had done, God had every right to send the severe judgment He had promised. Instead, He patiently worked with them over and over again.

Judges and Ruth at a Glance

Authorship: Anonymous

Date of writing: Probably in the very early years of the monarchy

Date of events: Either about 1375–1050 B.C. or about 1200–1050 B.C., depending on the date of the Exodus

Purposes:

1. To explain this disastrous period in Israel's history (Judges)
2. To describe God's faithfulness to righteous individuals (Ruth)

Form: Narrative

Part of God's plan: To show how disobedience would disrupt God's plan, but could not destroy it; God continued to bless faithful people

Key elements of God's character: Justice, patience

---

application questions

1. What other examples of God's justice and patience can you see in these books?
2. How does God balance His justice with His patience?
3. Can you think of ways God has been patient with you?

questions for study and discussion

1. Read Judges 1–4.

   a. How could the Israelites have fallen so far so fast?

   b. Why didn't God appoint another leader like Joshua?

2. Read Judges 6–7. Why did God want Gideon to have such a small army?

3. Read Judges 13–16.

   a. Why was Samson such a failure?

   b. Does Samson's death at his own hand mean that God approves of suicide? Why or why not?

4. Read Ruth.

   a. Identify the ways Ruth lived out the truth of her words to Naomi in 3:5.

   b. Why did the women say, "Naomi has a son" (4:17)?

   c. Why might God have included this book in the Bible?

5. What else can we learn about God's plan from these books?

6. What other characteristics of God do you see in these books?

endnotes

1. Some scholars take the view that Jephthah did not kill his daughter but dedicated her to God's service for life.

2. The laws on gleaning can be found in Leviticus 19:9; 23:22; and Deuteronomy 24:19–21.

chapter twelve

Order Out of Chaos
1 and 2 Samuel

SUGGESTIONS FOR READING 1 AND 2 SAMUEL

Narrative passages predominate in 1 and 2 Samuel. Read these stories in their historical context, remembering that God was accommodating himself to that time and culture. Ancient histories like this one do not always record events in strict chronological order. The author of 1 and 2 Samuel appears to sometimes rearrange events in order to convey his point.

Also read these stories in their literary context. Because these books contain some of the more familiar material in the Old Testament (e.g., David and Goliath), people tend to read these stories out of context, isolated from their place in the bigger story of Israel and God's great plan. Samuel and David are heroic figures, but they are not given to us as role models. They are only great when they carry out God's sovereign will. The heavenly King is the only real hero in these books.

INTRODUCTION

These books begin as the book of Judges ends, with chaos and catastrophe caused by Israel's disobedience. As they end, God has reintroduced order through the work of men like Samuel and David. Along the way, 1 and 2 Samuel mark a significant step forward in God's plan.

OVERVIEW

If only for the literary beauty and clear style of 1 and 2 Samuel, this two-part history of early Israel deserves a careful reading. As with all the Historical Books in the Old Testament, the writer was more interested in telling what God was doing than in just relating facts. The historical facts are here, but they are arranged to describe how God transformed Israel from squabbling, disorganized tribes to one nation under His chosen king, David.

Originally one book, 1 and 2 Samuel were divided for convenience. Nowhere in the books is the author identified. Some scholars maintain Samuel wrote them because he plays such an important role in their

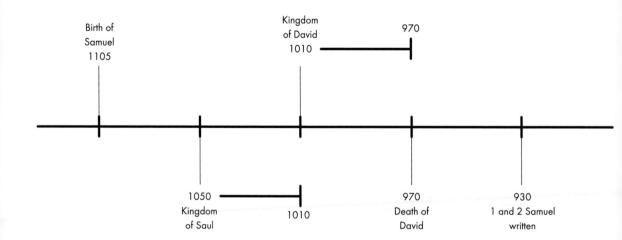

Birth of
Samuel
1105

Kingdom
of David
1010

970

1050
Kingdom
of Saul

1010

970
Death of
David

930
1 and 2 Samuel
written

1 and 2 Samuel
Unless otherwise noted, all dates are B.C.

Why did God allow Israel to have a king?

Some passages make it sound as if the Israelites were wrong to ask for a king and that God only reluctantly gave them what they asked for. In other passages, having a king sounds like God's idea. Israel did ask for a king because they feared the Philistines and wanted to be like the neighboring nations that were ruled by monarchs. In spite of Samuel's warning (1 Samuel 8:10–18), they persisted in their request. But having a king was also God's plan for them. He had talked about it years before in Deuteronomy. God planned to use David and other kings to help accomplish His purposes. Many psalms celebrate the earthly king as God's representative.

If having a king was God's idea, why was He so upset with the Israelites for asking for a king? Apparently, God disapproved of their motives. What they wanted was someone who could deliver them whenever they were in trouble. This sounds harmless, but it falls short of God's ideal. Their troubles had come because of disobedience; they wanted relief from their difficulties without solving the real problem. That is like taking an aspirin to deal with a headache caused by a brain tumor.

chapters. Samuel might have kept records that were later used as sources, but he could not have written the books because they describe events that occurred after his death. First and 2 Samuel were probably written sometime after 930 B.C. First Samuel 27:6 mentions that the town of Ziklag belonged to the kings of Judah. This description only makes sense well after Israel split into the Northern Kingdom (called Israel) and the Southern Kingdom (Judah), a split which occurred about 930 B.C.

How could an evil spirit come from the Lord? (1 Samuel 16:14–23)

As a way of recognizing God's superiority to all other gods and humans, the Israelites sometimes described God as causing something when He only allowed it to occur. We saw an illustration of this in Exodus. God was said to harden Pharaoh's heart when really Pharaoh himself was to blame. This may be the case here. God allowed this "evil spirit" to come to Saul; He did not send it.

Some have understood the "evil spirit" to be a demon, an evil supernatural being. Others suggest Saul had a mental illness that included paranoia. Either way, Saul brought this suffering on himself by his disobedience.

The Rocky Road to Monarchy

The opening seven chapters of 1 Samuel describe the rocky transition from the period of the judges to the monarchy. Overseeing this transition was the man for whom these books are named, a man who blended the roles of judge, prophet, and priest: Samuel. His miraculous birth, his dedication to the service of the Lord, and God's unusual call on his life reveal a unique role for this young man. According to the closing verses of 1 Samuel 3, a powerful prophet had come to all Israel.

Samuel arrived just in time. In a chapter that sounds like it could have come out of the book of Judges, the Philistines defeated Israel in a devastating battle (1 Samuel 4). Worse than the deaths of the high priest and his two sons was the capture of the ark of the covenant by the Philistines. The ark, which symbolized God's presence, had been taken by the enemy. Had God failed?

First Samuel 5 and 6 make it clear that the Israelites, not God, had failed. He withdrew His protection to show Israel His displeasure with their disobedience. God also showed the Philistines He was no one to mess with. Before long, they were eager to return the ark. It was not returned to the

Tabernacle at Shiloh; perhaps the Philistines had destroyed the Tabernacle. Instead, it was brought to the little town of Kiriath Jearim, where it stayed for about twenty years. The symbol of God's presence had returned to Israel but was not yet in its rightful home.

When the Israelites saw that Samuel was growing old and his own sons were not suitable replacements, they decided they needed a king to lead them. Samuel protested but they persisted; eventually, God instructed Samuel to give them a king.

Saul: Portrait of Failure

The narrative now shifts from Samuel to Saul, a tall, shy young man with great potential (1 Samuel 9–15). God instructed Samuel to anoint this man as Israel's first king. Although initially successful, Saul soon showed the weakness of character that would destroy him. In 1 Samuel 13, with the Philistines again threatening to attack, Saul panicked and offered sacrifices before battle. To us this seems insignificant, hardly worth the scathing rebuke he received when Samuel arrived. But Samuel had been late on purpose. God

Why did God strike Uzzah dead? (2 Samuel 6)

Uzzah's death at God's hand seems terribly unfair. After all, he was only trying to help, wasn't he? In fact, God had demonstrated considerable patience with Uzzah and his family. This "help" was likely the last straw in a long history of the wrong attitude toward God's holiness. The Law clearly specified that the ark should have been carried on poles supported by priests. Putting it on a cart demonstrated disregard for God's instructions. Although Uzzah's death was tragic, it served as an important reminder to all, including David, that God must be treated with deep respect and obedience. Such a lesson was needed at this important moment in Israel's history.

was testing Saul to see if he would rely on his own strength or on God's. Saul tried to have it both ways: He offered the sacrifices to win God's help, but because he was losing military advantage he disobeyed Samuel's instructions to wait. God is never pleased with behavior like this, especially when practiced by the king of Israel. Because King Saul was not willing to rely entirely on God, he failed the test.

The next two chapters demonstrate that Saul's failure was no momentary lapse, but evidence of a deeply flawed character. His foolish decree in 1 Samuel 14 weakened his army and nearly cost him his son. Chapter 15 offers the last straw when he disobeyed the clear instruction of God. From this point until his suicide in 1 Samuel 31, Saul provides a hideous portrait of failure.

If God knew He would regret the decision to make Saul king (1 Samuel 15:35), why did He do it? Some things needed to happen to reinforce important lessons. Saul needed to be king to show the Israelites the importance of obedience and the serious consequences of disobedience. They needed to see that a king was not just someone to rescue them from danger, but God's earthly representative. They needed to see that the actions of the king would have consequences for his subjects.

David: A Man after God's Heart

Although Saul remained king for several years, the focus of the story shifts to David and remains there until the end of 2 Samuel. We follow David from his hometown of Bethlehem into Saul's service. We learn of his friendship with Saul's son and heir, Jonathan. Chased from Saul's court, David remained a fugitive from the king (through 1 Samuel). As Saul's condition and kingdom deteriorated, David grew increasingly powerful. His obedience to God brought blessing, both in fighting strength and influence among the Israelites. He was so obedient to God that he refused to kill Saul, even though Saul was trying to kill him. Twice David had the chance but didn't follow through because, in his words, Saul was "the LORD's anointed" (1 Samuel 24:10). David believed God would punish Saul; it was not for him to take revenge (26:9–11).

What went wrong with David's census? Part 1

What does it mean that God incited David to commit a sin (2 Samuel 24:1)? To say that God causes people to sin, then judges them for sinning, would contradict passages that speak of God as holy and just. Instead, this is an example of the biblical writer tracing an event all the way back to its ultimate cause, as when Pharaoh's heart was hardened and the evil spirit came to Saul.

God had given David the victories described in 2 Samuel 21-23, victories that may have made David overly proud and prompted him to number the fighting men. Considered this way, God was ultimately the cause for prompting David to take the census. This may sound to us like a stretch, but explaining it this way emphasizes God's sovereignty without taking the blame away from David. (For another version of this episode, see 1 Chronicles 21.)

The author of these books makes it clear that David did not take Saul's throne away—God did. Even Jonathan understood this (1 Samuel 23:17). Not only did David refrain from killing Saul when he had the chance, but he grieved publicly and sincerely when he learned that Saul had died. The man who tried to take credit for Saul's death (and so win David's favor) only earned an early grave (2 Samuel 1:16). The same fate awaited those who killed Saul's successor to the throne and David's rival (2 Samuel 4). The death of Ish-Bosheth brought an end to civil war; David was anointed king over all Israel in 1003 B.C. Almost immediately, David marched on Jerusalem, a city that had stubbornly resisted Israelite conquest since Joshua's day. He defeated the non-Israelite inhabitants and set up his kingdom there. Since the city had not belonged to any tribe, it served as a suitable capital for a united Israel.

The Ark of the Covenant

Of all David did to establish his hold on the kingdom—defeating Israel's enemies, accumulating wealth, forming strategic alliances, showing kindness to Saul's family, governing justly, and building a fine palace for himself—the most significant involved the ark of the covenant. All during the reign of Saul, the ark had remained in partial exile—out of enemy hands but not yet in its proper place. David resolved to remedy this by bringing the ark to Jerusalem and placing it in the tent he had made for it. While there may have been political gain from such a move, David's primary motive seems to have been faithfulness to God (2 Samuel 6). Disaster scarred David's first attempt to bring the ark into Jerusalem. One of the men who had been caring for the ark, Uzzah, died after touching it. David's second attempt months later was more successful.

Having brought the symbol of God's presence to Jerusalem, David now determined to build a house for God. God declined the offer but promised instead to build a "house"—that is, a dynasty—for David. Overwhelmed by gratitude, David sat in front of the ark and expressed his thanks to God (2 Samuel 7).

Not Exempt from Sin

Although the author wanted to describe the establishment of David's dynasty, he was not willing to overlook David's failures. Obedience results in God's blessing and disobedience brings disaster, even for David. His adulterous affair with Bathsheba (2 Samuel 11) and the murder of her husband set off a chain of events that would haunt David for the rest of his life. His daughter would be raped, four of his children would die early deaths, a rebellion would force him to flee Jerusalem—all of these events can be traced directly to his sins. God forgave him but did not remove the consequences of those sins. Unlike its opening chapters, 2 Samuel's closing chapters are tinged with sadness and struggle. Sin has again proven to be a powerful poison.

GOD'S GREAT PLAN IN 1 AND 2 SAMUEL

In Genesis, God made a covenant with Abraham in which He promised descendants and a land where they could live. At Mount Sinai, God formed these descendants into the nation of Israel and gave them the Law by which to live. Eventually, through the leadership of Joshua, the Israelites reached that Promised Land. In 1 and 2 Samuel, God further elaborates on His plan for this people. They would be ruled by a righteous king whose dynasty would continue so long as it was characterized by righteousness. These books describe how God prepared His people for the monarchy and chose the one who would be king. God revealed His plans to David (2 Samuel 7) after David brought the ark to Jerusalem and offered to build a Temple to house it.

Another Step toward Reconciliation

God did not intend the covenant He made with David to replace His covenant with Abraham, but to supplement it. The new covenant represented one more step in God's plan to reconcile all the world to himself. Under David and his son Solomon, Israel grew to its largest and most powerful. Solomon built the Temple where God would be worshiped and the covenant blessing of God's presence most fully realized. Through David's descendants, God preserved His covenant people. Other passages in the Old Testament celebrate the covenant with David as one of Israel's greatest blessings. During the dark days before and after their exile to Babylon, the Israelites anticipated that God would send a king from the dynasty of David who would rescue them from their difficulties (Jeremiah 33:15–18).

The early Christians believed that Jesus was this king. The angel who announced His birth promised, "The Lord God will give him the throne of his father David, and he will reign over the house of Jacob forever; his kingdom will never end" (Luke 1:32–33). God's covenant with David was an important step closer to the fulfillment of God's plan. Through it God sent the Messiah, the Son of David, who would eventually reconcile the world to God.

WHAT WE LEARN ABOUT GOD FROM 1 AND 2 SAMUEL

God Is Sovereign

Throughout these books we see God working sovereignly to accomplish His will. Nothing can stop Him; He can even turn human error to His advantage. Because of their disobedience, the Israelites lost the ark of the covenant to the Philistines, who placed it in the temple of their god. But God showed His power by humiliating the Philistines and their god (1 Samuel 5). Later, when the Israelites trifled with the ark, God's power again exploded against the curious people in Beth Shemesh (1 Samuel 6:19) and against Uzzah (2 Samuel 6:6–7). In contrast, those who showed proper respect for the ark found abundant blessings (2 Samuel 6:11).

We also see God's sovereignty in the many ways He brought victory to His people. When the Philistines drew near to attack the Israelites, God sent "loud thunder against the Philistines and threw them into such a panic that they were routed before the Israelites" (1 Samuel 7:10). A young boy armed with only a sling and a few stones defeated a seasoned and sizable warrior in full armor because the sovereign God was on the boy's side (1 Samuel 17).

God showed His sovereignty by raising up the right leaders at the right time. He miraculously provided Samuel to lead Israel into the monarchy and to restore the priesthood, which had been defiled under Eli's sons. God used Saul to rescue Israel and even used his failures to teach His people what a king should be. God chose David to be the model king. In amazement, David asked God, "Who am I, O Sovereign LORD, and what is my family, that you have brought me this far? And as if this were not enough in your sight, O Sovereign LORD, you have also spoken about the future of the house of your servant. Is this your usual way of dealing with man, O Sovereign LORD?" (2 Samuel 7:18–19).

His Sovereignty Requires Our Obedience

How should we respond to a sovereign God? First, we must recognize His sovereignty over our lives. We acknowledge that sovereignty by our obedience, no matter what He asks of us. Saul's ruin and even David's failures reveal what happens when we fail to do so. Then we wait for Him to sovereignly work out His plan for us. David had to wait several years between the time he was chosen king by Samuel (1 Samuel 16) and the time he finally was acclaimed king by all the people (2 Samuel 5). Remembering God's sovereignty allows us to remain faithful in spite of obstacles and delays.

---

1 and 2 Samuel at a Glance

Authorship: Anonymous

Date of writing: Unknown, but probably around 930 B.C. (see 1 Samuel 27:6)

Date of events: 1105–970 B.C. (birth of Samuel to death of David)

Purpose: To describe the beginning of the Davidic monarchy

Form: Narrative

Part of God's plan: To show how God establishes a covenant with David and his descendants

Key element of God's character: Sovereignty

---

application questions

1. How else do you see God's sovereignty in these books?
2. In what ways have you seen God's sovereignty in your life?
3. How will remembering God's sovereignty help you deal with the situations you are facing right now?

questions for study and discussion

1. Read 1 Samuel 1–11, 13–18, 24–26, 31.

    a. Why did Samuel's mother give him to Eli?

    b. Why might God have waited so long to send Samuel to Saul?

    c. Why did God not immediately replace Saul with David?

    d. What does 1 Samuel 25 add to the story?

2. Read 2 Samuel 1–18.

    a. How are God's covenants with David and Abraham alike? How are they different?

    b. What role did the prophet Nathan play in David's court?

    c. If Saul was punished for disobedience, why wasn't David?

    d. What were the effects of David's sin on his family?

3. What else do these books tell us about God's plan?

4. What else do these books tell us about God's character?

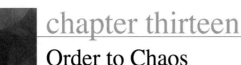

chapter thirteen

Order to Chaos

1 and 2 Kings

SUGGESTIONS FOR READING 1 AND 2 KINGS

As with 1 and 2 Samuel, most of what you will find here are historical narratives. Understand these in their historical and literary context, keeping in mind that these accounts were arranged and written for a theological purpose. Specifically, they retell the history of Israel's monarchy to explain the reasons and remedy for the defeat of God's people. Given Israel's role in God's redemptive plan, the Exile has implications for the larger story.

Kings and prophets move across the stage of these books, setting examples both noble and horrible. Their actions and destiny are all within the hands of the sovereign God. Although He maintains a low profile in these books, He is presented as the true hero of 1 and 2 Kings.

INTRODUCTION

Reading 1 and 2 Kings can be depressing. Forty-seven chapters filled with a few bright spots, but mostly with accounts of disobedience and disaster—this is hardly light reading. But God's light of hope shines through these pages, illuminating His plan and His character.

OVERVIEW

The books of 1 and 2 Kings, originally composed as one, were written by an anonymous author during the Exile. First Kings takes up the story of Israel's history from where 2 Samuel left off, at the end of David's reign.

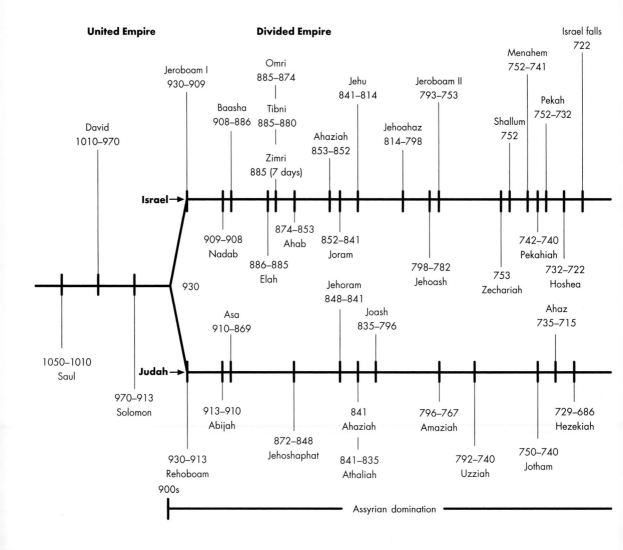

The last event described in 2 Kings took place around 560 B.C., so these books were probably written shortly after this. The author relied on several sources, some of which he names: the book of the annals of Solomon (1 Kings 11:41), the book of the annals of the kings of Israel (17 times), and the book of the annals of the kings of Judah (15 times). These were probably official court histories.

After describing the glorious days of King Solomon, the unknown author describes how Israel split into two countries, the Northern Kingdom of Israel and the Southern Kingdom of Judah. Alternating between these two, the book recounts the successes and failures of their kings down to the destruction of both countries. The author wanted to help the Israelites understand why they had been defeated by Babylon and to show them how to return to full fellowship with God.

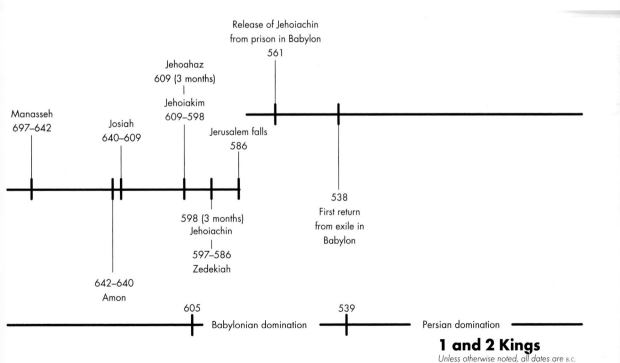

Release of Jehoiachin
from prison in Babylon
561

Jehoahaz
609 (3 months)

Jehoiakim
609–598

Manasseh
697–642

Josiah
640–609

Jerusalem falls
586

538
First return
from exile in
Babylon

598 (3 months)
Jehoiachin

597–586
Zedekiah

642–640
Amon

605   Babylonian domination   539   Persian domination

1 and 2 Kings
Unless otherwise noted, all dates are B.C.

MAP 7 The Kingdoms of Israel and Judah

The Great Sea
(Mediterranean Sea)

Sidon

Damascus

PHOENICIA

Mt. Hermon

SYRIA
(ARAM)

Tyre

Dan

Hazor

Acco

Sea of
Chinnereth

Mt. Carmel

Mt. Tabor

Jordan River

Megiddo

Scale of Miles

0   20   40

Scale of Kilometers

0   10   20   150

ISRAEL

Samaria

Shechem

Bethel   Gilgal

Jericho

Gath

Gibeon

Aijalon   Jerusalem

Ekron

Ashdod

Adullum

AMMON

Dead
(Salt)
Sea

Ashkelon

PHILISTIA

Lachish   Hebron

Gaza

Debir?

JUDAH

MOAB

Beer-sheba

EDOM

Negeb

Formula for a King

These books were named for their primary focus, the kings of Israel and Judah. Most of the kings are described in a similar way. First, we learn the king's name, his father's name, and when he became king. Then we are told how old he was when he began to rule, how long his reign lasted, and the name of his capital city. After this, the author evaluates the king as pleasing or displeasing God. Finally, the author tells his sources, relates the death and burial of the king, and provides information about the king's successor.

For examples of this formula, look at the account of Rehoboam in 1 Kings 14:21–31. Verse 21 tells us his name and that Solomon was his father. We learn that he was forty-one years old when he became king and that he ruled seventeen years in Jerusalem. We also learn his mother's name, something omitted from the accounts of the northern kings. The moral quality of his reign is described in verses 22–28; the news is not good. Rehoboam led his subjects into immorality, for which God sent the Egyptians to punish them. In verses 29–31, we are told that this information was taken from the book of the annals of the kings of Judah. After prolonged fighting between Judah and Israel, Rehoboam died and was buried in Jerusalem. Again we are told of his mother and that he was succeeded by his son, Abijah.

Why does the author focus attention on the kings? Because the king was the one person most responsible for preserving the covenant God had made with the Israelites. More than anyone else, the king, by his example and policies, could influence the Israelites toward greater obedience or greater disobedience.

The Beginning of the Downfall

In the opening chapters of 1 Kings, the prospects looked bright. After some initial struggle, Solomon was designated to rule in place of his father, David. One of the first things he did was to ask God for wisdom to rule justly. Another was to build the Temple of God in Jerusalem. That the author devotes several chapters to the building and dedication of the Temple indicates its importance to the Israelites. As the Tabernacle in the wilderness had symbolized God's presence with the wandering Israelites, the Temple represented that presence now that God had brought them to their land. They considered it God's palace. So long as it stood, it represented God's blessings to them.

God was so pleased with Solomon that He graciously offered to continue his dynasty for years to come, if only Solomon and his descendants would obey Him (1 Kings 9:1–9). But at the height of his success came the beginning of Solomon's downfall. In order to secure alliances with other nations, Solomon had married many foreign women who turned his loyalty from Yahweh to their gods and goddesses. Partly because of Solomon's disobedience, the kingdom was torn apart, with David's descendants ruling only a small part of their original territory (1 Kings 11).

At Solomon's death in 931 B.C., the ten tribes to the north asserted themselves. They agreed to follow his son Rehoboam only if he would make certain concessions. They objected to the fact that Solomon had forced them to work on his many building projects. When Rehoboam refused to change this policy, they rebelled and formed their own country, selecting Jeroboam as king. He and every one of his successors on Israel's throne received failing marks from God for their character. Although the Northern Kingdom of Israel was larger and grew to be more prosperous than the Southern Kingdom, it was never politically stable. Its nineteen kings from several dynasties ruled for only an average of eleven years each, many regimes ending in bloody palace coups. By contrast, the kings of the more stable country of Judah ruled for an average of more than seventeen years and included only one dynasty, that of King David.

Eventually, both countries were destroyed because of moral corruption, social injustice, and idolatry. The location of these two kingdoms on a land bridge crossed by several well-used trade routes brought prosperity to Judah and Israel. Increasing wealth brought increased oppression of the poor by the rich. First and 2 Kings only hint at this oppression, but prophets such as Amos, writing within this time period, reveal not only the amount of oppression but also how much God hated it.

What is a prophet?

In the Old Testament, when God wanted to communicate a message to His people, He often spoke through a prophet. Before the monarchy, the leader of the people might also serve as the prophet, like Moses, Deborah, and Samuel. In the early years of the monarchy, prophets served as advisors and conscience for the king. The prophet Nathan brought David God's promise of the Davidic covenant. He also rebuked David for his sin with Bathsheba. Elijah and Elisha advised several kings, although their advice was not always welcomed.

About 800 B.C., the role of the prophet changed from advisor to commentator. Prophets like Jeremiah, Amos, and Hosea usually addressed their messages to the crowds, calling for repentance, warning about disobedience, and promising God's blessings for faithfulness. Some of these messages, called oracles, were written down and preserved in the prophetic books we will study later.

The Snare of False Gods

Jeroboam, the first Israelite king after the split, started that nation on the road to idol worship, a road they never left. Jeroboam knew that if his people continued to worship at the Temple in Jerusalem, their loyalties would be divided between their new country and their old one. To prevent this, he built two sanctuaries in Israel, one in the northern boundary city of Dan and the other near the southern boundary, at Bethel. At each of these shrines he placed a golden calf, which he identified as a symbol of Yahweh. Whatever Jeroboam called these calves, God considered them idols. He harshly condemned Jeroboam for erecting them, and all his successors for leaving them standing.

Another snare for both the Israelites and Judeans was the worship of Baal, the fertility god worshiped by their neighbors. They believed Baal was the

157

Whatever happened to Israel?

In keeping with Assyrian policy, large numbers of Israelites were deported from their homeland and resettled in other parts of the empire. There seems to have been some attempt in this deportation to wipe out any sense of Jewish identity among the exiles. Intended or not, this was the result. The exiled Israelites intermarried with their new neighbors and eventually disappeared from history, never to be seen again. Meanwhile, back in Israel, the Assyrians resettled non-Israelites, who intermarried with the Israelites remaining in the land.

The name Israel was originally given to Jacob, then to the descendants of his twelve sons, and then to the ten tribes that broke away under Jeroboam. After Assyria destroyed the Northern Kingdom, the name Israel began to be used again to refer to all of God's people.

one who sent the rain that watered the crops. Lightning was his weapon and the clouds were his chariot. Baal worship was a nasty affair involving ritual sexual intercourse, sex with animals, and possibly child sacrifice (Jeremiah 19:5). Always a temptation, Baal worship received official approval when King Ahab of Israel married Jezebel of Phoenicia, a strong supporter of Baal.

Because God's people disobeyed Him, oppressing the poor and worshiping idols, God let them be defeated by their enemies. As in the time of the judges, Israel's unfaithfulness was the cause for these defeats, not God's weakness. But just as God was not idle during the days of the judges, He was not idle in these difficult days. Sometimes, as on Mount Carmel (1 Kings 18:16–46), God openly displayed His power. Just as He used the plagues to show His superiority over the Egyptian gods at the Exodus, on Mount Carmel He proved He was mightier than Baal.

No Contest

The people who assembled on the high, fertile mountain heard the challenge from God's prophet Elijah: Let the god who ignited a sacrifice with fire be acknowledged as the true god. This contest gave Baal the home field advantage since he was usually worshiped on mountaintops and this was an especially fertile one. The use of fire is significant, since fire and lightning were Baal's favorite tools. Elijah even allowed Baal's prophets to go first. From morning until evening they did everything they could to get Baal to send fire, but nothing happened, not even a spark. When it was God's turn, Elijah soaked the sacrifice and altar with water to make it more difficult to ignite. Then he prayed and God answered with fire—probably lightning. The strike incinerated the sacrifice, wood, water, stones, even the soil under the stones. Operating on Baal's home field and using Baal's favorite weapons against him, God easily prevailed. Baal could not hold a candle to God.

And not only on Mount Carmel. One scholar has pointed out other ways in the book of Kings that demonstrate God's superiority over Baal. Baal was supposed to be the god of fertility, but God sent a drought in response to Elijah's prayer (1 Kings 17:1). While the rest of the nation struggled with famine, God miraculously provided food (2 Kings 4:1–7, 42–44). Baal was said to have the power of life and death, but God healed the sick and even raised the dead (1 Kings 17:7–24; 2 Kings 4:8–37; 5:1–20).[1]

God's Messengers: The Prophets

In 1 and 2 Kings, God ministered to His people through His prophets. There are a dozen such individuals mentioned in these books, but the two most prominent are Elijah and Elisha. Elijah represented God in the Northern Kingdom of Israel during the troubled days of Ahab's reign (1 Kings 17–2 Kings 1). Before his unusual departure to heaven, Elijah appointed his successor, Elisha, whose ministry is described in 2 Kings 2–13.

Elisha's ministry opened with a series of miracles meant to demonstrate God's kindness. Elisha purified undrinkable water (2 Kings 2:19–22), helped a widow pay her debt (2 Kings 4:1–7), restored a young man to life (2 Kings

4:8–37), neutralized poisoned food (2 Kings 4:38–41), and multiplied food to feed one hundred men (2 Kings 4:42–44). When the commander of an enemy army developed leprosy, God used Elisha to heal him (2 Kings 5). The prophet even miraculously found a lost axhead (2 Kings 6:1–7). Why did the author of 1 and 2 Kings pay so much attention to such insignificant events? Because they demonstrate how God, through His prophet, cared for the needy—even needy foreigners—while Israel's corrupt rulers oppressed the poor (read 1 Kings 21).

These books also describe God punishing wicked kings and rewarding righteous ones. We saw that the kings of Judah, who tended to be more righteous, ruled an average of six years longer than their less righteous counterparts in Israel. Each of the eight Judean kings identified by the author as morally upright ruled an average of thirty-three years! When we look at individual cases, however, righteousness did not always lead to longer reigns. The most wicked Judean king, Manasseh, ruled fifty-four years, longer than any other. Josiah, who earned the highest commendations of all the kings (2 Kings 23:25), ruled only twenty years.

The Law of Retribution

What can we learn from this? We see, first, that God applied the law of retribution—obedience brings blessing and disobedience brings disaster—as a general principle. He did not intervene at each moment of obedience or disobedience but allowed events to take their course. The longer tenure of the righteous kings was a by-product of the healthy, just environment that righteousness created. Immorality and injustice carried the seeds of its own destruction.

Second, we see that God kept His promise to David. Except for a few years, one of David's descendants ruled continuously over Judah until the Babylonian exile.[2] Finally, God did eventually punish disobedience with disaster. Israel survived for just over two hundred years. Then, in 722 B.C., the Assyrian army destroyed the capital city of Samaria, imprisoned the Israelite king, and deported the people. Judah lasted for another century and a half until the Babylonians destroyed Jerusalem in 586 B.C. They broke down the walls, burned every important building, including the Temple, and forced the people of Judah to leave their land. The order seen in the opening chapters of Kings has given way to the chaos of the Babylonian exile.

GOD'S GREAT PLAN IN 1 AND 2 KINGS

As with the book of Judges, these books show the seriousness of sin. God had blessed Israel with a good law, a good land, and a good leader. They reached their golden era under a righteous monarch. But success brought disobedience in the form of idolatry. God's people were divided and struggled against each other. The rich became richer at the expense of the poor. Even the efforts of righteous kings could not reverse sin's destructive effects. A poison as fatal as sin requires a strong antidote. Nothing less than God's plan of redemption was needed.

Shaping the Future

We learn something else about God's plan when we step back to consider the author's purpose for 1 and 2 Kings. God inspired him to write for the Jews in exile, explaining the disaster that had befallen them.[3] Why would they need an explanation unless God still had a purpose for them to fulfill? These books not only explain why the Exile happened, but show the Jews how they could return to the Promised Land and to their God. God inspired the lengthy evaluation of the nearly forty kings who ruled Israel and Judah, not just so His people would know their history, but to remind them that obedience brings blessing and disobedience brings disaster. The Temple was built and inhabited through obedience, but destroyed through disobedience. With such knowledge, they could shape their future to please God once again.

Making It Personal

More than regret, God wanted these memories to produce repentance. Through repentance, God wanted to restore His people, but not to life as they knew it. He wanted to bring them into a more personal relationship with himself. They had trusted in the land and in the Temple as if these were good luck charms. God wanted them to trust Him as a child trusts a father. The prophet Jeremiah, writing during the closing years of the monarchy, described the new covenant God sought. It would not be written on stone tablets but on the human heart, and each one would know God personally (Jeremiah 31:33–34). The discouraging report of 1 and 2 Kings is actually a message of hope as well as warning. God wanted His people back and was showing them the way. His plan was not destroyed. It accompanied His people into exile in order to be restored to a new and better form after the brief time of punishment was over.

WHAT WE LEARN ABOUT GOD FROM 1 AND 2 KINGS

Because God is holy, He would not tolerate Israel's repeated disobedience. He had to punish them with exile, although He patiently postponed that punishment as long as He could. Because He is forgiving, He provided the history lesson of 1 and 2 Kings.

He Is the God of Second Chances

God was giving His people another chance. Throughout the Bible, we meet this God of the second chance. He forgave Abraham when he lied about Sarah. He pardoned the Israelites for their rebellion in the wilderness. And He gave David another chance to rule God's people, even after he committed adultery, murder, and deception.

Forgiveness doesn't eliminate the painful consequences of sin. Abraham was humiliated and Israel spent extra years in the desert. David lost several children and nearly his kingdom for what he had done. But with repentance comes God's forgiveness. Because of sin, Israel lost its land, Temple, and freedom. Through 1 and 2 Kings, God offered them a second chance.

He Has No Hidden Agenda

Some people forgive out of a sense of hidden guilt. When David forgave Amnon's rape of Tamar and Absalom's murder of Amnon, he was acting out of guilt, not love. Because he had committed murder and adultery, he found it difficult to punish his sons as they deserved. This hollow forgiveness helped no one and added only heartache. Others forgive because they have a hidden agenda; perhaps they want to control the person they have forgiven. When a holy God forgives, He has no hidden agenda. He wants fellowship with His people; only forgiveness can make this possible. These books show God offering a second chance to the Jews. One day that offer would be extended to every person in every nation, through the death and resurrection of Jesus Christ. Through that act, God provides everyone with a second chance at fellowship with Him.

WHERE TO FROM HERE?

Before continuing the history of Israel during the period of the Exile and beyond, we turn back for a closer, more personal look at what life was like as God's covenant people. The next several chapters allow us to explore Job, Psalms, Proverbs, Ecclesiastes, and Song of Songs and to observe Israel worshiping, contemplating, and falling in love.

Then we'll explore the writings of the prophets during the two centuries before the Exile. From their beautiful words—sometimes comforting, sometimes harsh—we can better understand how diligently God worked to prevent the Exile, but why, in the end, it had to be. After these two informative detours, we'll accompany the Israelites as they return from exile.

---

1 and 2 Kings at a Glance

Authorship: Anonymous

Date of writing: Probably during Exile

Date of events: From 970 (David's death) to 561 B.C., release of Jehoiachin from prison in Babylon

Purposes: To provide a theological account of Israel's history from the reign of Solomon to the Babylonian Exile, explaining the reason and remedy for exile

Form: Narrative

Part of God's plan: To show the dangers of disobedience and the way back to fellowship with God

Key elements of God's character: Holiness, Forgiveness

---

application questions

1. How has God given you a second chance to have fellowship with Him?
2. Does God ever stop forgiving? Why or why not?

questions for study and discussion

1. Read 1 Kings 1–6. How was Solomon's Temple similar to the Tabernacle? How was it different?
2. Read 1 Kings 10–22 and 2 Kings 1–25.
   a. Why did Solomon become disobedient?
   b. Who were the eight good kings from Judah? List the qualities that made them good.
3. What else can we learn about God's plan from these books?
4. What else can we learn about God's character from these books?

endnotes

1. Leah Bronner, *The Stories of Elijah and Elisha* (Leiden: Brill, 1968) as cited in Andrew E. Hill and John H. Walton, *A Survey of the Old Testament* (Grand Rapids, Mich.: Zondervan, 1991), 211.

2. God kept His promise to David, even during this brief period, by keeping alive the rightful king until he was old enough to regain the throne from the person who stole it (2 Kings 11).

3. Before the exile to Babylon in 586 B.C., the Old Testament refers to God's chosen people as Israelites. After the Exile, they are also called "Jews."

Suggestions for Reading the Next Section: A Window into the World of God's Covenant People

The book of Ruth provides a personal perspective on life in the time of the Judges. In the same way, these next several books allow us to better understand what the Israelites were doing while the kings ruled. In the book of Job, we hear the Israelites question why the righteous suffer. Psalms shows us God's people at worship. In Proverbs and Ecclesiastes, we break into the Israelites' thoughts on matters as diverse as wealth, words, marriage, and meaning. Song of Songs allows us to hear Israel in love. These books provide a window into the world of God's covenant people.

Wisdom: A Common Well

All these books, except for Psalms, say little about the Law, the Temple, sacrifices, or the Promised Land—themes found throughout the books we have studied so far. In fact, Job, Proverbs, Ecclesiastes, and Song of Songs don't sound all that different from the writings of the ancient Egyptians and Mesopotamians. When we consider the nature of this literature, however, we shouldn't be surprised. Ancient books written on themes like suffering, common sense, the search for meaning, and love sound very similar from culture to culture. Such writings—what scholars call wisdom literature—tend to avoid historical details specific to one country. Wisdom was understood to be something shared by all; every culture drew from a common well. By the ancient definition, if it was specific to one culture, it wasn't wisdom.

Wisdom and the Fear of God

Israel's wisdom literature was unique in at least one respect. The Israelites knew who had dug the common well. They knew their God had created the universe to run by certain rules, such as those found in Proverbs. If other nations discovered those same rules, that only showed the graciousness and superiority of Israel's God. All people, ancient and modern, have struggled with questions about suffering and meaning, Israel included. Because the Israelites had a personal relationship with their God, those struggles led to faith, not to despair. Although this literature sounds like the literature of Israel's neighbors, it begins from a different assumption about God. Israel knew there was only one God, not many, and that this God wanted a relationship with His people, a relationship characterized by reverence or respect that translated into obedience to God. Old Testament wisdom literature emphasized this relationship, which it called the "fear of God." The wise person is not characterized by intelligence, age, or experience, but by his or her "fear of God."

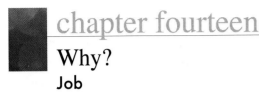

chapter fourteen

Why?
Job

SUGGESTIONS FOR READING JOB

Job combines at least three types of literature. The book begins (Job 1–2) and ends (Job 42) with narrative passages requiring us to attend to the historical and literary contexts. Poetry pervades the passages in between (Job 3–41), so handle the metaphors properly. For example, if you interpret God's description of creation in Job 38–40 too literally, you will misunderstand God's relationship with His creation.

The book of Job is an example of wisdom literature. Other ancient Near Eastern cultures also wrote wisdom literature; some even probed the problem of suffering. Comparing Job to those examples reveals some similarities, but also demonstrates Job's unique and comprehensive insights. We will avoid misunderstanding if we read all the material in context. For example, you must read the speeches of Job's friends in light of God's criticism in Job 42:7. Job's early speeches must be read in light of his later words. Since Israelite wisdom literature emphasized the fear of the LORD, pay close attention to this phrase in Job. Also, keep your eyes open for what you can learn about God.

INTRODUCTION

Who hasn't struggled with questions about suffering? We see innocent people in pain and wonder how a loving God could allow this. The ancient book of Job explores this question and provides some remarkably relevant insights. Job addresses the question of theodicy, how a God who is both all loving and all powerful could allow suffering. Although it does not resolve this question, Job clarifies it by emphasizing God's wisdom. We learn that an all-loving, all-powerful God may allow suffering when His wisdom decides it is needed.

OVERVIEW

While the book of Job never identifies its author, it seems clear that he was an Israelite: He speaks of only one God and calls Him Yahweh. The author chose to set his story at the same time as the book of Genesis. Like others from this period, Job's wealth was measured in livestock and he lived a very long life. Also, the book of Job never mentions the Law of Moses, the Tabernacle, or the priesthood, which would seem likely if it was written after Moses' day. The final version of the book was not completed until close to the Babylonian exile, evidenced by its inclusion of terms and concepts unknown among the Israelites until that time. Although set in the patriarchal period, Job's message is timeless.

Over and over, the Historical Books emphasize the law of retribution: Disaster comes from disobedience, but righteousness brings blessing. But what happens when the righteous suffer? Does this mean the law of retribution has been overturned? Has God become too weak to enforce it? Job was written to help Israel make sense of undeserved suffering and to show how to react when suffering comes.

The Quality of Righteousness

The opening two chapters describe a wealthy, righteous man whose world collapsed suddenly and without explanation. In rapid succession, he lost his property, children, and health. Yet, in spite of his agony, Job remained

Did the events of this book really happen?

Some have suggested that this book is really a parable rather than a historical account of an actual person named Job. Many elements in the story, they say, sound too ideal to be real. Job has the perfect number of sons (seven) and is described as the greatest man of the East. When God finally restores Job's wealth, He gives him exactly double of everything (Job 42:10). They also point out that the description of Satan and the heavenly court (Job 1–2) makes more sense in light of other Bible passages when read as a parable. How else could Satan come before God and then leave God's presence (Job 1:6, 12; 2:1, 7)?

The strongest reason to read this book as a parable seems to be the way God restores Job's family at the end. Losing a child is the most painful experience a parent can know. To lose ten children, then receive ten replacements—making everything "even"—sounds unrealistic, even coldly clinical, unless it is only a parable. Calling Job a parable, of course, does not negate its divine inspiration. Jesus used parables to teach and no one denies their authority.

On the other hand, this book usually has been treated as history, not as a parable. Just because the descriptions sound ideal doesn't mean they lack historical truth. Some would argue that when understood as historical, the book of Job makes an even greater impact.

righteous. Out of the dust of Job's tragedy, two conclusions emerge. First, God allows but does not bring suffering. Although suffering was not part of God's original plan for humanity, He allows it to touch His people. The second conclusion is that suffering is not always because of sin. Several times the author repeats that Job was righteous and he suffered.

Here is our first clue that the law of retribution is not a foolproof rule, but a principle. Just because a person suffers does not mean that person is wicked. God allowed Job to suffer in order to test the quality of Job's righteousness. Was he righteous for the right reasons? Did Job really want to obey God or did he just enjoy the blessings righteousness brought him? The only way to prove Job's motives was to remove the rewards of righteousness and see how righteous he remained.

Three friends learned of Job's suffering and came to comfort him. Then, after a week of compassionate silence, they began to speak to Job. Although each approached the problem in slightly different ways, their messages were essentially the same: Job was suffering because he had sinned. The friends misunderstood the law of retribution. They were using it both as a test to determine who was really righteous and as a club to beat the suffering person for his sins.

Debate or Trust?

Why does it take thirty-five chapters for the author to make this point? Perhaps to demonstrate a truth often overlooked: Suffering cannot be

Why did Elihu wait until all the others had spoken?

Elihu's speech seems out of place. If he were going to speak to Job, why did he wait so long? Some scholars consider this a later addition to the original story, which, they say, only included the three friends. Indeed, God never mentions Elihu in Job 42:7. More likely, Elihu did speak but waited until his elders had finished. Being the youngest in a culture that honored the wisdom of the aged, he let them go first. When he saw that Job continued to justify himself and that they had nothing more to say, he angrily entered the discussion, but added nothing new since nothing new really can be said about suffering.

resolved by discussion. As the words increased in number, so did the hostility of the friends and Job's assurance that he was innocent. Debates on the subject of suffering tend to drive the participants toward extremes and overstatements, not toward understanding. For dilemmas like this, only faith in God's wisdom can help. That is why at the heart of this book the author places a chapter that celebrates God's wisdom and provides the key to

Why was God so hard on Job?

If this is how God treated the most righteous person alive, no wonder so many choose to be wicked. Job's problems began when God pointed him out to Satan, not once but twice (Job 1:8; 2:3). Following Satan's assault, a suffering Job found the heavens silent to his cries of agony. He summoned God to defend himself, but when God arrived, He neither defended himself nor comforted Job. Instead, He hammered Job with two rounds of questions that showed His superior wisdom. This doesn't seem fair.

God's treatment of Job makes more sense if we keep the long view. First, God's people need to understand the "whys" and "hows" of suffering. The only way for God to teach these lessons is through the suffering of a person. In other words, God used Job's pain to help relieve yours. Second, for Job (or any of us) to survive suffering, he had to understand what God was really like. Comfort would come, but first Job had to learn that he was not God's equal. He needed to learn the importance of trusting God in the dark. If God turns on the lights before the lesson is learned, He has done us no great favor. Finally, Job's experience in suffering has been repeated by many others. When we need God the most, we often feel farthest from His presence. We can gain hope by remembering that just as Job found comfort in trusting God, so will we.

obtaining it. "The fear of the LORD—that is wisdom, and to shun evil is understanding" (Job 28:28). At a time like this, words cannot replace the fear of the Lord. When nothing else makes sense, when no one else agrees, cling to God's character.

Throughout this lengthy debate, Job begged God to appear and explain himself. When God did arrive, He completely ignored Job's appeal. Instead, He challenged Job to admit the vast superiority of His wisdom (Job 38–41). For seventy-two verses God blasts away at Job's inability to understand and control the natural world. Pausing briefly for Job's stumbling apology, God launches two more chapters of blistering questions. Job's reply to this was not as a challenger but as a wounded worshiper. His suffering had raised questions about God's justice; this painful encounter reminded Him that God knows what He is doing.

The epilogue (42:7–17) provides the rest of the story. God scolded Job's three friends and only by the intercession of their righteous friend, Job, did they get out of hot water. Job was abundantly rewarded with twice what he had lost. Later he died a contented old man. In this happy ending, we learn that Job was righteous for the right reasons. What is more, we see that the principle of retribution really does work: The humble and obedient are rewarded while the wicked are punished.

This book ends without God explaining to Job why he had to endure all that suffering. Strange as this may seem, it actually reinforces an important teaching of the book: In undeserved suffering, explanations are of little help. What we really need is humble trust in God's wisdom.

GOD'S GREAT PLAN IN JOB

Books like Judges and Kings show how sin can destroy a nation. Job reveals another side of sin's destructive power. Pain and suffering had no place in God's original design but entered when the original plan was spoiled by sin. Now even the innocent person suffers. Nor is suffering just something that happens to people. It is a tool in the hands of our enemy. We must wait until the New Testament to learn more about this supernatural foe, but the

What are behemoth (Job 40:15–24) and leviathan (Job 41)?

No one knows exactly what creatures God was referring to here. Behemoth is a Hebrew term meaning land animal. If the author has a specific animal in mind, the most likely choices are the hippopotamus or elephant. Some consider the behemoth to be a type of dinosaur. Others think behemoth refers not to any particular creature but to a legendary animal—the composite of the greatest qualities of all creatures, the ultimate land animal.

Similarly, the precise animal described by leviathan is unknown. Among the suggestions are a dinosaur—perhaps Tyrannosaurus Rex—or the crocodile. The ancient world spoke of a fierce sea creature called Lotan who, according to the myths, fought against the god Baal and lost. The Bible alludes to this animal and this battle, but sees Yahweh, not Baal, as the victorious monster killer (cf. Job 16:12–13; Psalm 74:13–14). God may be referring to Lotan in Job 41, but the description does not quite fit. According to the myth, Lotan was dead, but this animal still frolicked and frightened in Job's day. If behemoth refers to the ultimate but unspecified land animal, perhaps leviathan is the ultimate but legendary sea creature.

book of Job reveals Satan's malicious plan to hinder righteousness through suffering.[1] With such an enemy wielding such a weapon, we definitely need God's plan!

In the book of Job, God reveals more about the nature of His plan. We see clearly that being a part of God's covenant people does not immunize us against suffering. We must endure the effects of sin, even while God works to reverse those effects. Job also reminds us of the need to fear God. From the Historical Books we learn the importance of obedience. Job makes this lesson more personal, pointing out that obedience does not automatically bring blessing. We need to obey even while suffering and even when we don't understand why.

Finally, the book of Job suggests that God will accomplish His plan through a mediator. Several times while suffering, Job sought someone who could negotiate with God on his behalf (Job 5:1; 9:33; 16:18–22; 19:25–27; 33:23). Ultimately, no mediator was needed for Job, but God may have been hinting at an important element in His ultimate plan. God would eventually reconcile an alienated humanity to himself through someone who would stand in the gap between people and God. Jesus was this go-between. As the apostle Paul put it: "For there is only one God and one Mediator who can reconcile God and humanity. He is the man Christ Jesus" (1 Timothy 2:5 NLT).

WHAT WE LEARN ABOUT GOD FROM JOB

Ironically, we learn much about God's wisdom from a book in which He is mostly silent and invisible. When God does appear (Job 1–2, 38–41), He asks far more questions than He answers. His questions do not even answer Job's questions. Yet we leave this encounter with God as Job did, humbled and aware that God knows much more than we do. In these questions, God reveals His great wisdom by pointing Job toward the natural world. All the questions show that only One so wise could create and sustain the world Job knew. God's wisdom became the most obvious, undeniable fact of Job's existence. He could not deny it, for he saw its evidence everywhere.

The Faith Perspective

The same world surrounds us. The same evidence that made a believer out of Job faces us every moment. In fact, all the scientific discoveries about the natural world provide even more evidence of God's wisdom. We too must choose to believe God made and sustains this universe. Only by faith can we discover God's wisdom in nature. Many people—even brilliant scientists— examine the natural world and see nothing of God's wisdom. Only those looking from the right perspective—the faith perspective—can see it. Nor does suffering automatically show us God's wisdom, only suffering viewed from the perspective of faith.

If we ever need to remember God's wisdom, it is when we are suffering. If you must take terrible-tasting medicine, it is at least reassuring to know that your wise doctor prescribed it. When you cannot understand how suffering can help you and when you ask why God won't remove it, these are times when you most need to remember that God knows what He is doing. Even more than an explanation of why, those who suffer need to know that *God knows why*. A God whose vast wisdom made and sustains this world deserves our reverence; this is all the reason we need to "fear Him." With this attitude we have found the key to becoming wise ourselves (Job 28:28).

Job at a Glance

Authorship: Anonymous

Date of writing: Late monarchy, possibly exilic or post-exilic

Date of events: Patriarchal

Purposes: To help Israel understand why the righteous suffer and how to respond

Form: Narrative, poetry, wisdom

Part of God's plan:

1. To show how much God's plan is needed
2. To further clarify the nature of God's plan by showing that the righteous may suffer, that God wants our reverence, and that God will carry out His plan through a mediator

Key element of God's character: Wisdom

---

application questions

1. If God is so wise, why doesn't He figure out a way to prevent suffering?
2. What else can you learn about God's wisdom from this book?
3. How does knowing of God's wisdom help you face your problems?

questions for study and discussion

1. Read Job 1–3, 28, 38–40, 42.
   a. Do you think this book is a parable or a historical account? Why?
   b. How does Job 28 fit with the overall message of Job?
   c. How could a too-literal interpretation of God's description of creation in chapters 38–40 lead to misunderstandings about God and His relationship with creation?
   d. Why didn't God tell Job His reasons for what happened to him?
   e. What have you learned from Job that will help you help someone who is suffering?
2. What else can we learn from this book about God's plan?
3. What else can we learn from this book about God?

endnote

1. In Job, Satan is a title with a definite article ("the Satan"), not a proper name, as in the New Testament. In fact, we know virtually nothing about Satan from the Old Testament.

chapter fifteen

Singing the King's Praises

Psalms

SUGGESTIONS FOR READING PSALMS

In addition to giving attention to the parallel structure and heavy use of metaphors in the Psalms, remember their literary context. For the most part, interpret each psalm on its own. To find out what a psalm means today, start by asking what it meant to the ancient Israelites. For example, what did they understand when they heard that the wicked "will not stand in the judgment" (Psalm 1:5)? When they sang about the "Anointed One" in Psalm 2:2, who were they thinking of?

Most important, ask what you can learn about God, the subject of every psalm. Asking this question not only will help you better understand what the psalm meant to ancient Israel, but also what it means to you today.

INTRODUCTION

Job provides a window into the suffering of God's covenant people. With the Psalms, we have a window into their worship. We hear the psalmist praising God for who He is and what He has done. We listen as he complains about his problems and asks God to intervene. Although we no longer worship as the Israelites did, whom and why we worship has remained the same. Therefore, the Psalms provide rich insights into God's character and a wealth of ways to sing our King's praises.

OVERVIEW

Look in most church sanctuaries and you will find a hymnbook, a collection of the songs used by that congregation to worship God. The book of Psalms was originally Israel's songbook for worship in the Temple. Many of the psalms contain clues to their musical role: "a song," "for the director of music," "with stringed instruments," "for flutes," "to the tune of."[1] Some psalms refer to the Temple or to the worship performed there, such as those that speak of sacrifices.

Who wrote these psalms? David's name appears in the title of seventy-three of the 150 psalms. This could mean that he wrote or collected these psalms, or that these psalms had been dedicated to him. Since we read elsewhere of David's musical ability (1 Samuel 16:14–23; 2 Samuel 22) and interest in Israel's worship (2 Samuel 6), he could well have written the psalms that mention his name. Clearly he did not write all 150 psalms since other names are also listed: the Sons of Korah, Asaph, Solomon, Heman, Ethan, and Moses. One-third of the psalms appear with no name attached.

At some point, individual psalms were compiled into small collections. We have evidence for many such collections, such as the psalms of David and "psalms of ascent." Over time, these collections were joined to others. The 150 psalms were divided into five books (Psalms 1–41, 42–72, 73–89, 90–106, and 107–150) with a brief doxology (a statement of praise to God) added to the end of each book. No one has given a convincing explanation

for this five-fold division. Perhaps it was to parallel the five books of the Pentateuch or to link these books to five successive stages of Israel's history.[2] Since the latest psalms seem to have been written during or just after the exile in Babylon (for example, Psalm 137), the final collection probably took shape after the first group of Israelites returned from Babylon in 538 B.C. They rebuilt the Temple and worshiped God using this book, which they called the "Book of Praises."

Reflecting God's Authority

As you read, you will notice that most psalms either praise God or complain about a problem. Sometimes they praise God's character, as in Psalm 103. At other times they focus on His praiseworthy actions, such as in Psalm 77, or they express praise by stating their confidence in God (like Psalm 23). Sometimes they praise God indirectly, such as when they praise His Law (Psalm 19), His Temple (Psalm 84), or His appointed king (Psalm 45).

Do the Psalms talk about Jesus?

No and yes. When the psalmist spoke of the king, he meant the human ruler who sat on the throne in Jerusalem as God's representative, not Jesus. Occasionally, the psalmist would describe this earthly king in larger-than-life terms, such as ruling over the whole earth (Psalm 2:8) or living forever (Psalm 72:5). People in the ancient Near East commonly exaggerated in these ways when describing their kings.

In another sense, though, the psalms do speak about Jesus. The psalmist may not have been thinking of Jesus when he wrote, but God, the ultimate Author, certainly was. He knew that Jesus one day would take the throne as "king of kings" (Revelation 19:16). He also knew that during His life on earth Jesus would experience many of the situations found in the psalms. As the psalmist felt abandoned by God (Psalm 22:1), so did Jesus (Mark 15:34). The psalmist was betrayed by a friend (Psalm 41:9), and so was Jesus (John 13:18). Because the earthly king became a preview of what God intended for Jesus, the New Testament writers described the psalms as predicting Jesus (as in Acts 2:25-28).

When reading the Psalms, ask first what these psalms had to say to their original audience. Jumping too quickly to discover predictions about Jesus will cause us to miss much that God wants us to see. Read the Psalms as you read the rest of the Old Testament—to learn about God's character and His plan.

When the psalmists complained, it was usually about other people who had made life difficult for them (Psalm 22:7–8). At times they complained about their own sin (Psalm 39:8) or even about God (Psalm 22:1). These complaints usually close with a statement about how the psalmist still trusts in God in spite of his difficulties.

Both the praises and complaints agree on one important assumption: God is the heavenly King. He rules the world because He created it. "The earth is the LORD's, and everything in it, the world, and all who live in it; for he founded it upon the seas and established it upon the waters" (Psalm 24:1–2). When the psalmists wrote, Israel was the only nation that had acknowledged God's rule. But the Psalms also emphasize God's plan to bring the whole world back into fellowship with Him. Psalm 47 summons all nations to praise God, "the great King over all the earth" (verse 2). "God reigns over the nations; God is seated on his holy throne. The nobles of the nations assemble as the people of the God of Abraham, for the kings of the earth belong to God; he is greatly exalted" (verses 8–9).

Psalms of Praise

Most of the psalms were written to celebrate God's rule. Some praise God for His character or specific deeds of mercy. Other psalms describe the confidence the psalmist feels living under God's rule. A good example of the latter is Psalm 23, in which the psalmist compares himself to one of God's sheep, feeding in green pastures by quiet streams. Sometimes the psalmist praises God indirectly, by celebrating some aspect of His rule. Several psalms speak glowingly of God's Law. The first psalm describes the blessing that comes from obedience to this Law. The longest psalm, Psalm 119, devotes 176 verses to the virtues of the Law. Some psalms praise the king (Psalms 2, 110); one even celebrates his marriage (Psalm 45). Others praise the city of Jerusalem (Psalms 46, 87).

What makes these things special is their selection by God. Take an ordinary toothbrush worth one dollar and put it in the medicine cabinet of a celebrity. Later, that same toothbrush (now used) will sell for $100,000 at an auction.

Appoint an ordinary man to serve as God's human representative, and he becomes extraordinary. Establish an ordinary city as God's capital, and it becomes a praiseworthy city. The value of the man and the city rests in God; any praise received by them ultimately glorifies God.

Psalms of Complaint

When the psalmists were not praising God, they were complaining to Him. It was the job of the king in the ancient Near East to ensure a just society. Israel's kings were especially obligated by God to enforce His Law (not their own), which set a high priority on fairness and justice. The king was to immediately put a stop to any oppression or abuse. He was to ensure that merchants charged fair prices and that courts provided fair, honest decisions.

Unfortunately, even a good king could not always guarantee justice. Some forms of oppression, particularly slander, were impossible to prevent or remedy. Most of us have known firsthand the frustration and damage caused by a false rumor. No amount of protest can stop its spread; even an apology cannot undo the pain. Where did the Israelites go when their king could not or would not right their wrongs? They went to God. The complaint psalms represent the anguished cries of those who were unjustly suffering and who had no recourse in any human court. This is one reason why so many psalms complain specifically of slander and ask God to restore the psalmist's good name.

A few times the psalmist complains not about an enemy, but about himself. He admits to having sinned and asks for God's forgiveness (see Psalm 51 for a good example). More commonly, the psalmist complains to God about God. He contends that God had not done what He promised to do, or had unfairly treated the Israelites. "Why, O Lord, do you stand far off? Why do you hide yourself in times of trouble?" (Psalm 10:1). In Psalm 44, the people complain to God that He has treated them unfairly. Some might read these passages and criticize the psalmists for disrespect or a lack of faith. In fact, these psalms demonstrate it is precisely because the people have faith and a deep respect for God that they complain to Him. He had made certain promises to Israel and when these promises were not kept, the Israelites asked God why. If they had no respect for Him or lacked faith in Him, they would not even have bothered to complain. By holding God to His promises, they showed how much they believed in those promises.

Was this hymnal misnamed when it was called the "Book of Praises"? Shouldn't the ancient Hebrews have called it the "Book of Praises and Complaints"? No, because complaining to God, even complaining to God about God, is an act of praise. By taking these matters to God instead of taking revenge, the Hebrews acknowledged that He was in charge. By exercising their faith in His Word, they showed that His Word was worth believing. By trusting Him to intervene, they showed their confidence in Him.

GOD'S GREAT PLAN IN PSALMS

Israel's hymnbook has much to teach us about God's plan to restore fellowship with the world. The Psalms rehearse many of the important elements of this plan. They speak often of God's covenant with Abraham. They assert that God chose Israel to be "the people of his pasture, the flock under his care" (Psalm 95:7) and through Israel, to accomplish His plan. We hear frequent echoes of God's promise to make Abraham's seed a source of blessing to all the nations. By His work in and through Israel, God would make known His "salvation among all nations" (Psalm 67:1–2). The psalmists also refer frequently to God's covenant with Moses, which established Israel as a nation. When the psalmist wanted to illustrate how much God loved Israel, he often turned to the Exodus (as in Psalm 77). Several psalms celebrate the Law God gave Israel on Mount Sinai (such as Psalm 19).

We also see God developing the nature of His covenant still further by establishing the dynasty of David. The many psalms that arose from the life of David or speak of his dynasty were meant to celebrate this Davidic covenant.[3] The book of Psalms is a rich review of how God worked with His people from the original agreement with Abraham to His relationship with King David and his descendants.

185

What about the psalms that contain cursing?

At times, the psalmist's words sound vicious and very ungodly. Psalm 137:8-9 is a good example: "O Daughter of Babylon, doomed to destruction, happy is he who repays you for what you have done to us—he who seizes your infants and dashes them against the rocks." How can we reconcile this with Jesus' command to love our enemies?

First, recognize that these are literary expressions that make their point by overemphasizing that point. The psalmist was not as bloodthirsty as he sounds. Second, he sought justice, not revenge. Baby brains are what the Babylonians left behind when they destroyed Jerusalem. Confident that God would not allow this injustice to go unpunished, the psalmist anxiously awaited that day. In fact, God had promised to punish Israel's enemies; the psalmist was just holding God to His word.

These harsh passages highlight a very important truth: Those who oppose God's people oppose God. The psalmist was not concerned for himself. If these enemies went unpunished, something more important than his personal happiness was at stake. God must intervene to preserve His reputation and plan.

Are we allowed to use these curses? If we are angry at sin and our only motive is for God's honor, yes, we can. The inability to become angry at sin is no virtue. On the other hand, in the mouth of someone seeking personal revenge, they are sinful words. What should you do with the injustices you experience? Remember that what God does not vindicate in this life, He will handle in the life to come. Because the Israelites thought this life was all they had, they looked for God to intervene in the present. When we look ahead to the end of the story as described in the New Testament, we see that Jesus himself will be the one who brings about the full and complete justice God promised.

This book also teaches us about the nature of God's reconciling plan. As we hear Israel praise God for who He is and what He has done, we see the worthiness of God and His plan. The complaint psalms reveal the depths of human cruelty. The sin that so poisoned human relationships desperately needs the antidote of God's intervention. The Psalms offer a window to Israel's relationship with God. The rich fellowship they knew hints at what God has in store for all of us when His plan is fully realized. Finally, this book anticipates the part that would be played by Jesus. Just as Job hints at Christ's role as mediator, Psalms emphasizes His role as King. This is why the early church so often turned to the Psalms to explain Jesus' life and work.

WHAT WE LEARN ABOUT GOD FROM PSALMS

The Psalms teach about God as Creator, Redeemer, Warrior, and One who deserves praise. Each psalm supplies another glimpse of His marvelous character. However, the one image that stands out more than any other, the picture that unites the Psalms, is God as King.

God rules the universe because He created it. Out of all the nations, God chose to rule over Israel in order to bring the other nations under His righteous control. From the Israelites, God brought Jesus, whose death made it possible for all people to be reconciled to God. He will continue to work out His plan until He brings history to a conclusion and harmony is restored.

God's rule is more than a theological statement; it is a life-changing reality. If God is the rightful King, you and I need to be His loyal subjects. We need to fear God, accepting His right to rule over us. We need to live our lives according to His commands, not our own wishes. We need to make His pleasure, not ours, the highest goal. We exist to serve Him, not the other way around.

Taking God as our King also means we can and must take our problems to Him. We don't need to take them inside ourselves, turning bitterly resentful. We don't need to take them out on our enemies in vengeance. We can take them up to God in prayer. Even if our problems seem to come from God himself, we have the right, as His loyal subjects, to bring our concerns to

Him. God would rather hear honest words of complaint from a reverent, loyal heart than words of praise from an unbeliever.

Such a King is well worth praising. Whether we look back at what God has done throughout history, look around to see what He is doing today, or look ahead to see what He will accomplish through His plan, we find plenty of reasons to praise. With the psalmist we can say, "The LORD reigns, let the earth be glad" (Psalm 97:1).

Psalms at a Glance

Authorship: Various people
Date of writing: Earliest may have been by Moses, latest is exilic or post-exilic with most from the time of the monarchy. Psalms was probably combined into its present form in the post-exilic period.
Date of events: Mostly monarchy, some exilic
Purpose: To encourage Israel to praise God as heavenly King
Form: Poetry
Part of God's plan: To review the important elements of God's plan and clarify additional insights
Key element of God's character: King

---

application questions

1. Evaluate your prayer life. Do you pray as honestly and boldly as the psalmists? If not, why not?
2. What else does God as your King mean? What areas of your life still need to be put under His direction?

questions for study and discussion

Read Psalms 1–2; 3; 8; 19; 22–23; 46; 51; 99–100; 103; 110; 121; 137; 139; and 150.

1. Aside from the Law, Temple, and earthly king, how else is God indirectly praised in the Psalms?

2. What can you learn about praise from the Psalms? How can you apply this in your own worship?

3. What can you learn about prayer from the Psalms? How can you apply this in your own prayers?

4. Why do you suppose the Psalms contain so little confession of sin?

5. Do you think Christians should use the cursing Psalms? Why or why not?

6. What else do you learn about God's plan from the Psalms?

7. What else do you learn about God's character from the Psalms?

endnotes

1. Scholars still puzzle over the meaning of many of these musical terms, such as *selah*, *shiggaion*, *higgaion*, *gittith*, *sheminith*, and *miktam*.

2. John Walton suggests that the first book describes David's conflicts with Saul; the second book, David's kingship. The third book concerns Israel's struggles with Assyria, while the fourth concerns the destruction of the Temple and the Babylonian exile. The fifth book reflects the early days of the post-exilic era.

3. Thirteen psalms contain titles that refer to some event from David's life.

chapter sixteen

God at Home

Proverbs, Ecclesiastes, Song of Songs

SUGGESTIONS FOR READING PROVERBS, ECCLESIASTES, AND SONG OF SONGS

Remember that proverbs are principles, not promises. They state what usually happens, not what God guarantees is going to happen. As with Job, interpret each part of Proverbs and Ecclesiastes in light of its overall message. Reading one proverb in isolation from the others or only "hearing" part of Ecclesiastes can lead to misunderstanding.

Since Song of Songs is a collection of love poems, read it using the guidelines for poetry. Pay attention to the parallelism and heavy use of imagery. Also, watch the context. Although comparing the woman's neck to a tower might sound strange to us, she would have been flattered by the compliment. Each of these books, even Song of Songs, can teach us about God and His plan.

INTRODUCTION

Look inside the windows provided by these three wisdom books and you will see the many ways God relates to His covenant people. Proverbs shows God's knack for orderliness and sensibility. Quite a different picture emerges from the sober words of Ecclesiastes. In Song of Songs (also called Song of Solomon), we find two lovers frolicking through the pages of Scripture, celebrating the joys of romantic love. The same God who controls the tide of human history is just as much "at home" at home.

OVERVIEW OF PROVERBS

We learn from 1 Kings that Solomon was famous for his wisdom and that he collected three thousand proverbs (1 Kings 4:32). Probably under the direction of King Hezekiah (715–686 B.C.; see Proverbs 25:1), some of Solomon's sayings were combined with the work of other authors to form the book of Proverbs.

The Best Path

In the first nine chapters we listen in as parents encourage their son to choose the path of wisdom.[1] They tell him of the dangers of making the wrong choice and the blessings that follow the right one. Folly leads to violence and self-destruction; wisdom brings honor, safety, and God's blessing. The parents point out how wisdom can be found by those who eagerly pursue it. Those who go after other things, such as sexual gratification, ease, and wealth, will lose both the chance for wisdom and their lives. These parents earnestly plead for their son to choose wisdom.

In Proverbs 8, Wisdom, described as a woman, issues her invitation. Again we hear of the tremendous benefits that come to those who choose her. "Riches and honor, enduring wealth and prosperity" are found with her (Proverbs 8:18). More than this, she brings life itself and the blessing of God's favor (8:35). The final chapter in this introductory section contrasts Lady Wisdom's invitation with that of Lady Folly (Proverbs 9). Such a comparison leaves no doubt about the best path to choose.

A Matter of Common Sense

Having issued the invitation, the rest of Proverbs reveals what wisdom looks like. After such an extensive introduction, we might expect the wisdom we encounter in the rest of the book to be something deep, mysterious, or philosophical. Instead, we find proverbs—short, pithy sayings addressing things as ordinary as how to be a good neighbor. It's not that the other kind of wisdom doesn't matter; we'll get some of this in Ecclesiastes. But God knows how much true wisdom has to do with everyday common sense.

Why does Proverbs seem so black and white?

This young man's parents see the choice as very simple: Either you walk in the path of wisdom or you choose folly. Life is more complex than this, with lots of gray to go along with the black and white. Why doesn't Proverbs reflect the gray?

It isn't that the writer is naïve and ignorant of life's complexity. His goal is not to explore the nuances; he wants to persuade the young man to choose wisdom. There is too much at stake to bother with subtleties. Life and death hang in the balance and every moment of delay is a moment lost.

In some sense, life is simple. Even with all its complexities, the most important question is very basic: Will you choose to follow God or won't you? We may dispute many things about this question—what it means to follow God, how one makes that choice—but finally, it comes down to either yes or no.

These proverbs sound very similar to proverbs found elsewhere in the ancient Near East. Some even may have been borrowed from Egypt or Mesopotamia. What makes these proverbs special is not what they say or where they came from, but why they are to be obeyed. Elsewhere in the ancient Near East, people chose the wise path in order to succeed. For Israel, true wisdom began with a proper relationship with God, what the biblical writers called the "fear of the LORD" (Proverbs 1:7). The person who feared God chose to do the right thing out of obedience to God. If I bring my wife flowers so she'll let me buy a big screen TV, I might succeed but my motives would be wrong. How much better if I bring home flowers because I love my wife. I may still get the TV, but that wasn't my goal.

Important Themes

Several themes show up again and again in Proverbs. We learn more about God's role in creation from this book than almost any other, except Genesis. When the introduction claims that wisdom played a part in creation (Proverbs 3:19–20; 8:22–31), it means that everywhere you look, you can find proof of God's wisdom. Whether in the simplest flower or the vast galaxies, God displays His creativity and skill. Just as surely as He created the law of gravity, He designed human beings to act and interact in certain ways. When these laws are obeyed, happiness and wholeness result. To disobey those laws brings pain. Medical science and the collective experience of humanity have confirmed the truth of these laws. Patience works better than anger (Proverbs 14:29), heartache crushes the spirit (15:13), self-discipline and

Does God condone bribery?

Certain proverbs seem to suggest that bribery is OK with God. Proverbs 21:14 reads, "A gift given in secret soothes anger, and a bribe concealed in the cloak pacifies great wrath." A similar thought is also found in Proverbs 17:8 and 18:16. Does God approve of this?

As we saw earlier, interpreting proverbs requires us to read the passage in its context. When we do, we see that God does not approve of bribery. He has clearly condemned it in passages like Proverbs 17:23, since it runs counter to His character as a just God. If both Proverbs 21:13 and 21:15 command justice, how could we interpret the verse in between to condone injustice?

We must admit, though, that bribery does work. Although God's people must never use their resources to pervert justice, such as through bribery, this verse encourages us to do everything legitimate and in our power to accomplish what is fair.

diligence are crucial to success (21:5), justice improves society (21:15). Who can deny the truth of this wisdom?

Although God created this world to operate by certain laws, He also remains personally interested in all that happens among His creatures. "The eyes of the LORD are everywhere, keeping watch on the wicked and the good" (15:3). When necessary, God will do more than watch; He will intervene. "He who mocks the poor shows contempt for their Maker; whoever gloats

Why does Ecclesiastes seem so cynical?

Several passages in Ecclesiastes sound too cynical to be in the Bible: "Man's fate is like the animals. . . . As one dies, so dies the other . . . man has no advantage over the animal" (Ecclesiastes 3:19). "As a man comes, so he departs, and what does he gain, since he toils for the wind? All his days he eats in darkness, with great frustration, affliction and anger" (5:16–17). "Do not be overrighteous, neither be overwise" (7:16).

With wisdom literature like Ecclesiastes, it is especially important to read everything in the book before deciding what each part means. If we had not done that with Job, we would think the friends were right and Job was wrong; only the end of the book tells us the truth. So too with these passages. The Teacher's cynicism is not our model. His journey through cynicism leads him to find meaning in reverence for God. This is what we are to embrace.

Having said this, we must also admit that life is frustrating, especially when limited to the human point of view exemplified in Ecclesiastes. We must avoid the temptation to make sense of everything, trying to find logical explanations for what has no apparent reason. We must fear God, even when life doesn't make sense.

over disaster will not go unpunished" (17:5). More than likely, this punishment will not be a lightning bolt from the heavens, but the inevitable consequence of the action. This is the way God designed the world to operate. The wicked person falls into the very trap he laid for his victims (see Proverbs 1:18–19).

Proverbs not only commends wisdom, it condemns folly. Don't think of the fool as simply dumb, uneducated, or simple-minded. Foolishness as described in Proverbs refers to a moral, not a mental weakness. The fool is stubborn, rude, quarrelsome, lazy, and headed for trouble. He doubts the very existence of God, if not by his words, then by his choices.

Other themes play a prominent role in this book. Many proverbs refer to speech. Words have great power either to bring harm or good (Proverbs 12:18, 25; 18:21), but with all their power, they can't hide one's true character (26:23–28) or take the place of proper behavior (14:23). Words should be honest (16:13), limited (17:28), calm (17:27), and well chosen (25:11). Sexuality is also frequently mentioned. Exercised within the proper bounds, sexual love is celebrated as one of life's greatest blessings (5:15–23; 18:22). Use it outside those bounds and you might as well dump hot coals into your lap (6:27; 7:6–27). For a patriarchal society, women play a surprisingly important role in this book. Wisdom is characterized as a woman and many proverbs emphasize the wife's importance in the marriage. The ideal wife, playing a powerful and influential role, is even given "last word" in the book (Proverbs 31:10–31).

OVERVIEW OF ECCLESIASTES

The twelve chapters of Ecclesiastes trace one man's search for meaning through all the places he expects to find it: wisdom, wealth, pleasure, accomplishments. Finally, he learns that meaning has always been close at hand. Although the book never identifies its author, several clues point to Solomon. According to the first verse, these are "the words of the Teacher, son of David, king in Jerusalem." This Teacher elsewhere describes himself in terms that sound like Solomon (Ecclesiastes 1:12, 16; 2:4–11).

The Question of Authorship

However, there are significant reasons to doubt that Solomon actually wrote Ecclesiastes. First, the book never names Solomon as the author. Second, the author describes rampant oppression in the kingdom but seems powerless to prevent it (Ecclesiastes 3:16; 4:1–3; 5:8–9). King Solomon would certainly have used his considerable influence to accomplish a goal as important as justice. Third, the language doesn't sound like the Hebrew used in Solomon's day. It sounds more like the Hebrew that was spoken around the time of the exile to Babylon. Just as modern English is very different than the English spoken by Shakespeare, exilic Hebrew would have been different than what was spoken four hundred years earlier in Solomon's day.

If Solomon didn't write this book, the anonymous author may have chosen to identify himself with Solomon in order to strengthen the book's message.[2] If meaning could be found in wealth, women, or wisdom—three places most people still look for it—who would be better able to find it than Solomon, who had all he could want of each? But since even Solomon couldn't find meaning in these places, no one will.

The Question of Meaning

Ecclesiastes is depressing reading. How else could we describe a book that begins "Meaningless! Meaningless!"? It's depressing to watch the Teacher search for meaning in one place after another, only to come away empty-handed. We feel the Teacher's frustration as he discovers that life is not as simple as Proverbs makes it seem. You can almost see his shoulders slump as he counsels the reader to make the best of a bad situation. Even the scattered arrangement of Ecclesiastes adds to its depressing tone.

By the time we reach the "conclusion of the matter" (Ecclesiastes 12:13), we've discovered that life is hard and meaning hard to find. Just when we've exhausted all other sources, meaning meets us in wisdom's motto: Fear God. These two words put the whole book into perspective, transforming it from discouraging to hopeful. Life is hard, but don't let that drive you from God. Life has its joys, which should be enjoyed as God's gifts to you. Meaning is missing from the world as we see it, but it can be found in a life lived in relationship with God.

OVERVIEW OF SONG OF SONGS

Reading the wisdom books is like looking through a window into the world of God's covenant people. When we come to Song of Songs, we feel like "peeping Toms," for here we have a book about physical love and human romance. What is it doing in the Bible?

The Song as Allegory

Throughout the history of the church and Judaism before that, many have denied that the Song is about physical love. Instead, they considered it an allegory about God's love for His people. God was the bridegroom and His people were the bride. Those who defend this approach point out that the book makes no explicit mention of God. On the other hand, most literature that was meant to be allegorical provides some hint of the proper way to read it. In *Pilgrim's Progress*, we have this clue that the book is an allegory of the spiritual life: The main character is named Christian. But Song of Songs gives no hint that it should be interpreted allegorically. The real reason people prefer the allegorical approach is that they cannot understand why the Bible would contain a book about sex.

Love as Celebration

God included this book to celebrate the goodness of physical love within a marriage relationship. Sexual intimacy is one of God's best gifts when used properly. More than just the way to produce children, God provided sex as a way for one person to experience close intimacy with another. Sin has destroyed human relationships, making it harder for us to relate to each other. Through the physical intimacy celebrated in Song of Songs, we regain something of what sin destroyed.

Song of Songs tells of a love relationship in a series of poems arranged to highlight the anticipation, agony, and ecstasy of love. Very similar examples of this kind of poetry have been found elsewhere in the ancient Near East.[3] As with Ecclesiastes, we must regard the Song of Songs as anonymous. Solomon's name appears in the title but this could mean simply that the Song was dedicated to him or was written about him, perhaps because of his great interest in women (read 1 Kings 11:3). If not written by Solomon, our best guess for the origin of this song would be some time during the monarchy.

Whoever the author is, he describes this love in very sensual terms. Though clear, the description is not graphic. The terms are delicately presented behind the veil of symbolic language. Most of the symbols are taken from nature, like apple trees, flowers, and animals. Some comparisons sound anything but flattering: Her nose is like a tower and she reminds him of a horse. Following the standards of ancient Near East love poems, however, these are high compliments.

The apparent lack of a plot has led some to conclude that these eight chapters represent an anthology of individual love poems. Although we don't have a clear story line, we do find the same two characters appearing throughout. We even have something like a plot with two invitations (Song of Songs 2:8–17 and 7:11 —8:4) and two dreams (3:1–5 and 5:2—7:10) surrounding the moment when their relationship is consummated (4:16—5:1).[4]

GOD'S GREAT PLAN IN PROVERBS, ECCLESIASTES, AND SONG OF SONGS

These wisdom books not only provide a window into the lives of God's people, they also clarify God's plan to reconcile the world to himself. In Proverbs we catch a glimpse of what life will be like under God's plan. By living according to Proverbs, God's people can live in harmony under God's blessings. Interpersonal conflict and self-destructive behavior are minimized. By obeying, one makes wise choices that lead to better marriages, better business relationships, and a more just society. If this is possible in a world still infected with sin, how much greater will it be when sin is removed and God's plan is fully realized!

Sin not only destroys relationships (as we saw in Judges, Kings, and elsewhere) and causes suffering (as we saw in Job), it also robs people of a sense of meaning. Ecclesiastes documents one man's struggle to regain that meaning and reinforces the need for reconciliation with God. By locating the source of meaning in our relationship with God, the book also hints at the blessings we will experience when we are fully reconciled to God.

Even a book about human love teaches us about God's plan. Remember that one of the relationships that suffered as a result of sin was the relationship between Adam and Eve. Song of Songs shows how God can, through His gift of human intimacy, partially restore that relationship. If God can provide such joy and harmony now, imagine what life will be like when all relationships are fully reconciled!

WHAT WE LEARN ABOUT GOD FROM PROVERBS, ECCLESIASTES, AND SONG OF SONGS

God's Wisdom Is Practical

We came to know something of God's wisdom through the struggles and questions of Job. Proverbs, Ecclesiastes, and Song of Songs help to further clarify this wisdom. Proverbs shows its practical side. God designed this universe to operate according to certain laws, both natural and social. When we obey these laws, things generally go well. When we violate these laws, we eventually suffer for it. Like an oak tree inside an acorn, our blessings or punishments reside within our actions. Every day in a thousand ways we prove true the principles of Proverbs. Every day we gain more reasons to honor the wisdom of the God who designed the world to operate this way.

God's Wisdom Requires Trust

We see a different aspect of God's wisdom in the book of Ecclesiastes. Although much in this book confirms the wisdom of Proverbs, finally the Teacher has to admit, "As you do not know the path of the wind, or how the body is formed in a mother's womb, so you cannot understand the work of God, the Maker of all things" (Ecclesiastes 11:5). How true! Perhaps part of his frustration arises from the paradox of knowing that God is wise but not always being able to see His wisdom in operation.

So much of life perplexes the Teacher. What he thought would bring a sense of fulfillment fails to do so. Those who should be successful fail. Those who should fail succeed. "The race is not to the swift or the battle to the strong, nor does food come to the wise or wealth to the brilliant or favor to the learned; but time and chance happen to them all" (Ecclesiastes 9:11). What can be done with a world like this? "Fear God and keep his commandments" (12:13). God remains wise, even when we don't understand His ways.

God's Wisdom Preserves Us

As a wise mother knows best what her crying infant needs, so God shows His wisdom by giving us what we need. Song of Songs describes one of God's wise gifts, physical intimacy. He knows how it can help to restore the relationship sin destroyed. He knows how this intimacy can shelter us against the wild winds of adversity and preserve us from disastrous detours. He knows how much pleasure sexual intimacy brings to His people when used properly. Although this book never explicitly mentions the name of God, it reveals His wisdom by describing His gracious gift.

Proverbs at a Glance

Authorship: Solomon and others

Date of writing: Monarchy

Date of events: Monarchy

Purpose: To produce good, orderly lives by living according to the fear of the Lord

Form: Poetry, wisdom

Part of God's plan:

1. To reveal nature of God's wisdom
2. To demonstrate blessing that comes from living according to God's plan

Key element of God's character: Wisdom

Ecclesiastes at a Glance

Authorship: Anonymous

Date of writing: Exilic or post-exilic

Date of events: Unknown

Purpose: To show that meaning comes from the fear of God

Form: Poetry, wisdom

Part of God's plan:

1. To show the need for God's plan because sin deprives us of sense of meaning
2. To emphasize the true source of meaning found in proper relationship with God

Key element of God's character: Wisdom

Song of Songs at a Glance

Authorship: Anonymous

Date of writing: Monarchy

Date of events: Solomon's reign

Purpose: To celebrate the goodness of physical love within marriage

Form: Poetry

Part of God's plan: To show, in the husband-wife relationship, the joy and harmony God intends for all relationships

Key element of God's character: Wisdom

application questions

1. In what ways have you found the proverbs to demonstrate God's wisdom?
2. If God is so wise, why doesn't this world make more sense?
3. If sexual intimacy is so great, why did God place restrictions on it?
4. How would Song of Songs apply to an unmarried person?

questions for study and discussion

1. Read Proverbs 1–9, 10, 31.
   a. List the rewards that come with choosing wisdom according to Proverbs 1–9.
   b. List the dangers of choosing folly.
   c. Choose three of the proverbs in Proverbs 10 and summarize them in your own words.
   d. Why is it appropriate for the book of Proverbs to end with 31:10–31?
   e. What else do we learn about God's plan from Proverbs?
   f. What else do we learn about God's character from Proverbs?

2. Read Ecclesiastes 1, 3, 11–12.

    a. Why is wisdom a heavy burden according to 1:12–18?

    b. Summarize what the author is saying in 3:1–8.

    c. What is the writer describing by the allegory in 12:1–8? How does it fit into his overall message?

    d. What else do we learn about God's plan from Ecclesiastes?

    e. What else do we learn about God's character from Ecclesiastes?

3. Read Song of Songs 1–3.

    a. What can we learn about romantic love from these chapters?

    b. What else do we learn about God's plan from Song of Songs?

    c. What else do we learn about God's character from Song of Songs?

endnotes

1. Although sons are specifically addressed, both men and women need this wisdom. The author probably focused on sons because this was a patriarchal society. Some suggest that this material may have been used to instruct young men entering the king's service.

2. This type of literature, known as royal fiction, is found elsewhere in the ancient Near East.

3. Consider this example from Egypt:

    The voice of the swallow speaks and says: "The land has brightened—What is thy road?"
    Thou shalt not, O bird, disturb me! I have found my brother in his bed,
    And my heart is still more glad, when he said to me: "I shall not go afar off.
    My hand is in thy hand, I shall stroll about, and I shall be with thee in every pleasant place."
    He makes me the foremost of maidens. He injures not my heart.

                          ANET, 467–469

4. David A. Dorsey, *The Literary Structure of the Old Testament: A Commentary on Genesis–Malachi* (Grand Rapids, Mich.: Baker, 1999), 199–213.

chapter seventeen

A Vision of the Holy One
Isaiah

SUGGESTIONS FOR READING ISAIAH

Reading the prophetic books can be challenging for several reasons. First, these are mostly oracles, with little historical or geographical background. A good study Bible can fill in these gaps. Second, most of the oracles are written in poetry using hyperbole, so it isn't always easy to know how literally to interpret a passage. When Isaiah speaks of captives being freed and prisoners released (61:1), does he mean this literally or symbolically?

Third, we struggle to know when these prophecies were fulfilled. In my opinion, most of what Isaiah and the other prophets predicted has already been fulfilled by the Jews' return from exile in Babylon, by Jesus, or by the early church. The glorious restoration Isaiah promised, especially in Isaiah 60–66, is being symbolically fulfilled today in the lives of Christians and will ultimately be fulfilled in heaven. Remember that the prophets were primarily God's spokesmen, not fortune-tellers. That is, their primary concern was to motivate Israel to obey God, not predict the future. Instead of focusing on when these oracles will be fulfilled, ask what God was telling ancient Israel about himself and His plan. Then learn what you can about God.

When reading Isaiah, pay special attention to his literary artistry. He communicates God's message using a greater variety of words than any other Old Testament writer. He skillfully employs many literary devices, such as personification (Isaiah 44:23), sarcasm (44:9–20), word play (5:7), and alliteration (24:7).

INTRODUCTION

Prophets were nothing new to the Israelites. From their earliest days as a nation, they were familiar with the prophetic ministry of Moses. Samuel served in this role, as did many others during the monarchy. Beginning around 800 B.C., prophetic messages, also called oracles, began to be preserved in writing.[1] The most famous of the writing prophets was Isaiah. None of the others can match the beauty of his poetry or the breadth of his thought. We know very little about the man Isaiah, only that he lived in or around Jerusalem during the 700s B.C. He was married and had at least two children (Isaiah 7:3; 8:3). A well-respected prophet, he served as counselor to the king of Judah (37:1–7).

OVERVIEW

Isaiah, the greatest of the writing prophets, prophesied for about sixty years, from 740 to 681 B.C.[2] He preached a message of warning and hope, primarily to the nation of Judah. If Judah persisted in disobeying the covenant, God would punish her with exile. But God still loved His people and promised to restore them after a time of punishment.

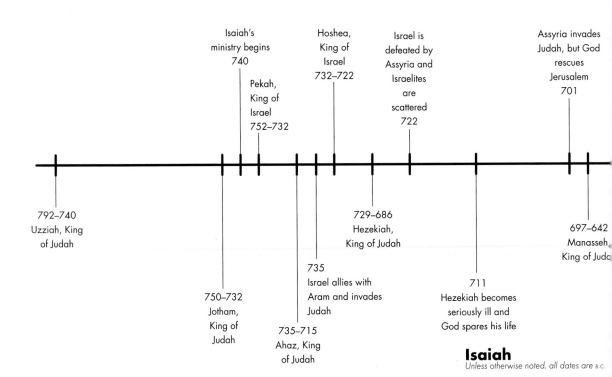

Isaiah's ministry begins 740

Pekah, King of Israel 752–732

Hoshea, King of Israel 732–722

Israel is defeated by Assyria and Israelites are scattered 722

Assyria invades Judah, but God rescues Jerusalem 701

792–740 Uzziah, King of Judah

729–686 Hezekiah, King of Judah

697–642 Manasseh, King of Judah

735 Israel allies with Aram and invades Judah

750–732 Jotham, King of Judah

711 Hezekiah becomes seriously ill and God spares his life

735–715 Ahaz, King of Judah

Isaiah
Unless otherwise noted, all dates are B.C.

MAP 8 The Assyrian Empire

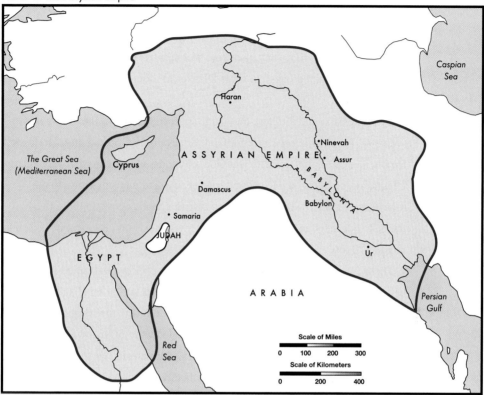

The book of Isaiah falls into three sections. Chapters 1–35 primarily contain messages of warning to God's people and to the surrounding nations. In Chapters 40–66 we primarily find messages of hope, promising salvation and restoration. The four chapters in between (36–39) describe two incidents from the history of Judah that illustrate the earlier chapters of warning and anticipate the salvation to come.

Judgment and Hope

Isaiah 1 provides a good overview of Judah's sins and the response God threatened. God's people had forgotten who called them and why (verses 2–4). Even when God disciplined them (verses 5–9), they still failed to remember Him. On the surface, everything looked great. People still brought

209

sacrifices to the Temple, celebrated the holidays, even prayed (verses 10–15), but something was terribly wrong. They had neglected the very important matter of justice, oppressing the very people God had commanded them to protect (verses 15–17). They also were worshiping other gods besides Yahweh. The "sacred oaks" in verse 29 refer to idolatrous and immoral practices.

By oppression and idolatry, they had "spurned the Holy One of Israel" (verse 4), Isaiah's favorite title for God. Since a holy God cannot tolerate sin, He threatened to punish them. But God's holiness also means that He cannot tolerate sin's effects, so He offered forgiveness and a bright future to the repentant (verses 18–19). The next sixty-five chapters contain these two themes, judgment and hope, with a greater emphasis on judgment in 1–39 and hope in 40–66.

These two themes also emerge in the account of how God called Isaiah to be a prophet (Isaiah 6). In a vision, Isaiah saw God sitting on His throne while seraphs called, "Holy, holy, holy is the LORD Almighty; the whole earth is full of his glory" (verse 3).[3] Isaiah, suddenly made aware of his own sin, cried out for mercy; God's holiness always reveals human sin (verse 5). We see the other side of God's holiness as He immediately pardoned Isaiah's guilt and commissioned him as prophet to His people (verses 6–10). God knew Isaiah's message would be ignored, but the Holy One of Israel would not give up on His people. A small remnant would be preserved, and through this remnant God would continue to accomplish His plan (verses 11–13).

Although most of Isaiah's messages concerned Judah, he also spoke about other nations. In Isaiah 13–23, God announced judgment on Babylon, Assyria, Philistia, Moab, Syria, Israel, Cush, Egypt, Edom, Arabia, and Phoenicia. Many of these nations had opposed Judah, but they were probably singled out because they were the significant powers in the ancient Near East. God was not just in charge of Judah, but all the nations.

Isaiah 24–27 extends this still further to describe God's judgment on the whole earth, the restoration of His people, and their response of praise. These chapters describe more than the return from exile in Babylon. They

Who wrote Isaiah?

Many scholars argue that at least two and possibly three authors are responsible for the book of Isaiah. They point to the very different tone and theme of chapters 1–39 as compared to chapters 40–66. The earlier section is very accusing and warns of a coming exile, while the latter section is very consoling and speaks as if the people are already in exile. It seems to make more sense, these scholars argue, for chapters 40–66 to have been written during the period of the Exile. If so, this could not have been Isaiah, who would have been long dead. Those who speak of several authors also point to the difficulty of someone writing in the 700s referring by name to Cyrus, the Persian king who lived in the 500s.

Those who consider the whole book to come from the prophet Isaiah in the 700s see no problem with the different tone and theme. If God changed the theme from judgment to hope, they contend, the tone would necessarily change as well. Furthermore, describing the first half solely as judgment and the second solely as salvation overlooks the messages of hope in the first half and those of judgment in the second. Reference to Cyrus by name in advance of his birth is only a problem if one denies the possibility that God inspired the writing, which the book clearly claims.

Both sections frequently call God by an unusual name, the Holy One of Israel. While this title appears only six times outside Isaiah, it is found twelve times in the first half of Isaiah and fourteen times in the second half. As well, both halves share many common words and ideas. All the evidence from early Hebrew copies of Isaiah supports the idea of a single author, as does the evidence from the New Testament.

summarize how God will accomplish His plan, once and for all. God
promises supernatural judgment (Isaiah 24:21), universal worship (25:3, 6),
even the destruction of death (25:7–8).

Lessons from History

Isaiah 36–39 retells two episodes from Judah's history. The first (chapters
36–37) describes how God rescued Judah from the Assyrians. After Assyria
defeated Israel in 722 B.C., it turned its sights on Judah, surrounding
Jerusalem and preparing to destroy it in 701 B.C. King Hezekiah and his
people were understandably frightened. They knew about Assyria's reputation
and had seen what that ruthless enemy had done to Israel and many Judean
towns. In response to Hezekiah's prayer for help, God sent Isaiah to the king
with a promise of deliverance. Shortly after, God miraculously rescued
Jerusalem.

The second episode, chapters 38–39, actually happened about a decade
earlier, in 711 B.C. Hezekiah, seriously ill, prayed for God to spare his life.
God did so and Hezekiah responded with a lovely psalm of deliverance.
When the Babylonians, a rising rival to the Assyrians for power in the Near
East, heard about Hezekiah's illness and recovery, they sent him letters and a
gift. Flattered to the point of carelessness, Hezekiah threw open the doors to
his treasury and showed the Babylonian messengers all that he possessed.
Isaiah scolded him for this foolishness, predicting that one day Babylon
would return to plunder that treasury. This promise came true less than 150
years later. Isaiah retold these stories to illustrate his prophecies. When
Hezekiah trusted God, powerful Assyria was miraculously defeated and a
mortal illness healed. But giving way to self-confidence invited judgment in
the form of Babylonian conquest and exile.

Salvation and Restoration

Chapters 40–66 are as optimistic as the first thirty-five chapters are
pessimistic. Most of these oracles announce the good news that God would
save His people. Salvation would come in three steps: First, God would bring

What was the historical background of Isaiah's prophecy?

When Isaiah began his ministry around 740 B.C., King Uzziah had just died. Uzziah had ruled for more than half a century, providing stability and godly leadership to Judah. The stability of Uzziah's rule, that of his son, Jotham, and that of his grandson, Ahaz, probably fostered the moral carelessness that Isaiah criticized.

Around 735 B.C., the Northern Kingdom of Israel and its ally, the nation of Aram, invaded Judah. They may have been trying to force King Ahaz to join their revolt against the Assyrians. Ahaz responded by hiring the Assyrian army to come to his rescue. The Assyrians, a rising power in the Near East, accepted Ahaz's offer and lived up to their reputation as a ruthless and powerful enemy. They defeated and took control of Aram and Israel. When Israel tried to escape from Assyrian control in 722 B.C., Assyria destroyed its capital, Samaria, and scattered the Israelites throughout the vast Assyrian Empire. Although Isaiah says little about these events (except in chapters 7–12), the threat of an Assyrian invasion of Judah probably added emphasis to Isaiah's judgments against idolatry.

Ahaz's successor, Hezekiah, was a very good king. He purified the country of the idolatry fostered by his father and reorganized worship in the Temple, reforms Isaiah probably supported. Hezekiah disagreed with his father's pro-Assyrian policies and joined a revolt against Assyria. Assyria responded by invading Judah in 701 B.C. Although many Judean cities were attacked and destroyed, God answered Hezekiah's prayer by destroying the Assyrian army camped outside Jerusalem. This story is told in Isaiah 36–39 and 2 Kings 18:17–37.

His people back from exile; next, God would reestablish Israel as part of His ultimate plan; and, finally, God would accomplish that plan. The first step involved bringing the Israelites back from exile in Babylon. Although promising restoration before the Exile actually happened sounds strange, it certainly would give God's people a reason to hope. Many passages describe this return as a new exodus. The announcement to prepare a way for the Lord in the desert (Isaiah 40:3) reminds us of Israel's travels through the wilderness. The Red Sea and Jordan may be in mind in Isaiah 43:2, which speaks of passing through waters and rivers; this is certainly the picture in Isaiah 43:16–17.

Even more than restoring Israel to its homeland, God wanted to restore the people's relationship with Him. They remained His people throughout the Exile, but needed to be reminded of what this involved. God promised a relationship every bit as close as what they had ever known, one that was personal and life changing. God also spoke of their role in His plan. They understood that their disobedience had prevented them from fulfilling God's design: "We have not brought salvation to the earth; we have not given birth to people of the world" (Isaiah 26:18). But God was not finished with them. He would still use them to be a "light to the nations" (42:6 RSV) so that the whole earth could find God's house to be a "house of prayer for all nations" (56:7). "The Sovereign LORD declares—he who gathers the exiles of Israel: 'I will gather still others to them besides those already gathered'" (56:8).

God's Servants

In Job and Psalms we have seen that God intended to accomplish His plan through an intermediary. Isaiah tells us much more about this intermediary, the Messiah. He would arise from the Israelites, particularly from the family of King David (Isaiah 11:1–9). Although ruling as a king, the Messiah would also suffer on behalf of others (52:13—53:12).

Isaiah also looks ahead to the day when God would accomplish His plan. As we saw in chapters 24–27, Isaiah blurred the distinction between the return from Babylonian exile and God's ultimate victory, using heavily symbolic language. We know that the return from exile was not the end of God's plan, only one part of it. In Isaiah's picture of the end, we see that God will completely judge sin and those who choose it (Isaiah 63:1–6). With the end of sin will come a restoration of those relationships destroyed by sin (65:23–25).

GOD'S GREAT PLAN IN ISAIAH

God used Isaiah to reveal much of His ultimate plan to reconcile all the world to God. In particular, Isaiah emphasized Israel's role as a "light to the nations" (Isaiah 42:6 RSV). In Isaiah's vision of the "last days"—that time when God will accomplish His plan—he sees all nations streaming to the Temple in Jerusalem. They long to learn God's ways and obey them.

Who is the servant Isaiah speaks about?

The second half of Isaiah includes several passages that describe the "servants" God would use to carry out His plan. Some verses describe the nation of Israel as God's servant (Isaiah 41:8; 44:1). Other verses refer to the righteous group that remains after the rest of the Israelites are punished (49:1-7). Some passages speak about Cyrus, the Persian king who would release the Israelites from captivity and allow them to return home to Jerusalem (44:28).

Several passages describe the servant as the future, ideal king from David's line (42:1-7; 49:5-6). One lengthy passage (52:13–53:12) describes a suffering servant whose death brings forgiveness to others. The New Testament writers saw this passage as referring to Jesus (Luke 1:32b; Acts 8:30-35). Historically, not one but several servants would accomplish God's purposes. But only one, the Messiah, would bring salvation to the world.

Universal peace will prevail as the nations "beat their swords into plowshares and their spears into pruning hooks" (2:4). Following this symbolic description of a reconciled world, God emphasizes Israel's important role by calling her to "walk in the light of the LORD" (2:1–5). Although when this would happen and what it would look like is unclear, Isaiah's prophecies leave no doubt that God would reconcile the world by using Israel.

The Servant as Messiah

We also learn that God would accomplish this reconciliation through a very special servant. Isaiah's audience learned that this servant would be a king born into the family of David under remarkable circumstances (Isaiah 7:14). His reign would bring victory, justice, and peace to God's people (32:1–20). Some of Isaiah's prophecies suggest that this king would be more than human; He would be none other than God himself come to live among His people. Isaiah names this servant Immanuel, which means "God with us" (7:14). Later he refers to this servant by the titles "Wonderful Counselor, Mighty God, Everlasting Father, Prince of Peace" and predicts that His reign will be eternal (9:6–7). This servant came to be known as the "Messiah," a Hebrew term that refers to His having been anointed with oil, as a king was anointed when he took the throne. In the Greek language, "Anointed One" is translated "Christ."

The picture of the Messiah as triumphant king is not the only image Isaiah uses to describe Him. In Isaiah 52:13 — 53:12, we see that the king would also suffer unfairly on behalf of His people. Only after dying as a "guilt offering" would He be made alive to bring victory. When you read this passage, you can understand why the early church saw this as a prediction of Jesus Christ.

Finally, Isaiah helps us better understand what life under God's plan will be like. Figuring out whether passages such as Isaiah 11:1 — 12:6 and Isaiah 60–66 will be literally or symbolically fulfilled is less important than realizing the joy that comes from fellowship with God. Reconciliation with ourselves, with one another, with nature, and with God—this is what

God has wanted and what we will someday see, regardless of what it might look like.

WHAT WE LEARN ABOUT GOD FROM ISAIAH

Like many of the prophets, Isaiah describes a sovereign God who is able to control the destiny of His people and all other nations. We also meet a loving God who, even before the Exile, comforts His people. The prophet's most striking picture of God is captured in his favorite name, Holy One of Israel.

The Holy One of Israel

Isaiah may have liked this title because it expresses the two main themes of his message: judgment and salvation. God's holiness could not tolerate Israel's sin and had to judge it. Worshiping other gods and mistreating fellow Israelites were sins that had to be punished. Many of the oracles in the first half of the book warn against this coming judgment.

God's holiness also meant hope for God's people. First, He had promised to preserve Israel in order to accomplish His plan; His holiness required that He keep that promise to His people. He was, after all, the Holy One *of Israel*. Israel's salvation, described so beautifully in Isaiah 40–66, was just as much an act of God's holiness as the judgment pictured in Isaiah 1–35.

A Picture of Sinlessness

Second, God's holiness would not be content just to punish. Sin itself must be destroyed. How God would accomplish this destruction, the role the Messiah would play, what such a sin-free world would look like—these are themes to which Isaiah often returns, themes close to the heart of the Holy One of Israel.

Isaiah at a Glance

Authorship: Isaiah

Date of writing: 740–681 B.C.

Date of events: 740 B.C. to the completion of God's plan

Purposes: To warn Israel of coming judgment and comfort her with the certainty of God's salvation

Form: Prophetic oracles in poetry

Part of God's plan: To reveal the universal nature of God's plan, the role of the Messiah, and what this plan will look like

Key element of God's character: Holiness

application questions

1. The Old Testament often tells us to be holy as God is holy. In light of this description of God as the Holy One of Israel, what does this command mean to you in terms of warning? Comfort?

questions for study and discussion

Read Isaiah 1–12, 24–27, 40, 51–66

1. Try to put yourself in Isaiah's place in Isaiah 6. What would you have thought and done?
2. Why did God use an intermediary like the Messiah?
3. Isaiah's favorite title for God is "Holy One of Israel." What title would you give God?
4. What connections can you find between Isaiah 52:13—53:12 and Jesus' experience as described in the Gospels?
5. Do you think chapters 56–66 have already been fulfilled in the Jews' return from exile? If they will still be fulfilled, will it be literally or symbolically? Defend your answer.

6. How would Isaiah have been read differently by a Jew just after the return from exile?

7. What else can we learn about God's plan from Isaiah?

8. What else can we learn about God from Isaiah?

endnotes

1. An oracle was a message from God delivered to one of His spokespersons, the prophets. The prophet then passed along that message to those God intended to hear it.

2. These dates are based on passages such as Isaiah 1:1; 6:1; and Isaiah 36–39.

3. A seraph is a winged, supernatural creature whose appearance resemble a flame (seraph means "burning" in Hebrew). The Bible mentions seraphs only here.

chapter eighteen

Minor Books—Major Message
More Prophets of the Eighth and Seventh Centuries

SUGGESTIONS FOR READING THE MINOR PROPHETS OF THE 8TH AND 7TH CENTURIES

Since most of these books contain prophetic oracles written in poetic form, the guidelines for both prophecy and poetry must be kept in mind. In particular, the more you understand the historical background of the books, the more you will understand the prophets' words. Also, remember that prophecy is more about what God wanted to say to the original audience than what will happen in the future. What was predicted has mostly been fulfilled in Israel's history or is being fulfilled now through God's new covenant people, the church. For the greatest benefit, ask what these prophets can teach you about God.

INTRODUCTION

Isaiah wasn't the only prophet at work among God's people in the eighth century B.C. The Bible contains the writings of seven more: Hosea, Joel, Amos, Obadiah, Micah, Nahum, and Zephaniah, and a story about an eighth prophet, Jonah. Although classified as Minor Prophets, these books have a major message to deliver.

What are the Minor Prophets?

The dozen brief prophetic books found at the end of our Old Testament first circulated together about a century after the last of the books was written. When identified as "minor prophets" several hundred years later, minor referred only to their size, not their message. They are arranged in roughly chronological order, although several of these books cannot be dated with certainty.

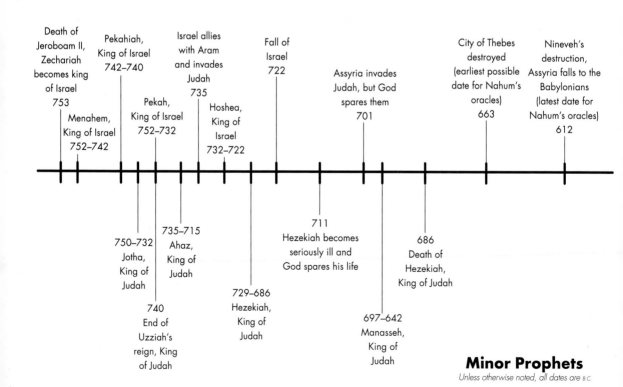

Death of Jeroboam II, Zechariah becomes king of Israel
753

Pekahiah, King of Israel
742–740

Menahem, King of Israel
752–742

Pekah, King of Israel
752–732

Israel allies with Aram and invades Judah
735

Hoshea, King of Israel
732–722

Fall of Israel
722

Assyria invades Judah, but God spares them
701

City of Thebes destroyed (earliest possible date for Nahum's oracles)
663

Nineveh's destruction, Assyria falls to the Babylonians (latest date for Nahum's oracles)
612

750–732 Jotha, King of Judah

735–715 Ahaz, King of Judah

740 End of Uzziah's reign, King of Judah

711 Hezekiah becomes seriously ill and God spares his life

729–686 Hezekiah, King of Judah

697–642 Manasseh, King of Judah

686 Death of Hezekiah, King of Judah

Minor Prophets
Unless otherwise noted, all dates are B.C.

MAP 9 Israel and Judah in the Days of Jeroboam II and Uzziah

OVERVIEW

Hosea: God's Ties of Love

While Isaiah was preaching to Judah, another of God's prophets addressed the Northern Kingdom of Israel. Hosea faced major challenges from a resistant audience there, but none greater than the challenge he faced from God. In order to illustrate how much He loved Israel, His unfaithful covenant partner, God commanded Hosea to marry a prostitute. The opening two chapters describe this marriage and the birth of three children, as well as the

Did God really make Hosea marry a prostitute?

Asking a prophet to marry a prostitute doesn't seem like something God would do. After all, He had forbidden priests to marry prostitutes (Leviticus 21:7); wouldn't He require the same of prophets? Some have suggested that the marriage was only symbolic and never took place, but this seems to contradict the clear message of the passage. Others argue that Gomer was not personally immoral, only born into the sinful, idol-worshiping society of Israel. Still others believe she did become a prostitute, but after she married Hosea, not before. While this may be possible, it only pushes the problem back one step: Why would God ask a prophet to marry a woman who would become a prostitute?

It seems more likely that Gomer was a prostitute when Hosea married her. She may even have been a "sacred" prostitute, one of the women hired to have sex with male worshipers of Baal. The Bible nowhere forbids a prophet to marry a prostitute, and such a marriage would certainly have delivered a powerful message to the Israelites about God's love for sinful Israel. By now we are not surprised to learn that God may ask His people to do some very difficult things.

What happens in a locust invasion?

Few natural disasters were more feared than an invasion by locusts. These small cricket-like insects bred in Africa and blew north. With their voracious appetites, they could eat their body weight in grass, leaves, plants, and other vegetation every day. When they ate tree bark, the trees often died and those that survived were less productive.

Such destruction had lasting consequences. The people not only lost the crops from that year, they also lost the seed to plant for the year to come. Many seasons could pass before new trees replaced the trees that had been killed. If these prolific insects had time to lay their eggs, another invasion could happen the following year.

spiritual lesson God sought to teach. Some time later, after Hosea's wife deserted him and returned to her immoral lifestyle, God instructed the prophet to bring her home and love her once again (Hosea 3). The rest of the book describes how God had done the same for His "bride," Israel. He took her back even after she committed spiritual adultery by worshiping other gods.

Because of idolatry and other sins, God threatened to punish His people with defeat at the hands of their enemies. These harsh words cannot hide God's deep love for His people, pictured in Hosea 11:1–11 as clearly as anywhere in the entire Old Testament. God concludes this book with an invitation to the Northern Kingdom to repent and return to Him (14:1–9). Because Israel rejected this invitation, the Northern Kingdom received destruction at the hands of the Assyrians instead of abundant blessings from God.

Joel: Judgment through Locusts

The introduction to the book of Joel tells us almost nothing about the prophet or when he wrote. The content of his prophecy suggests he was an eighth-century prophet who addressed Jerusalem with words of deep concern. Through an invasion of locusts, Joel saw judgment coming on Judah. God may have helped him to make this connection by reminding him of Deuteronomy 28:42: If His people disobeyed, God warned that

What was the historical background of this period?

The first half of the eighth century marked the golden age of the Northern Kingdom of Israel. During the long reign of Jeroboam II, Israel became a large, powerful, and wealthy nation. But all was not well spiritually, for Jeroboam continued the wicked practices of the Israelite kings before him. The thirty years following his death in 753 B.C. saw Israel slide quickly from security to total destruction.

Judah also enjoyed peace and prosperity during this time. Uzziah, toward the beginning of the eighth century, and his great-grandson, Hezekiah, at the end, were two of Judah's greatest monarchs. But as the writings of Isaiah and the other prophets make clear, spiritual problems were present here too.

Within this period, both Israel and Judah came under Assyrian control. At times the prophets criticized reliance on Assyria instead of on God (Hosea 5:13; 7:11; 8:9). They sometimes spoke of the coming divine judgment, with Assyria as God's instrument (8:1; 9:3; 10:6; Amos 5:27). Such passages would be painfully realized when Israel was destroyed in 722 B.C.

Israel's hatred of the Assyrians forms the background for the book of Jonah; Nahum and Zephaniah predict God's judgment on Assyria. At least one passage in these books may predict Judah's deliverance from Assyria in 701 B.C. (Micah 5:5-6).

"swarms of locusts will take over all your trees and the crops of your land."

As destructive as a locust invasion might be, God's judgment would be worse. When the "day of the LORD" arrived, that day on which God would judge the wicked, nothing would be spared. Hope remained if only Judah would humble itself and return to God (Joel 2:12–17). God would then restore His people (Joel 2:18—3:21).

Amos: Love for Neighbor

Unlike Joel, Amos tells us several things about himself. He was "one of the shepherds of Tekoa," a city just south of Jerusalem (Amos 1:1). We later learn he took care of fig trees, a tedious task performed by common laborers (7:14). Although from Judah, God called him to prophesy to the Northern Kingdom of Israel.

Amos began by condemning Israel's neighbors for their sins against God's people (1:3—2:5). No doubt this message was very popular with the Israelites. Before too long, however, Amos turned his accusing finger onto Israel's own sins, accusing Israel of oppressing the poor and of immorality (2:6—6:14). Unless Israel repented, God would send judgment, described symbolically in a series of visions (7:1—9:10). This judgment was not meant to destroy but only to punish Israel. The book concludes with a picture of the blessings God has in store for His people (9:11–15).

Obadiah: Brother against Brother

About the only thing we know of Obadiah is that he was a man of few words. The Old Testament's shortest book condemns Edom, a neighboring nation related to Israel through Esau, Jacob's brother. Edom had been guilty of gloating over Judah's defeat (Obadiah 2–9). Some suggest this defeat was the Babylonian invasion that destroyed Jerusalem in 586 B.C. More likely it was an earlier invasion of Jerusalem by the Philistines and Arabs when Jehoram was king (853–841 B.C.; see 2 Chronicles 21:17).

Obadiah promised that God would punish the Edomites, even though they proudly trusted in their ability to protect themselves. The Israelites would be

227

restored to their former glory and Jerusalem would be rebuilt. God would even allow His people to take control of the land that had been Edom's.

Jonah: A Lesson in Mercy

The book of Jonah is unlike the other books of the prophets. They mostly contain messages spoken by the individual prophets, while Jonah is a narrative about the prophet and contains no oracles. The other prophets were sent to God's people, while Jonah was sent to the archenemy of God's people in the eighth century, the Assyrians. Each of the other books identifies its author, but the book of Jonah is anonymous. The other books portray the prophets as faithful and courageous; the book of Jonah leaves us with a different impression of the book's namesake.

God sent Jonah, a prophet from the Northern Kingdom, to preach to Nineveh, a major city of the Assyrians. We can hardly blame Jonah for

Did the events of the book of Jonah really happen?

Many scholars, even some committed to the divine inspiration of the Bible, question whether the events in the book of Jonah really happened. They argue it sounds more like a parable, longer but similar to the ones Jesus told. Just as Jesus' made-up stories are God's Word, so is the parable known as the book of Jonah.

Others point out that Jesus appeared to understand the book as historical, not as a parable (Matthew 12:40). For centuries, interpreters have understood Jonah as historical. The moral of the story would certainly be more pronounced if these events actually happened. Certainly, nothing in this book would be impossible for God to do. Whether a parable or historical account, the book has much to teach us about God and His plan.

MAP 10 Jonah's Travels

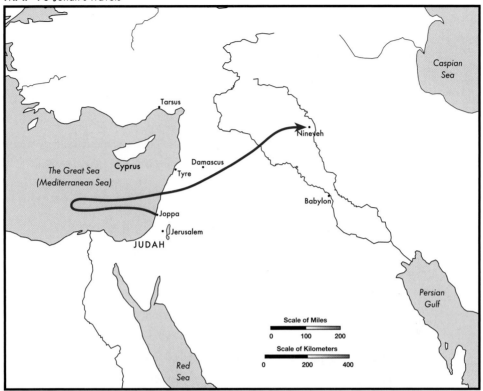

running away from this assignment. The Israelites hated the Assyrians and would have been happy for God to wipe them out. Even giving them a chance to repent was more than Jonah could stand. He would rather run away than obey (Jonah 1).

Unfortunately for Jonah, no one runs away from God. Jonah's efforts only landed him in very difficult circumstances (Jonah 2). Finally, he obeyed and went to Nineveh, where he preached God's message of coming judgment to an incredible response. When all the people from Nineveh turned from their sins, God spared them, which was exactly what Jonah was dreading (Jonah 3). The book ends with God teaching Jonah a lesson about His mercy. He took an ordinary vine and used it as an object lesson. Jonah became furious when the vine that had shaded him died. God pointed out that if Jonah could care so much about a vine he had not made, why couldn't God care about the Assyrians whom He had made and who needed His help (Jonah 4)?

More than just the last chapter, the whole book is about God's mercy. This mercy rescued Jonah from the big fish, gave him a second chance at obedience, and gave the Assyrians a chance to repent. Then God forgave the Assyrians and patiently instructed Jonah using the vine. Through this book, God reminded the Israelites that He was merciful. If they repented, they would find mercy as the Ninevites had. Because God was merciful, they were to be merciful too. God called them to be a light for the nations—even their enemies.

Micah: A Cry against Oppression

Although lesser known, Micah prophesied in about the same time period as Isaiah. He directed his message of judgment at the people (Micah 1:2—2:13), the leaders (3:1—5:9), and the whole nation (6:1—7:20). The people were guilty of oppressing their fellow Israelites and disregarding God's Word. The same could be said of the leaders "who despise justice and distort all that is right; who build Zion with bloodshed and Jerusalem with wickedness" (3:9–10). Like a prosecuting attorney, God accused His people of ignoring Him and cheating each other, then threatened them with punishment (6:1–7:7).

As with the other prophets, Micah offered not only judgment, but hope. He held out the promise of deliverance and restoration (2:12–13; 4:1–13; 7:14–20) and even promised that a "ruler over Israel, whose origins are from of old, from ancient times" would come from the town of Bethlehem (5:2).

Nahum: A Prophecy against Nineveh

Some time between 663 B.C. and 612 B.C., the prophet Nahum delivered oracles that predicted the destruction of Nineveh, capital of Assyria. We can be pretty sure about the earliest (663 B.C.) and latest dates (612 B.C.) of this book's writing. Nahum speaks about the Egyptian city of Thebes as already having been destroyed (Nahum 3:8–10), which occurred in 663 B.C.

Nineveh's destruction took place in 612 B.C., so Nahum's prophecies had to be delivered before this time.

Whatever revival had taken place as a result of Jonah's ministry a century earlier had long since evaporated. Assyria once again earned God's condemnation. Nahum's words would have been very reassuring to Judah, who had seen the Assyrians destroy the Israelites to the north (in 722 B.C.) and almost wipe them out too (in 701 B.C.). God would vindicate His people, even if He had to defeat the ancient Near East's mightiest power. As predicted, Nineveh and Assyria fell to the Babylonians in 612 B.C. after several years of decline.

Zephaniah: A Call for Reform[1]

With the death of Hezekiah in 686 B.C., Judah entered a long period of spiritual darkness. Manasseh, Hezekiah's son, worked hard to undo all the good his father had done. He rebuilt idol sanctuaries and participated in their worship, even to the point of sacrificing his own son (2 Kings 21:1–6). Only the zeal of his grandson, Josiah, prevented God's judgment from coming sooner (2 Kings 22:4–20).

Zephaniah prophesied during Josiah's reign and may himself have been a member of the royal family (Zephaniah 1:1). Perhaps it was Zephaniah's words and influence that encouraged Josiah to carry out his important reforms. Judah had survived to this point but was not immune to judgment (1:1—2:3). God's day was near (1:7–18), both for Judah and for other nations (2:4–15). The book ends with a message of hope to Judah (3:9–20).

GOD'S GREAT PLAN IN THESE BOOKS

The minor prophets who wrote in the eighth and seventh centuries reveal several important truths about God's plan to reconcile the world to himself. We see, first, the motive for that plan: God's love. Because these prophets often describe this love in a minor key, we can misunderstand and see only harshness and judgment. By listening carefully, we hear the reassuring strains of mercy and hope.

These books also make it clear that a plan for reconciliation was needed. In spite of Israel's external success and prosperity, sin's cancer had spread to every part of society. God's people had broken their covenant promises and worshiped other gods, even while pretending to follow Yahweh. Their greed had led them to oppress their brothers and sisters. Corruption was rampant (Amos 5:10), human life devalued (Amos 2:6), and the leaders were unconcerned (Amos 6:1). The seriousness of the sin problem begged for a remedy.

Righteousness and Restoration

We also see several things about the nature of God's plan. In the repeated picture of the Day of the Lord, we are reminded that God's plan will punish wrongs and reward righteousness. God's people are often unfairly treated, even persecuted. Truth doesn't always triumph. But when God completes His plan, righteousness will prevail. When we hear Obadiah predict judgment on Edom or Nahum on Assyria, and when we realize that judgment did come on these nations, we are reminded that, in the end, God wins.

We also see that God's plan included the restoration of God's people after exile (Hosea 11:11). From this remnant of God's people, God would cause the Messiah to be born in Bethlehem (Micah 5:2). These books symbolically describe the blessings experienced by God's people now and ultimately in heaven for eternity (Zephaniah 3:14–20). God's goal has always been to reconcile all nations back to himself. Israel was God's vehicle to accomplish this, a fact brought out in the book of Jonah and in Micah 4.

WHAT WE LEARN ABOUT GOD FROM THESE BOOKS

God loves the world. Even the harsh words of judgment contained in these books can't hide this truth. In fact, they emphasize it. Hosea presents in graphic terms how much God cares about His people. They cheated on Him and broke their promises, but God still loved them and wanted to be reconciled. He waited for them, giving them every opportunity to repent, but they ignored His passionate appeals.

For Israel's Good

Finally, punishment must come. The prophets made it very clear that God would bring this punishment, but they also made it clear that the punishment was for Israel's good. God knew they would never be happy in disobedience. For their own good, He had to bring them back to himself. When He saw that the only way they would return would be through discipline, He punished them. As the surgeon must wound in order to heal, God wounded His people in order to bring them back to their senses and back to Him.

For God So Loved the World

We can also see God's love in the judgment He brought on those who harmed His people. Obadiah specifically mentions Edom, and Nahum targets Nineveh, but these are only the more obvious examples of such warnings (for others, see Amos 1:3–15; Zephaniah 2:4–15). Israel's privileged status should not blind us to the fact that God loves all nations, even those He judges. Otherwise, He never would have sent Jonah to Nineveh in the first place, or bothered warning Nineveh the second time through Nahum.

Finally, we get a hint of the amazing extent of God's love in Micah 5:2, which predicts that the Messiah would be born in Bethlehem. In the New Testament, we can read about this birth and the life that followed. We learn how this Messiah died on the cross and how that death was God's way to accomplish His plan for reconciliation. When we see the cross, we understand more clearly how much God loves this world.

Hosea at a Glance

Authorship: Hosea

Date of writing: 750–723 B.C.

Date of events: 750 B.C. and beyond

Purpose: To affirm God's love for Israel

Form: Oracles

Part of God's plan: To show God's love as the motive for His plan

Key elements of God's character: Love, justice

Joel at a Glance

Authorship: Joel

Date of writing: Unknown

Date of events: Unknown

Purpose: To call Israel to repentance by describing coming judgment

Form: Oracles

Part of God's plan: To show the need for God's plan: problem of sin

Key elements of God's character: Love, justice

Amos at a Glance

Authorship: Amos

Date of writing: 760–750 B.C.

Date of events: 760 B.C. and beyond

Purposes: To warn against judgment for oppression, offer hope

Form: Oracles

Part of God's plan: To show the need for God's plan: oppression; and the nature of God's plan: justice

Key elements of God's character: Love, justice

Obadiah at a Glance

Authorship: Obadiah

Date of writing: Unknown

Date of events: Either 9th century or 6th century B.C.

Purpose: To promise the defeat of Edom

Form: Oracles

Part of God's plan: To reveal the nature of God's plan: Show importance of Israel

Key elements of God's character: Love, justice

Jonah at a Glance

Authorship: Anonymous

Date of writing: 8th century B.C.

Date of events: 8th century B.C.

Purpose: To reveal God's mercy for all

Form: Narrative

Part of God's plan: To reveal the nature of God's plan: Show God's love for all

Key elements of God's character: Love, mercy

Micah at a Glance

Authorship: Micah

Date of writing: 750–686 B.C.

Date of events: 750 B.C. and beyond

Purpose: To warn against judgment and offer hope

Form: Oracles

Part of God's plan: To reveal the need for God's plan: sin; and the nature of God's plan: promise of Messiah

Key elements of God's character: Love, justice

Nahum at a Glance

Authorship: Nahum

Date of writing: Between 663–612 B.C.

Date of events: 612 B.C.

Purposes: To predict and celebrate downfall of Nineveh

Form: Oracles

Part of God's plan: To reveal the nature of God's plan: vindication of God's people

Key elements of God's character: Love, justice

Zephaniah at a Glance

Authorship: Zephaniah

Date of writing: 640-630 B.C.

Date of events: 640 B.C. and beyond

Purpose: To announce God's judgment on Judah and other nations

Form: Oracles

Part of God's plan: To reveal the need for God's plan: sin

Key elements of God's character: Love, justice

application questions

1. In what ways is God's love like that of a parent whose child disobeys?

2. In what other ways is God's love evident in these books?

3. What does it mean to you to know that God loves you this much?

questions for study and discussion

1. Read Hosea 1–3. Do you think God really asked Hosea to marry a prostitute? Why or why not?

2. Read Joel.

   a. What does God tell the people to do in 2:12–17?

   b. What can you learn about the "day of the LORD" in this book?

3. Read Amos 1–2, 7–9.

   a. In chapters 1 and 2, why does Amos save his criticism of Israel until last?

   b. Summarize each of the visions Amos has in chapters 7–9.

4. Read Obadiah.

   a. What do you learn about the "day of the LORD" in this book?

   b. Why would such a small book about such an insignificant enemy be included in the Old Testament?

5. Read Jonah.

   a. Do you think this really happened? Why or why not?

   b. What does this book teach about God's mercy?

6. Read Micah. Does Micah 4 predict the rebuilding of a literal temple at some date still in our future? Why or why not?

7. Read Nahum.

   a. What sins is Nineveh accused of in this book?

   b. What does God's treatment of Nineveh tell us about Him?

8. Read Zephaniah. What is the "day of the LORD"?

9. What else can we learn about God's plan from these books?

10. What else can we learn about God's character from these books?

endnote

1. Although Habakkuk comes next in our Bibles, it probably was not written until the sixth century. We'll discuss it in the next chapter.

chapter nineteen

Disobedience Brings Disaster—Part 2

Jeremiah, Habakkuk, Lamentations

SUGGESTIONS FOR READING JEREMIAH, HABAKKUK, AND LAMENTATIONS

These three books present a wide variety of literary types. The poetry of Lamentations is very similar to the laments found in the book of Psalms. The first four chapters of Lamentations are alphabet acrostics: The first verse begins with the first letter of the Hebrew alphabet, the second verse with the second letter, and so on. Habakkuk is also poetry, but is written in dialogue form with the prophet asking questions, which God answers.

The book of Jeremiah contains numerous prophetic oracles; many are written in poetry, while others are written in prose (for example, Jeremiah 3:14–18 or 7:1—8:3). In several places throughout the book, we overhear Jeremiah complaining to God (for example, Jeremiah 12:1-4; 15:10-21; 20:7-18). A number of passages tell stories about Jeremiah or about the events surrounding the fall of Jerusalem in 586 B.C.

Pay attention to how the types of literature flow from one to the other, employing whatever guidelines are appropriate. Also keep the historical context in mind; prophetic material is notoriously difficult to understand otherwise. Most importantly, listen for insights about God's character.

INTRODUCTION

These books are not easy to read because they describe the terrible disaster that came to Judah in 586 B.C. for its disobedience to God. But all was not lost; God was still at work. Even in this dark hour of Judah's history, clear traces of hope shine through.

OVERVIEW

Jeremiah: Hope and a Future

Jeremiah had a difficult life. He was appointed while only a young man—perhaps just a teenager—to announce destruction on his own country. He was betrayed and rejected by his family, persecuted by the people, and imprisoned by the king. At times he even felt that God was against him. In spite of this, Jeremiah remained an honest, fearless spokesman for God.

He was called in 626 B.C., about the time the ministry of Zephaniah was ending. Like that prophet, Jeremiah was told to warn Judah and the surrounding nations about God's coming judgment. He continued to preach his unpopular message until that judgment fell on Jerusalem in 586 B.C.

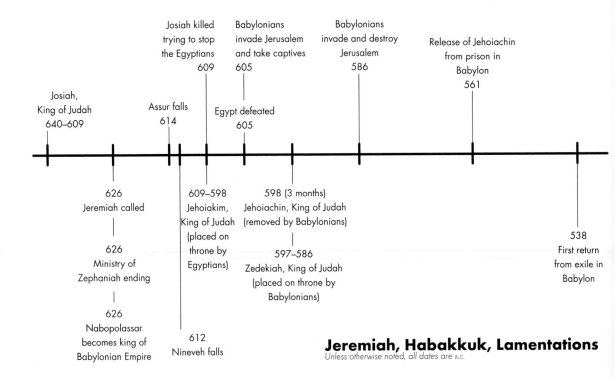

Jeremiah, Habakkuk, Lamentations
Unless otherwise noted, all dates are B.C.

MAP 11 New Babylonian Empire

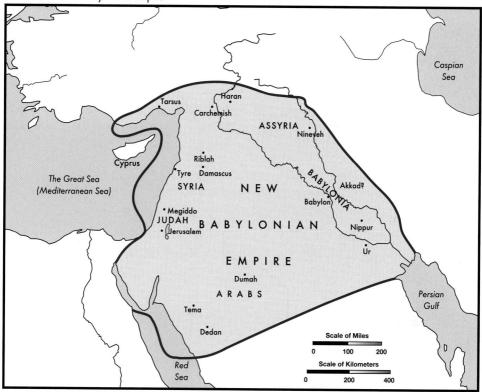

While often obscured by dark, ominous clouds, a message of hope designed to comfort God's people shines through Jeremiah's prophecies.

Most of Jeremiah's attention was consumed with the coming storm of God's anger. At his call, God appointed him "to uproot and tear down, to destroy and overthrow" (Jeremiah 1:10). Judah had abandoned God and turned to idols (1:16). When confronted with their sin, they denied it (2:35). When God tried to get their attention by withholding the needed rain, they acted as if nothing was wrong (3:1–5). Outwardly, everything looked fine. Josiah's reforms, as good as they were, left the people feeling self-righteous. The Temple became a good luck charm; they thought that as long as the building remained, God wouldn't let anything happen to them. Meanwhile, they continued to cheat God and each other (7:1–8).

241

MAP 12 The Campaign of Nebuchadnezzar against Judah

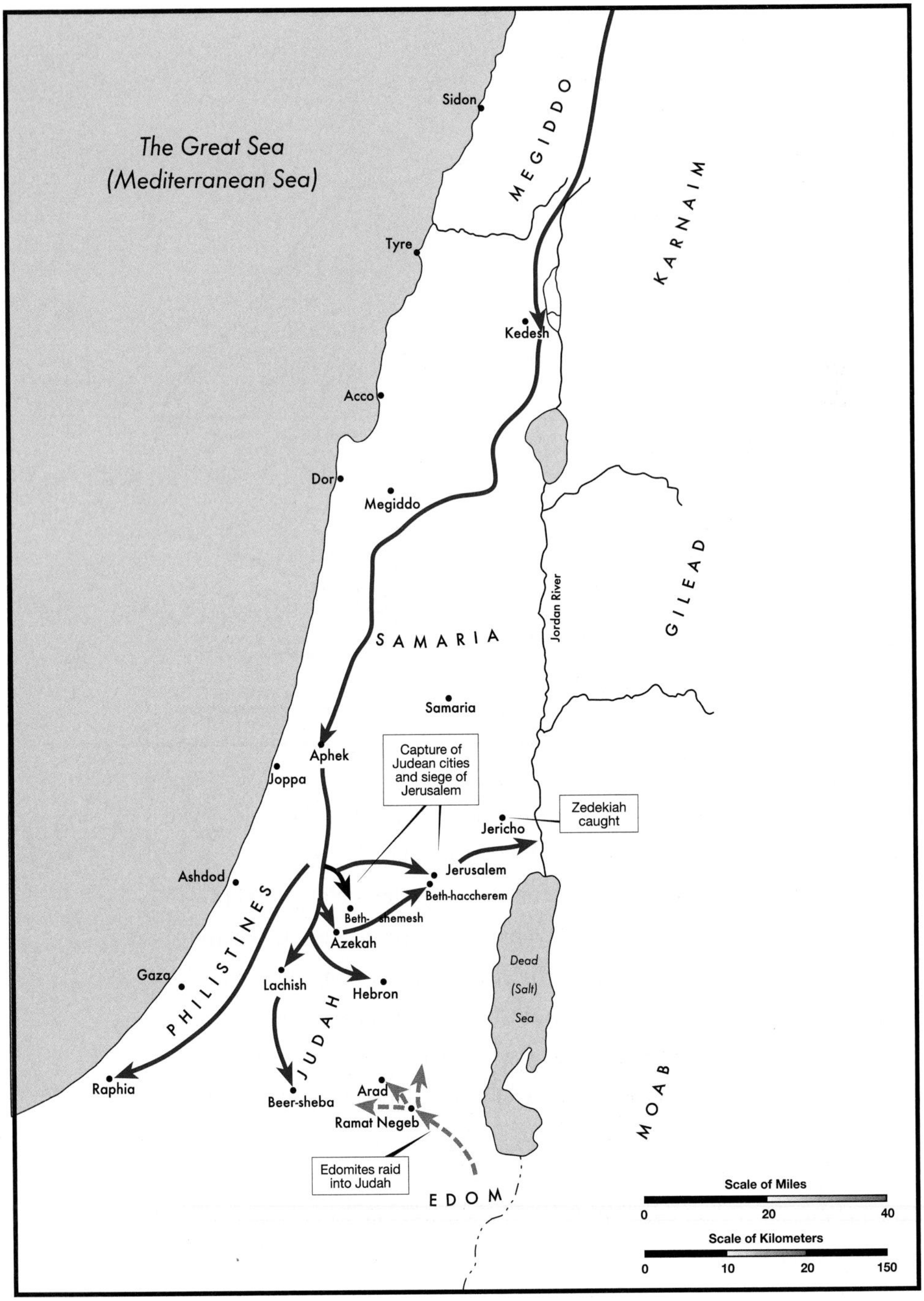

The Great Sea (Mediterranean Sea)

Sidon

MEGIDDO

KARNAIM

Tyre

Kedesh

Acco

Dor

Megiddo

GILEAD

Jordan River

SAMARIA

Samaria

Aphek

Joppa

Capture of Judean cities and siege of Jerusalem

Jericho

Zedekiah caught

Ashdod

Jerusalem

Beth-haccherem

Beth-shemesh

Azekah

PHILISTINES

Dead (Salt) Sea

Gaza

Lachish

Hebron

JUDAH

Raphia

Beer-sheba

Arad

Ramat Negeb

MOAB

Edomites raid into Judah

EDOM

Scale of Miles

0   20   40

Scale of Kilometers

0   10   20   150

Metaphors of Judgment

Several times, God instructed Jeremiah to announce judgment through a symbolic action. Jeremiah 13 explains how he was told to buy and wear a linen belt, bury it, and some time later, dig it up. When he did, he saw it was completely ruined. To those watching and listening, God provided the application: Judah had been the belt around God's waist, but because of its sin, it would be ruined. Another time God told Jeremiah to buy a clay pot and take it to a valley outside Jerusalem. There, after preaching a sermon announcing God's judgment, he broke the pot to symbolize Judah's destruction (Jeremiah 19). He made a wooden yoke, like those used to harness oxen for plowing, and wore it for some time to symbolize how Judah should surrender to Babylon, putting itself under the captor's yoke (Jeremiah 27–28).

Is there any order to the arrangement of the book of Jeremiah?

Though some have compared the lack of arrangement of passages in this book to broken and scattered pieces of pottery, perhaps the picture is not quite so random. When we look closely, we can see a few patterns among the pieces. First, we see that the book is arranged by themes, not by chronology. We also can observe that chapters 1–25 contain mostly prophecies against Judah and chapters 26–45 mostly stories about Jeremiah. Dated oracles of judgment seem to be clustered in chapters 21–29, and the heart of the book contains messages of future hope (chapters 30–33). Following this are more dated oracles (chapters 34–35) and stories about Jeremiah's sufferings (chapters 36–45). Prophecies against foreign nations are found in chapters 46–51 with a historical appendix attached in chapter 52. (For a thorough outline and explanation, see David A. Dorsey, *The Literary Structure of the Old Testament* [Grand Rapids, Mich.: Baker], 1999.)

Should Jeremiah have complained so much?

There is no denying that Jeremiah used some pretty strong language when speaking to God. He accused God of tricking him (Jeremiah 20:7) and compared Him to a brook that should contain water but doesn't (15:18). Was it okay for Jeremiah to speak to God like this?

We faced a similar problem in Psalms. As we noted there, complaints are appropriate under difficult circumstances if they come from a heart that is loyal to God. In spite of the physical and emotional distress Jeremiah was forced to endure, he continued to faithfully serve God. God never scolded him for his honesty.

God wanted Jeremiah and the people to know that Judah's destruction would be caused by its disobedience, not God's failure, so He sent Jeremiah to the potter's house to watch the pot-making process (Jeremiah 18). While the clay spun on the wheel, the potter discovered that the pot was not turning out as he wished, so he started again. God spoke to Jeremiah: "O house of Israel, can I not do with you as this potter does?" (18:6). Destruction would come, not because God lacked the power to protect Judah, but because of God's power to judge.

Announcing this judgment nearly killed the messenger. Several times Jeremiah complained to God about his task and its toll. Sometimes God reassured him (Jeremiah 15:19–21), but at other times we hear no heavenly reply. Jeremiah's experience reminds us that serving God does not assure us a rosy path of blessings. Faithful service to God can be tough.

The Light through the Clouds

Periodically, hope shines through the clouds, like in the letter Jeremiah wrote to those already taken into exile (Jeremiah 29:1–23). After telling them the bad news that the Exile would continue for a long time, Jeremiah promised it would not last forever. Yahweh would come to Babylon and escort them home to Jerusalem. God planned to prosper them, to give them hope and a future life (29:10–14). Then the clouds returned as Jeremiah told them about the difficulties that still awaited Jerusalem.

What is the historical background of these books?

In 626 B.C., about the same time God was calling Jeremiah to be His prophet, Nabopolassar became king of the Babylonian Empire. One of his first tasks was to wipe out the Assyrian Empire, then in decline. Assur fell in 614 B.C. and Nineveh in 612 B.C. When the Egyptian army marched north to defend Assyria (609 B.C.), Josiah, king of Judah, tried to stop them. On the plain outside the city of Megiddo, Josiah was killed in battle. Four years later, Egypt was defeated at the battle of Carchemish (605 B.C.) and the Babylonians became the absolute rulers of the ancient Near East.

Josiah's death meant the beginning of the end for the nation of Judah. His sons lacked the character and skills to preserve his spiritual gains and to deal with the Babylonians. One son ruled only three months before being replaced by the Egyptians in 609 B.C. Jehoiakim, his pro-Egyptian replacement, lasted eleven years. That he was no friend of God's can be seen in his treatment of Jeremiah, God's prophet. During Jehoiakim's reign, the Babylonians invaded in 605 B.C. and took captives. They were on their way to Jerusalem for a second invasion in 598 when Jehoiakim died. His son, Jehoiachin, ruled only three months before the Babylonians removed him from the throne. They replaced him with another of Josiah's sons, Mattaniah, who was renamed Zedekiah. When he rebelled against the Babylonians, they marched back to Jerusalem in 586 B.C., burned it to the ground, and led many of the people into exile.

For four chapters (Jeremiah 30–33), hope is all we see. God would restore His people to their land after the time of discipline had been completed (Jeremiah 30–31). By God's mercy, the original covenant God made with Abraham and modified under Moses and David still stood. God announced a new version, in which the covenant would be based on a more personal, individual relationship with God than what was known previously (31:31–34). Another symbolic action affirmed these promises. Jeremiah was told to purchase a field in his hometown just outside Jerusalem (32:6–15), even as the Babylonian army surrounded Jerusalem where the prophet sat in prison. In this way, God promised, "Houses, fields and vineyards will again be bought in this land" (32:15).

As great as was the return from Babylonian exile, God had something even better in mind. He would raise up the Messiah from the line of David to lead God's people to their appointed destiny (33:1–26). The storm of God's anger would still come, but a bright morning awaited the faithful.

Habakkuk: Trust in God's Power

The prophet Habakkuk shared Jeremiah's concern for the coming judgment. Instead of taking his concerns to the people, Habakkuk engaged in a dialogue with God. The result is something like the book of Job. Both include dialogue, although God actually answers Habakkuk's questions. Both books take on the same theme—God's justice—although Habakkuk raises the issue on a national rather than a personal level.

An Appointed Time

Like Job and Jeremiah, Habakkuk complained that God seemed unfair. "Why don't you maintain justice?" the prophet asked (Habakkuk 1:2–4, paraphrased), to which God replied, "I do, in My time" (based on 1:5–11). In his second complaint, Habakkuk asked how God could use the wicked Babylonians to punish the Judeans (1:12—2:1). As bad as God's people had become, they were still more righteous than these pagans. "Babylon will be repaid for her sins," God answered (2:2–20).

In the final chapter, Habakkuk prays for God's mercy, perhaps prompted by Judah's impending destruction at the hands of the Babylonians. His prayer concludes with Habakkuk's personal resolution to believe in spite of the worst (3:16–19). Few passages in all of the Bible so eloquently express what faith really means. The Jews who returned from exile must have found comfort in these words, for they used Habakkuk 3 in their worship, as the musical instructions at the beginning and end of this chapter imply.

Lamentations: A Funeral Song

Immediately following Jeremiah, we find a small collection of lament poems that mourn the destruction of Jerusalem and Judah. Although the book does not identify its author, it has long been thought to have been written by Jeremiah. Both books share a common theme and a common vocabulary. Whoever wrote Lamentations did so shortly after Jerusalem's fall in 586 B.C.

Order amid Chaos

As noted earlier, the first four chapters of Lamentations are alphabet acrostics. Each of the twenty-two verses in chapter 1 starts with the successive letter in the Hebrew alphabet.[1] The same is true for chapters 2 and 4. In chapter 3, verses 1 through 3 each begin with the first letter, verses 4 through 6 begin with the second letter, and so on. Perhaps the author used the acrostic form to make it easier to memorize this material. Or he may have wanted to imply how God can still maintain order (as suggested by the alphabet) even in the face of chaos (as suggested by the content of these poems).

In the first two chapters, we learn of the terrible devastation, including exile, destruction, starvation, cannibalism, plunder, and scorn. Even worse is the knowledge that God had done this because of Judah's sin. Chapter 3 continues to relate Judah's pain, but now through the voice of the author's personal agony. Tucked into the middle of this lament and in the middle of this book of laments is a beautiful statement of trust. Because God is faithful, His people will not give up in despair. God will come to the rescue of those who trust in Him (Lamentations 3:22–33). This realization does not change the circumstances, but it does provide hope for enduring those circumstances. The prophet returns to his lament in chapter 4, while chapter 5 reflects the Jews' anguished yet hopeful prayer for restoration.

GOD'S GREAT PLAN IN JEREMIAH, HABAKKUK, AND LAMENTATIONS

You can't read these books without being impressed by the seriousness of sin. Sin cost Judah its king, its land, its freedom, and its Temple. If bloodshed, famine, cannibalism, desolation, bitter tears, and agony were the symptoms, sin was the disease. The very thing that makes these books so hard to read also shows us the absolute necessity of God's plan.

Familiar Themes

Jeremiah highlights several things about God's plan that we have seen in other books. We hear that the Messiah will come from the line of David and be "a King who will reign wisely and do what is just and right in the land" (Jeremiah 23:5). His arrival will mean salvation and safety for God's people; "The LORD Our Righteousness" will be His name (verse 6). Jeremiah also reminds us that God's plan also includes other nations besides the Jews. After these nations are judged, God will show them compassion and restore them too. He says that if they embrace Him, "they will be established among my people" (12:16).

From Jeremiah, we learn something else about God's plan, something only hinted at in earlier books. We learn that this plan calls for a more personal relationship between God and His people. God had always loved people individually, but He had usually related to them as a group because this was how people understood themselves in the group culture of the ancient Near East. He also had maintained His distance, relating to them through priests, prophets, and others.

A New Covenant

Although this worked well, God's goal was to relate to each person individually and personally through His Holy Spirit. First, He would remove the sin problem (Jeremiah 31:34) that had prevented this full fellowship. Then He would put His Law "in their minds and write it on their hearts" (verse 33) so each person could understand what God wanted from him or her.

Jesus understood Jeremiah's prophecy to refer to His ministry. When eating the Last Supper with His disciples, Jesus raised a glass of wine and said, "This cup is the new covenant in my blood, which is poured out for you" (Luke 22:20). Using the language of Jeremiah (31:31), He was referring to His death on the cross, only a few hours away. The author of the book of Hebrews quoted Jeremiah 31:31–34 and specifically applied it to Jesus. By the cross, God would solve the sin problem (Hebrews 9:12; Romans 3:21–24). With sin removed, each person could know God through the Holy Spirit (Romans 5:1–2; 8:3–4).

Despite the dark clouds that linger over these books—perhaps because these clouds hang so low—God's faithfulness shines even brighter. Even with all Jeremiah's complaints, he continued to count on God. Habakkuk promised to trust Him, even if his world collapsed (Habakkuk 3:17–19). Right in the middle of one of the most depressing books of the Bible, Lamentations, you will read some of the most encouraging words ever written about God's faithfulness (Lamentations 3:19–24). We can be confident that such a faithful God will complete His plan and reunite the world to himself.

WHAT WE LEARN ABOUT GOD FROM JEREMIAH, HABAKKUK, AND LAMENTATIONS

Each of these books teaches us about God's faithfulness. It stands out most clearly at the heart of Lamentations, but also shines through in other places. Why did God ask Jeremiah to endure so much, if not to show His faithfulness? Why would God send Jeremiah as His prophet—even when He knew Israel wouldn't listen—if not because He was and is so faithful?

His Faithfulness Endures

God is so faithful that Jeremiah could voice his honest complaints without fear of punishment. Habakkuk could anticipate the worst things—"Though the fig tree does not bud and there are no grapes on the vines, though the olive crop fails and the fields produce no food, though there are no sheep in the pen and no cattle in the stalls"—and still "rejoice in the LORD," because he knew that God is faithful (Habakkuk 3:17–19).

Although God's faithfulness shines through in warming rays, God shows himself most clearly in these books as a disciplinarian. It isn't an easy picture to look at; no one likes to think about punishment. But the same God who loves us, the same God who from the very beginning has been seeking to have a relationship with us, the same God who sent Jesus to die on the cross for us—this God must sometimes punish His people.

The Babylonians broke down the walls of Jerusalem, carried off its inhabitants, and burned down the Temple because Judah had rebelled against their rule. But Babylon was only God's tool to discipline His rebellious children. They had broken *His* Law, disregarded *His* warnings, and brought this judgment on themselves. He did not want to punish them—no decent parent wants to punish a child—but He loved them too much to let them off the hook.

Discipline Tempered by Love

The Bible's frequent reference to punishment arising from God's anger makes us suspicious. Can an angry God really be holy? But God's anger is very different than human anger. We usually get angry for the wrong reasons: Our rights have been violated or our feelings hurt. Most of us find it difficult to maintain self-control while angry. However, God's anger is never selfish, only loving. He becomes angry when anger is the only proper response. He becomes angry only when love most demands it and when anything else would be the wrong reaction.

The best parents discipline because they must, not because they enjoy it. Only the long-term goal of raising a well-adjusted child would ever cause them to hurt that child. Just so, God would prefer not to discipline at all; He withholds discipline until it is absolutely necessary. The Bible calls Him "slow to anger; abounding in love" (Psalm 103:8). God would much rather forgive than punish, and show mercy than exact retribution, which is what the psalmist meant when he said that God's "anger lasts only a moment, but his favor lasts a lifetime" (Psalm 30:5).

Jeremiah at a Glance

Authorship: Jeremiah

Date of writing: 626 B.C. until just after 586 B.C.

Date of events: 626 B.C. and beyond

Purpose: To warn Judah and other nations about the coming judgment

Form: Prophetic oracles in poetry, prophetic oracles in prose, narrative, poetic laments

Part of God's plan:

1. To reveal the need for God's plan: Reveals serious nature of sin
2. To reveal the nature of God's plan: more personal relationship

Key elements of God's character: Faithfulness, disciplinarian

---

Habakkuk at a Glance

Authorship: Habakkuk
Date of writing: Near end of the 600s B.C.
Date of events: 605–586 B.C.
Purpose: To examine God's justice with nations
Form: Prophetic oracles in poetry
Part of God's plan: To show God's faithfulness to execute His plan
Key elements of God's character: Faithfulness, disciplinarian

Lamentations at a Glance

Authorship: Anonymous, but traditionally Jeremiah
Date of writing: Just after 586 B.C.
Date of events: 586 B.C.
Purpose: To mourn the loss of God's favor
Form: Lament poetry
Part of God's plan: To show the need for God's plan: reveals the serious nature of sin
Key elements of God's character: Faithfulness, disciplinarian

application questions

1. In what ways has God been faithful to you?

2. Have you ever experienced God's judgment in your life?

3. What have you learned from this material that will make it easier for you to deal with your difficulties?

questions for study and discussion

1. Read Jeremiah 1, 7, 11–20, 25–33.
   a. When is it wrong to question God?
   b. What role did Baruch play in Jeremiah's ministry?
2. Read Habakkuk. Why did the Jews use Habakkuk 3 for worship?
3. Read Lamentations. Why do you think the first four chapters of Lamentations were written as alphabet acrostics? Why wasn't chapter 5 written this way?
4. What else can we learn about God's plan from these books?
5. What else can we learn about God's character from these books?

endnote

1. Verse 1 begins with the first letter of the Hebrew alphabet, א (aleph); verse 2 begins with the second letter, ב (beth), and so forth through all twenty-two letters of the Hebrew alphabet.

chapter twenty
"They Will Know That I Am the Lord"
Ezekiel

SUGGESTIONS FOR READING EZEKIEL

Like several other books of prophecy, the book of Ezekiel contains both narrative and prophetic oracles. Most of those oracles are in prose rather than poetic form. As with all the prophets, pay close attention to the historical background behind the oracles.

What we find in Ezekiel is very different than anything we've seen so far in the prophetic books. This prophet experienced visions in which he was transported from one place to another or saw something quite unusual. Sometimes an angel had to explain what Ezekiel had seen. Continue to use the same guidelines for prophetic passages. Also, don't let the book's weirder aspects distract you from your main goals: learning what you can about God's plan and His nature.

INTRODUCTION

Ezekiel is unlike anything you've come across so far in your trip through the Old Testament. You'll see visions that defy description and hear some of the most depressing and some of the most hopeful words in Scripture. Although it is one of the more challenging books of prophecy to understand, Ezekiel is well worth the effort.

OVERVIEW

While Jeremiah's ministry in Jerusalem was concluding, another prophet in exile spoke God's message. Ezekiel had been brought to Babylon in 597 B.C., along with ten thousand of his fellow Jews, including King Jehoiachin and the royal family. Ezekiel was taken to live among other exiles at the Kebar River, an irrigation canal located near the city of Nippur in Babylon.

Four years later, God appeared to Ezekiel in a very unusual way and called him to be a prophet to his fellow exiles (Ezekiel 1–5). He had been born into a family of priests and would have taken up that task at age thirty had he remained in Jerusalem. Instead, in his thirtieth year, God called him to be a

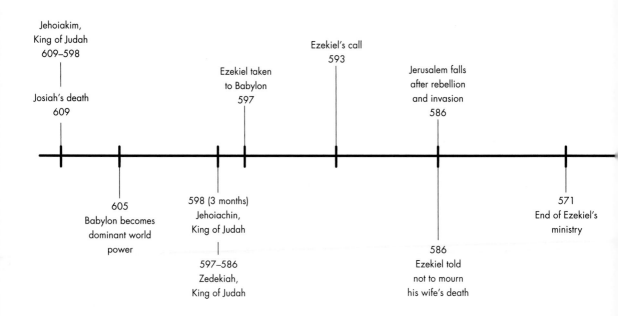

Jehoiakim,
King of Judah
609–598

Josiah's death
609

605
Babylon becomes
dominant world
power

Ezekiel taken
to Babylon
597

598 (3 months)
Jehoiachin,
King of Judah

597–586
Zedekiah,
King of Judah

Ezekiel's call
593

Jerusalem falls
after rebellion
and invasion
586

586
Ezekiel told
not to mourn
his wife's death

571
End of Ezekiel's
ministry

Ezekiel
Unless otherwise noted, all dates are B.C.

What is the historical background of this book?

Babylon became the dominant world power in the ancient Near East by 605 B.C. The Babylonians had already defeated Assyria and in 605 dealt a crushing blow to the Egyptians. King Josiah's death in 609 B.C. while fighting the Egyptians left Judah unable to deal with Babylon's rising power. Rebellion against Babylon led to several invasions and deportations before the final destruction in 586 B.C. Babylon took the best of Judah's society, including the leaders and craftsmen. The prophet Daniel was taken in 605 and a young man named Ezekiel was deported in 597.

Life in Babylonian exile was difficult but not impossible. Unlike exile under Assyria, these Jews were allowed to live together in communities and maintain their identity as Jews. They were free to own property and earn a living by manufacturing, farming, and business. The worst part was knowing that they had lost their land and Temple due to disobedience.

prophet. To explain what it meant to be a prophet, God had him eat a scroll that was to symbolize God's Word. He also explained to Ezekiel that being a prophet would be difficult but that he must obey; he must be a watchman announcing God's warning (3:1–21).

A Painful Warning

True to God's prediction, Ezekiel's ministry was full of challenges. The exiles were slow to accept the truth of his words, and his message was painful to deliver. Much of what he communicated was through symbolic actions, some of them quite bizarre. At one point God had him build a model of Jerusalem and then pretend to attack the model. Another time God had him lie on his side every day for more than a year, eat bread cooked over a fire

MAP 13 The Exile from Judah

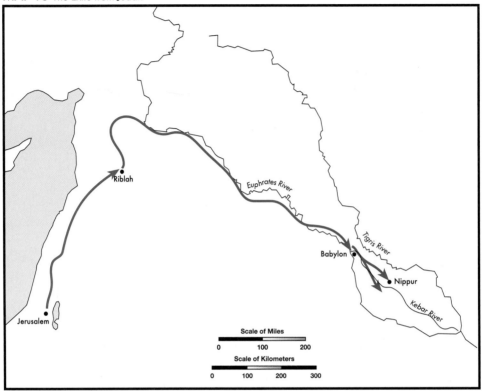

made from cow dung, and shave his head (4:1—5:4). Much of Ezekiel's message concerned the fate of the Temple as a symbol of God's fellowship with His people.

Ezekiel's ministry from his call in 593 B.C. until the fall of Jerusalem six years later was primarily a ministry of warning and condemnation. Ezekiel 1–24 contains these messages and symbolic acts of judgment. At the heart of this section is an account of Ezekiel's vision of the Temple in Jerusalem (Ezekiel 8–11). God showed Ezekiel the terrible idolatry happening right in the Temple courts. Ezekiel watched as God's throne rose and left the Temple.[1] God was abandoning His palace. What a painful vision for a priest to see! Just before Jerusalem was destroyed in 586 B.C., God gave Ezekiel his toughest assignment. His wife would die, likely of natural causes, but

Ezekiel was not to mourn her death publicly (24:15–27). In this way, God would symbolize the destruction of His beloved city and people.

Like other prophets, Ezekiel was given oracles to speak against other nations (Ezekiel 25–32). These nations were Judah's enemies who had participated in her defeat by Babylon, profited from it, or celebrated it. The longest section is devoted to Egypt, the proud nation that had promised to defend Judah against Babylon but had broken that promise.

Not Without Hope

From Ezekiel 33 on, the tone of the book changes from warning to encouragement. These messages, delivered between the fall of Jerusalem and the end of Ezekiel's ministry in 571 B.C., convey hope to God's people. Although the people were like a pile of bleached bones, God would bring them back to life again (37:1–14). The two nations—Judah and Israel—would be reunited under one leader, a king from the tribe of David (37:15–28).

In Ezekiel 8–11, God revealed Jerusalem's destruction by showing Ezekiel the terrible things that were happening in the Temple. When God wanted to symbolize Jerusalem's restoration, He showed this priest-prophet a vision of the Temple as it would be when restored to a glory even greater than it had previously known (Ezekiel 40–48). Ezekiel described his vision in great detail (the kind of detail a priest would have enjoyed), emphasizing how God's glory would return to this new Temple. Ezekiel saw a river flowing from the Temple, giving life everywhere it went, even enlivening the deepest and deadest place on earth, the Dead Sea (47:1–12).

GOD'S GREAT PLAN IN EZEKIEL

The book of Ezekiel reveals the great need for God's plan to remove sin from the world. The condemnation that pours from Ezekiel 1–33 is depressing and makes us long for something more pleasant and encouraging. But sin is depressing and its effects destructive. Every painful moment in Ezekiel has "Because of Sin" stamped on the bottom.

"The Lord Is There"

God also used Ezekiel to emphasize certain aspects of His plan and to reveal a few additional facets. We are reminded that God's plan includes all the nations, for even non-Jews are given a place among God's chosen people (Ezekiel 47:21–23). God will accomplish His plan through the Messiah, a Divine Shepherd from the line of David (34:1–31). Ezekiel reaffirms that the heart of this plan involves God enjoying fellowship with His people. That is one reason why so much attention is given to the restoration of the Temple and the return of God's presence. That is also why the restored city is given the name "The LORD is there" (48:35). Wherever God is, there is life, whether in the valley of dry bones (37:1–14) or the Dead Sea (47:1–12). When God removes sin, then we become fully alive.

When will chapters 38–48 be fulfilled?

Not everyone agrees on when and how these chapters will be fulfilled. Some see them as describing Judah's return from Babylonian exile in 538 B.C., speaking symbolically of how God would restore His people.

Others consider these chapters to refer to events still in the future. They believe God will literally rebuild the Temple and Israelite society in line with Ezekiel's description. Gog and Magog, the two enemies described in Ezekiel 38, are seen as future enemies of Israel. This view seems less likely because it has God restoring the sacrificial system (Ezekiel 43:13–27; 44:10–31), which He has now replaced by the cross (read Hebrews 10:11–14). Nor did the Jews who returned from exile in Babylon read Ezekiel as being fulfilled literally. When they rebuilt the Temple and reestablished Israelite society, they did not try to copy Ezekiel's plan.

Individual Responsibility

Ezekiel's prophecies explain two more aspects of God's plan, things alluded to elsewhere but made more specific here. First, Ezekiel emphasizes individual responsibility. Jeremiah made this point when he spoke about each person taking responsibility for his own sin (Jeremiah 31:30). Ezekiel makes the same point but more strongly and in more detail (Ezekiel 18:1–32). God values individuals and wants a personal relationship with each one. The good news is that we can each experience the best God's plan has to offer. The bad news is that we cannot hide behind anyone else; each of us must deal with God.

Reunited

Ezekiel also explicitly says that God will reunite Judah and Israel into one nation once again (37:15–28). Jeremiah had prophesied this (Jeremiah 3:18; 23:5–6) as had Hosea (Hosea 1:11) and Amos (Amos 9:11), but no one emphasized it like Ezekiel. This reunion happened during the post-exilic period, although in a very limited way. God may have meant this symbolically, describing the perfect reconciliation His plan would accomplish.

WHAT WE LEARN ABOUT GOD FROM EZEKIEL

More than any other divine characteristic, Ezekiel emphasizes God's sovereignty. He is able to accomplish His plan in spite of any obstacle. One phrase appears dozens of times in this book: "Then they will know that I am the LORD." God seemed intent on proving that He was in charge.

The Symbol of Sovereignty

Throughout this book a single vision recurs. We see it in Ezekiel 1 as the book opens, in Ezekiel 10 as God leaves the Temple, and again in Ezekiel 43 when God returns to the Temple. Although the description is too mind-boggling to fully explain, we know that we are looking at God's throne (Ezekiel 1:26; 43:7). What better way to emphasize God's sovereignty than to describe the glorious throne of God?

Jerusalem fell, not because God failed, but because the sovereign God was accomplishing His work of discipline. All the nations would know that God is "the Sovereign LORD" (Ezekiel 28:24). God's people would be restored because they served a sovereign God (36:22–32). Perhaps knowing that God was sovereign enabled Ezekiel to be faithful in spite of very difficult circumstances. He had the confidence to speak God's word and make a fool of himself, if necessary, because he knew that God could be trusted to do what He promised.

Ezekiel at a Glance

Authorship: Ezekiel
Date of writing: 593–571 B.C.
Date of events: 593 B.C. and beyond
Purpose: Announce judgment and future hope for Judah
Form: Narrative, prose oracles, poetic oracles
Part of God's plan:
1. To reveal the need for God's plan: problem of sin
2. To reveal the nature of God's plan: God's presence, individual responsibility, reconciliation

Key element of God's character: Sovereignty

---

application questions

1. How else do you see God's sovereignty in this book?
2. How does knowing of God's sovereignty encourage you?

questions for study and discussion

Read Ezekiel 1–5, 12, 18, 24, 37–39, 47.

1. One reason God concentrated on the Temple was because Ezekiel was a priest as well as a prophet. What other reasons might there have been?
2. Why did God have Ezekiel perform so many symbolic acts?
3. What can we learn from Ezekiel 18 about the way God works with individuals?
4. Why would God prohibit Ezekiel from mourning for his dead wife?
5. How do you think God will fulfill Ezekiel 38–48?
6. Is the river described in Ezekiel 47:1–12 going to be a literal river, or does it symbolize new life in God? Explain.
7. What else can we learn about God's plan from Ezekiel?
8. What else can we learn about God's character from Ezekiel?

endnote

1. This is the throne he had seen when God called him, as described in Ezekiel 1.

chapter twenty-one

Puzzling Over the Obvious

Daniel

SUGGESTIONS FOR READING DANIEL

The first six chapters of this book contain narratives, describing several events that occurred while Daniel was a captive in Babylon. Chapters 7–12 contain an unusual style of prophecy known as apocalyptic. Like the prophecies we have already seen, apocalyptic contains messages from God spoken through His messenger. But with apocalyptic there is a difference. True to its name (apocalyptic means "uncovering"), an apocalyptic message is revealed by God, generally through visions filled with very unusual symbolism. In fact, the symbols can be so puzzling that a heavenly interpreter must explain them. These messages were meant to encourage God's people, who were facing desperate circumstances. God himself would intervene if they would be faithful.

As with all types of biblical literature, be sure to read apocalyptic prophecy against the background of the historical context. Find out what it meant to the struggling community before asking what it means to you. Don't get bogged down in the symbolism, but seek the main point God was trying to convey through the image. As always, try to learn what you can from this material about the character of God.

INTRODUCTION

The book of Daniel is a curious combination of the familiar and bizarre. Some of the best-known Bible stories are found here (e.g., Daniel in the lions' den), as are some of the most puzzling visions in the Old Testament. The book also combines the complicated and the profound. Trying to figure out "who's who" in Daniel's visions requires heavenly help, but the main purpose of the book is profoundly simple. Daniel wrote to encourage God's people to be faithful by showing them that God is sovereign.

OVERVIEW

During the year 605 B.C., the Babylonian army under King Nebuchadnezzar invaded Judah and carried away some of Jerusalem's finest young men. Daniel was forcibly removed from his home and family and taken to live in captivity in Babylon. With God's help, he rose to a position of great power under Nebuchadnezzar. Though overlooked by later monarchs, he was recalled to the Babylonian court just in time to announce the end of that empire. His influence continued even after the Persians took over.

Jehoiakim
King of Judah
609–598

Babylon invades
Judah, Daniel
taken captive
605

Jerusalem falls
586

First return from
exile in Babylon
538

End of Daniel's
ministry
536

Authorship of Daniel
(late date)
165

598 (3 months)
Jehoiachin,
King of Judah

597–586
Zedekiah,
King of Judah

539
Persians conquer
Babylon

A.D. 70
Jewish Temple
destroyed by the
Romans
(perhaps part of
the fulfillment
of Daniel's
prophecy)

Daniel
Unless otherwise noted, all dates are B.C.

The first six chapters of this book describe several important events that took place when Daniel was in Babylon. We discover how he initially rose to power with God's help (Daniel 1–2). We learn how Daniel's three friends would have roasted because of Nebuchadnezzar's pride if God hadn't intervened (Daniel 3). Chapter 4 describes a sobering experience in the life of King Nebuchadnezzar. Daniel 5 and 6 relate events in Daniel's life at the very end of the Babylonian Empire and the beginning of the Persian Empire.

Daniel 7 through 12 describes a series of very unusual dreams and visions. Through an angel, Daniel learned what the future held for God's people and the rest of the world—from Daniel's day into the distant future. The purpose for this curious combination of exciting stories (Daniel 1–6) and puzzling visions (Daniel 7–12) was to encourage God's people by reassuring them that God was in charge. Exile and destruction did not mean God had forsaken them. He would still carry out His plan through them if they would be faithful to Him.

Acknowledging God's Sovereignty

We see God's sovereignty in His power to predict the future. Daniel is given the ability to interpret two of Nebuchadnezzar's dreams (Daniel 2; 4). He read the handwriting on the wall and announced that Persia was about to defeat Babylon (Daniel 5). Because God is sovereign, He could rescue His people from their difficulties, whether those might be a fiery furnace (Daniel 3) or a lions' den (Daniel 6).

The narrative portion also reveals God's sovereignty by showing His superiority over the mightiest of earthly kings. After his temporary insanity and recovery, Nebuchadnezzar himself testified of God's greatness: "How great are his signs, how mighty his wonders! His kingdom is an eternal kingdom; his dominion endures from generation to generation" (Daniel 4:3). These are remarkable words for a pagan king to confess about Israel's God, but he says even more several verses later: "His dominion is an eternal dominion; his kingdom endures from generation to generation. All the peoples of the earth are regarded as nothing. He does as he pleases with the powers of heaven and the peoples of the earth. No one can hold back his hand or say to him: 'What have you done?'" (Daniel 4:34–35).

What is the historical background of this book?

Daniel opens with the Babylonian Empire at the height of its power and the great king Nebuchadnezzar sitting on the throne. Nebuchadnezzar was famous for his military conquests against Egypt, Judah, and many other nations. He also carried out extensive building projects in Babylon, including military fortifications, canals, and one of the seven wonders of the ancient world, the famous hanging gardens.

None of Nebuchadnezzar's successors was his equal. The final king, Nabonidus, seems to have been the worst of all. He was very unpopular with his subjects, in part because he tried to shift their loyalty from their national god, Marduk, to another god. He even left the capital, probably to devote himself to the worship of this other god, and appointed his son, Belshazzar, to rule in his absence. Belshazzar was the ruler God confronted by writing a message on the palace wall (Daniel 5).

In 539 B.C., in fulfillment of God's predictions, the Persians conquered Babylon. Persia had been rising in power under the leadership of Cyrus the Great. Within twenty years of assuming the throne from his father, Cyrus extended the boundaries of the Persian Empire from the Aegean Sea in the west to India in the east. Then he turned his sights on Babylon. After a decisive victory north of the city, Babylon fell without a fight in October, 539 B.C. Cyrus treated the conquered Babylonians kindly and they quickly transferred their loyalties to the Persians.

MAP 14 New Babylonian Empire

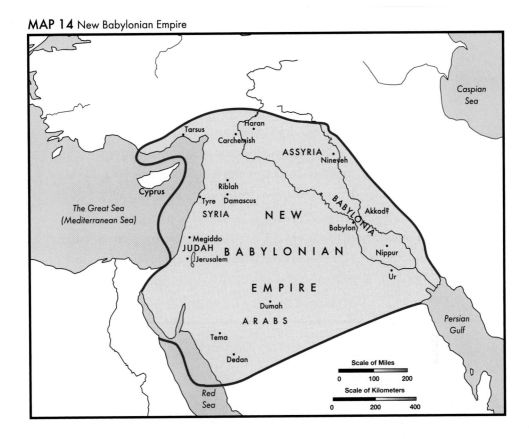

God spoiled Belshazzar's party by writing words of judgment on the palace wall (Daniel 5). Before Daniel interpreted those words, he criticized the ruler for dishonoring "the God who holds in his hand your life and all your ways" (5:23). Then he announced the judgment of this sovereign God: Belshazzar would die and the Babylonian Empire would be taken over by the Persians.

After Daniel had been released from the lions' den, Darius, the ruler of the Persians, issued a proclamation commanding that all his people must "fear and reverence the God of Daniel. 'For he is the living God and he endures forever; his kingdom will not be destroyed, his dominion will never end'" (Daniel 6:26). This pagan king also had to admit that God is sovereign.

269

An Everlasting Kingdom

The apocalyptic portion of Daniel (Daniel 7–12) demonstrates God's sovereignty by repeatedly picturing His triumph over all kingdoms. After watching the three beasts rise and fall, Daniel saw a fourth beast—"terrifying and frightening and very powerful" (Dan. 7:7). But then Daniel saw God powerfully and decisively defeat this fearsome beast (7:9–11). The angel predicted that "the sovereignty, power and greatness of the kingdoms under the whole heaven will be handed over to the saints, the people of the Most High. His kingdom will be an everlasting kingdom, and all rulers will worship and obey him" (7:27).

These repeated reminders of God's sovereignty were given in order to encourage God's people to be faithful. They would be tempted to

MAP 15 The Persian Empire

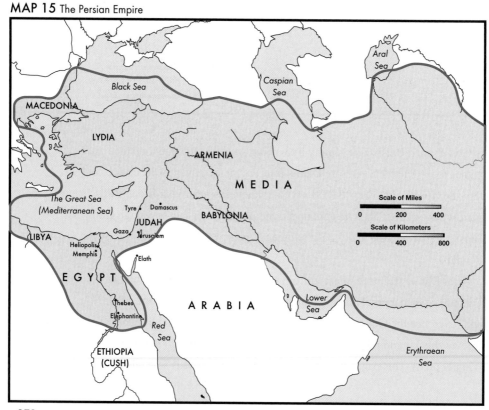

When was Daniel written?

Scholars disagree about when this book was written. If composed by the same person who was carried off to Babylon by Nebuchadnezzar, then it must have been written in the sixth century. Others claim that the real author wrote this book around 165 B.C.; the ancient figure of Daniel was just his pseudonym.

Those who prefer the second-century date point to the startling accuracy of the author's "predictions," especially those in chapters 2 and 11. This is very unusual for the Old Testament. The author could only have known such specifics from hindsight, they say. "Predictions" of events already past are one of the well-known characteristics of apocalyptic writings from the second century. These writings also were written under the pseudonym of a famous ancient figure.

The main problem with the second-century date is that it does not leave enough time for Daniel to be accepted as Scripture. The Jewish monks living near the Dead Sea began to copy this book shortly after 165 B.C. and considered it to be God's Word by 25 B.C. at the latest. No other book was accepted into the Old Testament canon that quickly. The specificity of Daniel's prophecies, while unusual, would not be impossible if God was truly the divine Author.

compromise God's Law, just as Daniel and his friends had been tempted to eat the king's food (Daniel 1). This book reminds them to remain faithful to the sovereign God who will protect them. The Jews would be tempted to worship other gods, just as Daniel and his friends were tempted to bow down to Nebuchadnezzar's image (Daniel 3). If the Jews found themselves at the mercy of plots against them, like Daniel in chapter 6, they had to remain faithful in order for God to rescue them. When they felt weak and insignificant compared to the mighty forces that had defeated and exiled them, they had to remain faithful, for their God is King over all kings. When they felt frightened by the ominous rumblings on the future's horizon, they had to remain faithful. The sovereign God—their God—controls the future.

GOD'S GREAT PLAN IN DANIEL

Many of the prophetic books have overlapped each other in what they say about God's plan. They show how much this plan was needed because of the

When were Daniel's prophecies fulfilled?

Many generations have interpreted Daniel's predictions in light of their own experience. The Jews who were persecuted by the Greeks in the second century B.C. believed they saw Daniel being fulfilled before their very eyes. So did the Jewish monks living at the Dead Sea around the time of Christ. The Jews whose Temple was destroyed by the Romans in A.D. 70 believed that Daniel not only was predicting events that happened two centuries earlier, but also prophesying events in their day. The early Christians considered Jesus to be the Son of Man whose coming Daniel predicted. Throughout history, people have believed Daniel predicted the events of their own day: Jews in the Middle Ages, Christians in the 1500s, Christians in the 1800s, and Christians today.

Were all these people wrong? Were all these people right? Though we cannot say for sure, two things seem clear. First, the prophecies are primarily concerned with the struggles experienced by the Jews in the centuries leading up to and including the first century A.D. Second, God may have left the predictions deliberately vague so that every generation of His people could picture themselves among the righteous and thereby anticipate God's victory for them.

seriousness of sin. They tell something of the nature of the plan: that it involves the Messiah, that it will bring fellowship with God, and so forth. Daniel also shows these things, but tells us much more.

Daniel sketches how God's plan will develop from the end of the Babylonian Empire to the coming of the Messiah in the first century A.D. He shows us that many years will pass, nations will rise and fall, the Jews will experience great persecution, and then the Messiah will come and suffer.[1] Daniel agrees with the rest of the prophets that God's plan definitely will succeed, thanks to the work of the Messiah (Daniel 7:13–14). While the book does not specify how the victory will take place, it leaves no doubt that God will win.

One of the primary reasons for the book of Daniel was to encourage God's people to be faithful. Problems will certainly come and God may take a while to accomplish His plan. Not seventy years, but seventy "sevens" (a period of undetermined length) will pass before the final end (Daniel 9:20–27). But God will win. Hang on!

WHAT WE LEARN ABOUT GOD FROM DANIEL

We have already seen that sovereignty is the overwhelming characteristic of God emerging from the pages of this book. In both the narrative sections and the apocalyptic visions, God is in charge. We also see that God's sovereignty is a very practical truth. Because we believe that God is all-powerful, we have the confidence that in the end, God will win. Certainty of God's victory gives us courage to be faithful to God.

Blessed Are the Faithful

Many who read Daniel become confused both by the visions and by trying to figure out when they will be fulfilled. The visions *are* confusing; even Daniel found this true (Daniel 8:27). No doubt, a certain amount of speculation is inevitable due to the innate curiosity of human nature. But the book itself cautions us at this point. It gives us just enough information to let us know that God knows exactly what will happen, but not enough so that *we* will know exactly what will happen. We get just enough information to know that God is in control, but not enough to put *us* in control. After all he had seen, Daniel wondered, "How long will it be before these astonishing things are fulfilled?" (Daniel 12:6). The angel answered his request for specifics with a vague prediction: "It will be for a time, times and half a time" (verse 7). Daniel pushed for more details, but the angel declined. His reply was again ambiguous, speaking symbolically of 1,290 days. Essentially, the angel only affirmed that the time would eventually come and God would be victorious. What was most important for Daniel (and us) to remember, the angel put in the form of a blessing: "Blessed is the one who waits for and reaches the end of the 1,335 days" (verse 12). In other words, blessed are those who are faithful until the end, whenever that might be.

Daniel at a Glance

Authorship: Daniel
Date of writing: 605–530 B.C.
Date of events: 605 B.C. to A.D. 70
Purpose: To display sovereignty of God to encourage faithfulness in difficulty
Form: Narrative and apocalyptic prophecy
Part of God's plan:
    1. To reveal more of God's plan
    2. To assure ultimate victory of God's plan
    3. To describe proper attitude for God's people
Key element of God's character: Sovereignty

---

application questions

1. Why are people so hungry for details about how the world will end?
2. How else do you see God's sovereignty in this book?
3. What does it mean to you to "be faithful"?

questions for study and discussion

Read Daniel 1–12.

1. The suggestions for reading Daniel at the beginning of this chapter identify several characteristics of apocalyptic prophecy. Identify two passages from Daniel for each of the following characteristics:
   a. revealed by God through visions
   b. visions filled with very unusual symbolism
   c. visions interpreted by heavenly interpreter
   d. addressed to God's people in difficulty
   e. includes call to be faithful
2. How might Daniel's prophecies have encouraged those, like Daniel, who were living in exile? How would they have encouraged those Jews who returned from exile under Cyrus in 538 B.C.?
3. What else can we learn from this book about God's plan?
4. What else can we learn from this book about God's character?

endnote

1. Some would argue instead that the book is *primarily* an account of the time leading up to the return of Christ, when God will complete His plan. See the discussion under the question "When were Daniel's prophecies fulfilled?"

chapter twenty-two

Israel after the Exile
Ezra, Nehemiah, Esther, Haggai, Zechariah, Malachi

SUGGESTIONS FOR READING THESE BOOKS

Three of these six books are primarily narrative: Ezra, Nehemiah, and Esther. Knowing the historical context will be very helpful for understanding them. Also remember to read these books in the context of the larger story of God's work with His people.

Haggai and Malachi contain mostly prophetic oracles written in prose directed to the Jews who had returned from exile. Read these messages "over the shoulders" of the original audience. Nearly all the prophets' predictions were fulfilled in their day, shortly thereafter, or by the time of Jesus.

Zechariah, with its bizarre symbolism and the use of a heavenly interpreter, sounds like the apocalyptic style of prophecy we met in the book of Daniel. As we cautioned there, try to see the overall message of the vision rather than picking it apart like a puzzle. For all these books, be sure to ask what you learn about the character of God.

INTRODUCTION

Although God kept His promise and allowed His people to return to their homeland, Israel was not yet out of danger. Would the people turn from their rebellious ways or head back down the path of disobedience to disaster?

OVERVIEW

These books share a common theme: homecoming. The Jews, in exile for more than half a century, were finally permitted to return to their land. Nearly fifty thousand made the initial journey, optimistic about the bright days ahead. However, the initial euphoria dissolved into the drudgery of rebuilding, one stone at a time. God used Ezra and Nehemiah to provide leadership during

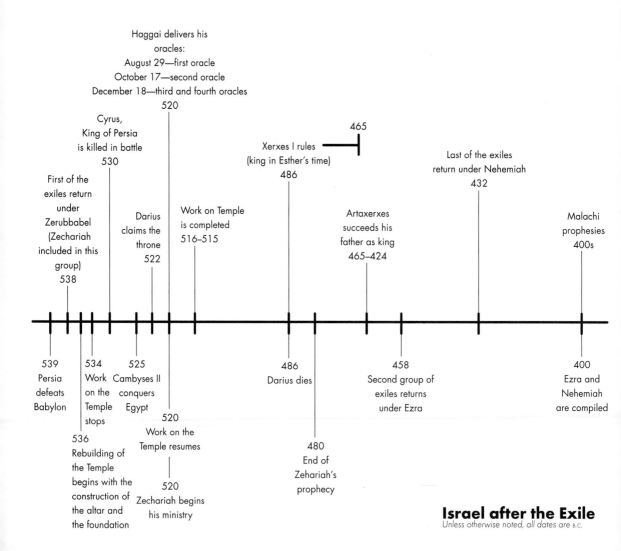

Israel after the Exile
Unless otherwise noted, all dates are B.C.

this long rebuilding process. Haggai, Zechariah, and Malachi were His spokesmen, announcing messages of direction, correction, and encouragement to the people. Meanwhile, back in Persia, God was watching out for the Jews who stayed behind, some of whom we meet in the book of Esther.

Ezra-Nehemiah: Rebuilding a Righteous Society

Most of what we know of Israel's homecoming we owe to the books of Ezra and Nehemiah. Originally written as a single book, these chapters were compiled anonymously around 400 B.C. from historical accounts of the initial return (538 B.C.) and from the personal memoirs of Ezra and Nehemiah, who returned several decades later. The author, who never identified himself, described the reestablishment of Israelite society between 538 and about 430 B.C. He made it clear that although Cyrus, king of Persia, was the man responsible for Israel's freedom, ultimately God should get the credit (Ezra 1:1). Israel appears to have understood her obligation to God. The Jews immediately began to rebuild the Temple in Jerusalem, starting with the altar and moving on to the foundation (Ezra 3). Opposition from neighboring nations and a loss of courage and focus by the Jews halted progress on the Temple for nearly two decades. As the project languished, so did Jewish society. Finally, inspired by the preaching of Haggai and Zechariah, the work was completed in 516 B.C. (Ezra 4–6).

More than half a century elapsed between the rebuilding of the Temple and Ezra's arrival in 458 B.C. Ezra, a priest and teacher of the Law, came to help Israel understand God's Word and its part in His plan (Ezra 7–8). Apparently, the Jews needed his instruction, for they had already drifted away from God to the point that they had begun to intermarry with their non-Israelite neighbors. It was this mistake years earlier that had caused them to rebel against God. Ezra led the people in the very difficult process of confession and repentance (Ezra 9–10).

Another decade of silence passes before we meet Nehemiah. Although an important official in the court of the Persian king, Nehemiah became concerned about the well-being and security of the Jews back home. He was permitted to return and began rebuilding the walls of Jerusalem, left in rubble by the Babylonians nearly 150 years earlier (Nehemiah 1–3). Opposition from Israel's neighbors threatened to halt the rebuilding, but under Nehemiah's leadership, the project was completed in record time (Nehemiah 4–6). Nehemiah was concerned about more than just Israel's physical safety; he wanted to create a just and righteous society. The rest of the book describes his efforts and those of Ezra and other leaders to make the Jews aware of the Law and to help them live by it (Nehemiah 7–13).

Haggai: First Things First

The first wave of Jews returned in 538 B.C. They began to rebuild the Temple in 536 B.C., only to give up in 534 B.C. due to opposition and discouragement. God used Haggai and Zechariah to motivate the Israelites to finish the work they had begun. When Haggai delivered his oracles in 520 B.C., the masons' tools had been silent for fourteen years.[1] The people even excused themselves, imagining that God preferred the Temple in ruins.

In his first oracle, delivered "in the second year of King Darius, on the first day of the sixth month" (Haggai 1:1; that is, August 29, 520), Haggai challenged them to consider if it was right for them to live in nice houses while God's house was in shambles. Could it be that the economic difficulties in which they found themselves had something to do with their failure to put first things first? The people responded obediently and resumed work on the Temple.

About a month later (October 17, 520), Haggai preached again. He encouraged the people by describing how God would bless this building. It must have been hard for the people to believe that "the glory of this present house will be greater than the glory of the former house," the one built by Solomon (Haggai 2:9), but God would keep this promise. More than five hundred years later, God himself would enter that Temple in the person of Jesus.[2]

In his third oracle, on December 18, 520, Haggai announced that because they had put God first and were rebuilding the Temple, God would reverse

MAP 16 The Return to Zion

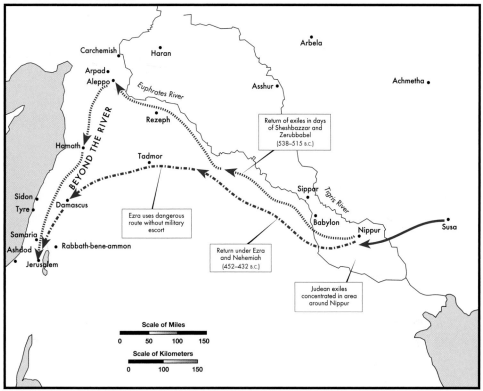

their bad fortune and bless them. Later that same day, Haggai delivered another message from God, this time concerning Zerubbabel, governor of Judah and descendant of King David. God would honor Zerubbabel with great authority. God may have been referring to the governor's role in rebuilding the Temple, but more likely He was announcing the restoration of King David's family line that would come with Jesus, the Messiah.

Zechariah: Visions of Things to Come

Like Jeremiah and Ezekiel before him, Zechariah was both a prophet and a priest. Born in Babylon, he returned with the first wave of exiles in 538 B.C. He began his ministry in 520 B.C., the same year of Haggai's ministry, but continued to prophesy until at least 480 B.C. The two men shared the same

What is the historical background of these books?

Under powerful King Cyrus, Persia defeated Babylon without a fight in the fall of 539 B.C. The next year Cyrus permitted all those taken captive by the Babylonians to return to their homes with the blessing and support of the Persian government. This included the Jews. Although Cyrus had political motives for this action, the Old Testament makes it clear that he was doing the will of God.

About fifty thousand Jews accepted Cyrus's offer and returned. They were established as a province of Persia under a governor. The rebuilding of the Temple began in 536 B.C. with the construction of the altar and then the foundation. The project stopped in 534 B.C. and languished for fourteen years. Thanks to the preaching of Haggai and Zechariah, the work resumed in 520 B.C. and was completed four years later.

After Cyrus was killed in battle in 530 B.C., he was succeeded by his son, Cambyses II, who conquered Egypt in 525 B.C. Only a few years later, Cambyses, away from home on a military campaign, learned of a rebellion back in the capital and apparently committed suicide. Darius, one of Cambyses' officers, claimed the throne in 522 B.C. and ruled until his death in 486 B.C. Darius's son, Xerxes I, who ruled from 486–465 B.C., was the king referred to in the book of Esther. At least during Xerxes' rule, if not the whole Persian period, the Jews enjoyed some freedom, but also had their deadly enemies.

Artaxerxes succeeded his father, Xerxes I, in 465 B.C. With the king's permission, Ezra led another group of Jews back to Jerusalem (Ezra 7:7), now to bring about a spiritual revival rather than a physical rebuilding. Twenty years later, Artaxerxes authorized another return to Jerusalem, this time led by Nehemiah (Nehemiah 2:1–6), who would rebuild the walls of Jerusalem.

passion and a similar message. Both wanted God's people to experience spiritual renewal, both felt that rebuilding the Temple was an essential ingredient in this renewal, and both encouraged the people toward this end by promising wonderful blessings to the faithful (Zechariah 8).

In spite of the similarities, the two prophets used very different approaches. Zechariah saw puzzling visions at night, which required interpretation by an angel.[3] In the first of these visions (Zechariah 1:7–17), God promises His blessing on the returning exiles. Subsequent visions describe their vindication (1:18–21) and the promise that Jerusalem would be rebuilt (Zechariah 2). The fourth and fifth visions (Zechariah 3–4)

Why would God make the Jews divorce their wives?

Ezra's command for the Jews to divorce their wives seems very harsh, but the sin of intermarriage with the surrounding nations was much more serious than we might imagine. It inevitably led to compromise on the matter of idolatry, as the Israelite spouse was seduced to worship the gods of the non-Israelite partner. This is why God so clearly prohibited the practice (Exodus 34:11-16; Deuteronomy 7:1-6). Such intermarriage was one of the causes of the Babylonian exile.

A serious disease calls for a drastic remedy. Those who had sinned in this way, although only a very small percentage of the population, were told to divorce their wives. Some scholars believe that any wife who agreed to convert to Judaism would have been exempted. To handle this matter fairly and see that the divorced women were properly cared for, a legal system was set in place in which each case was carefully considered (Ezra 10:16). As painful as this was for all involved, it was necessary if the Jews were to accomplish their God-given purpose.

promise the restoration of Temple worship. Israel's sin had brought about its punishment; the removal of this sin is described in visions six and seven (Zechariah 5). The final vision of four chariots celebrates the sovereignty of God (Zechariah 6:1–8). Zechariah also had much to say about the coming of the Messiah (especially in 9–14). His coming would give God's people many reasons to rejoice: Enemies would be defeated, sins would be forgiven, and the Messiah would take His throne and rule the whole earth.

Malachi: Looking Forward

Although Israel had listened to the messages of Haggai and Zechariah and rebuilt the Temple, the spiritual health of the people still left something to be desired. To remedy this problem, God would send Ezra, the priest and teacher of the Law in 458 B.C. But about a decade earlier, God also confronted His people through the prophet Malachi.

Malachi challenged the Israelites to live up to the Law of Moses (Malachi 4:4). Instead of showing their love to God by giving Him their best in worship, they offered crippled and diseased animals for sacrifices (1:6–14) and withheld what they owed Him (3:6–12). Instead of showing love to their

Why do Haggai and Zechariah date their prophecies so specifically?

Haggai and Zechariah were not the first prophets to provide such specific dates to their prophecies, but they did so more regularly than any others. Why? Probably to emphasize how God had kept His promises. Hundreds of years earlier, Isaiah had predicted that a king named Cyrus would rebuild Jerusalem and set the exiles free (Isaiah 45:1–13). By dating their oracles to the reign of a Persian ruler, Haggai and Zechariah emphasized how God had fulfilled this and other prophecies and how He could be counted on always to keep His word.

MAP 17 The Land of Judah in the Days of the Return

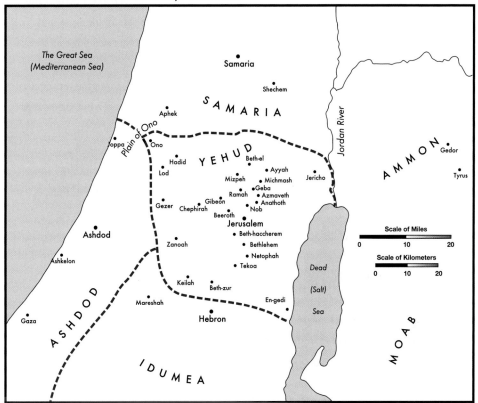

neighbors, they were unfaithful to their spouses (2:13–16) and mistreated others (3:5).

"Surely the day is coming," announced the prophet, and "it will burn like a furnace" (Malachi 4:1). Judgment would fall on those who did evil, but wonderful blessings would come to the righteous (4:1–2). The book ends with the prophet gazing ahead to that day.

Esther: A Story of Deliverance

The book of Esther takes us back to Persia for a look at the Jews who chose not to return with Zerubbabel in 538 B.C. It reveals that God was concerned not only for Jews in Jerusalem, but for those who lived far from there as well. A young Jewish girl was selected to marry the Persian king Xerxes. About this

285

same time, Haman, one of the king's favorites, became angry at a certain Jew named Mordecai. Haman decided to take out his anger on all the Jews and persuaded the king to issue a decree that would have meant death for all the Jews on a certain day. Mordecai, Esther's relative, persuaded her to appeal to the king on behalf of her people. Esther knew that to come into the presence of the king without being invited could mean death (Esther 4:11), but she agreed to risk her life for her people.

When Esther approached the king, he was overcome by her beauty and spared her life. Instead of appealing for her people, Esther invited the king and Haman to a private banquet just for the two of them. While at that

When were these prophecies fulfilled?

Christians disagree about when these prophecies of Haggai, Zechariah, and Malachi were or will be fulfilled. Some predictions appear to have been realized in the prophets' own day, following the rebuilding of the Temple (Haggai 2:10–19). If we allow for some literary exaggeration, perhaps many of these prophecies were fulfilled at that time (see Zechariah 1–6; 8:1–8). Others found fulfillment in the first coming of Christ (Haggai 2:9; Zechariah 9:9; Malachi 4:5–6).

What about the predictions that were not literally fulfilled, such as those in Zechariah 14? Some see them being fulfilled literally at Christ's future second coming. For example, they believe there will be a literal battle against Jerusalem during which God will intervene by physically standing on the Mount of Olives. Others look for a symbolic fulfillment, seeing in Zechariah 14 a general description of how God will triumph over evil in the end. While such questions are interesting, we must not lose sight of the fact that, for the prophets, the timing of the fulfillment was less important than the fact that God was in charge of history and would sovereignly accomplish His purposes.

MAP 18 The Persian Empire

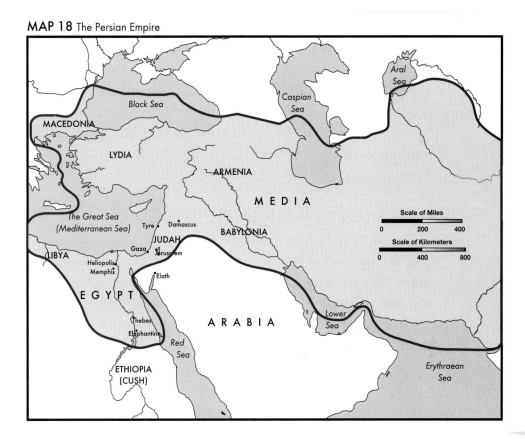

banquet, she made her request—that they come to another banquet the next day. That night the king could not sleep, so he called for his servants to read the historical records of his reign as an antidote for insomnia. Of all the passages for the servant to read, he selected one that described how Mordecai the Jew had rescued the king from assassins. The king determined to honor Mordecai and delegated that task to none other than Haman.

The next day, at the queen's banquet, Esther finally appealed on behalf of her people and identified Haman as the one responsible for the plot against them. After he was hanged on the gallows (or more likely impaled on a stake) he had built for Mordecai, the king issued a decree that overruled the earlier decree, and the Jews were spared. They continue to commemorate that deliverance during the Feast of Purim every spring.

Curiously, this book never mentions God by name. On the surface, Israel's deliverance had more to do with human courage and "coincidence" than with divine intervention, but this is just the point. God always protects His people. Sometimes that protection comes through dramatic miracles like the parting of the Red Sea. At other times it might be through human courage and "coincidence." Sometimes He protects us by keeping us safe from difficulties; at other times He keeps us safe while we go through difficulties. Either way, Esther reminds us that God is still at work.

GOD'S GREAT PLAN IN THESE BOOKS

What had the destruction of Judah and the exile to Babylon done to God's plan? This question had to be swirling in the minds of the Jews. Could they still be God's people and accomplish His will in a foreign country? If permitted to go home, could they ever regain their role as "light to the nations"? These books make clear that God was not done with the Jews. He still had a part for them to play in His plan and still longed for fellowship with them. Having them return to the land and reestablish society according to God's Law was an important step. The rebuilding of the Temple was especially significant. More than a building, the Temple symbolized God's presence with His people. What about those who remained in Persia? The book of Esther makes it clear that God cared about them as well; He would protect them. Although the Exile was not God's first choice, He proved His sovereignty and continued to work out His will in spite of it.

These books also provide more details about God's plan. From the beginning we see that God planned to reconcile the whole world to himself through the Jews. Haggai predicts that the wealth of the nations will be brought as an offering to God (Haggai 2:7). In several passages, Zechariah predicts the universal spread of the gospel (Zechariah 2:1–13; 8:20–23; 9:1–8).

Each of the prophetic books reveals more about the Messiah. Haggai predicts He would come to the rebuilt Temple (Haggai 2:6–9). Zechariah announces the Messiah's dual role as priest and king, as symbolized in the role of Joshua (Zechariah 6:9–15). This prophet also predicts Jesus' triumphal entry (Zechariah

9:9; see John 12:13–15), His rejection (Zechariah 13:7; see Matthew 26:31), the amount for which He would be betrayed (Zechariah 11:12–13; see Matthew 27:3–7), and His suffering (Zechariah 12:10; see John 19:34). From Malachi we learn that Elijah would come first, the role filled by John the Baptist (Malachi 4:5–6; see Matthew 11:10).

WHAT WE LEARN ABOUT GOD FROM THESE BOOKS

Among the several characteristics God reveals about himself in these books, we see that He is faithful. Ezra asserts that the return of the Jews in 538 B.C. may have been with Cyrus's permission, but it was God's doing (Ezra 1:1). In spite of Israel's unfaithfulness, God remained faithful and kept His promises to restore the people to their homeland.

Faithful in Every Detail

God usually shows His faithfulness through others. Cyrus released the captives and other Persian kings provided support to the returning Jews (Ezra 6:22; 7:27–28; Nehemiah 1). Esther describes how the Jews were spared destruction by the intervention of King Xerxes. Though God used others to show kindness and protect His people, every incident reveals His faithfulness.

Jealous for His Own

In addition to God's faithfulness, we also see His jealousy. We usually consider jealousy a bad quality and are often surprised to hear God described this way. But most of us would agree that jealousy is appropriate under the right circumstances. If I see someone trying to seduce my wife and I don't feel jealous, something is wrong with me. To say that God is jealous means He is unwilling for anyone or anything else to take His place in the hearts of His people. He loves them too much. The moment they begin to turn away, He becomes jealous for their affection. Ezra 9–10 describes a very serious moment in Israel's history. By intermarrying with non-Jews, the Jews had started down a road that could only spell disaster. Intermarriage would eventually lead the Jews away from God toward idolatry. God intervened, jealous for their affection, and required a costly sacrifice.

Sovereign at Every Level

Finally, we see again the sovereignty of God. The short book of Malachi refers to God twenty times as "LORD Almighty." Esther makes clear that He can "show off" His power without even showing himself. Using Esther's beauty and courage, the king's sleeplessness, and a remarkable series of "coincidences," God spared His people. Cyrus, the mighty king of Persia, was only a pawn in God's plan (Ezra 1:1). Israel's enemies sought to prevent the rebuilding of the Temple (Ezra 4–5), but God turned the tables. In the end, this sovereign God even made the enemies pay the cost of rebuilding the Temple they opposed (Ezra 6:8)!

Ezra-Nehemiah at a Glance

Authorship: Anonymous

Date of writing: 400s B.C.

Date of events: 538–432 B.C.

Purposes:

    1. To describe reestablishment of Israelite society after exile

    2. To demonstrate God's faithfulness

Form: Narrative

Part of God's plan: To describe recovery of God's plan by God's people

Key elements of God's character: Faithfulness, jealousy, sovereignty

Haggai at a Glance

Authorship: Haggai

Date of writing: 520 B.C.

Date of events: 520 B.C. and beyond

Purpose: To encourage Jews to rebuild Temple

Form: Prophetic oracles

Part of God's plan: To describe nature of God's plan

Key elements of God's character: Faithfulness, jealousy

Zechariah at a Glance

Authorship: Zechariah
Date of writing: 520–400s B.C.
Date of events: 520 B.C. and beyond
Purpose: To produce spiritual renewal evidenced by rebuilding Temple
Form: Apocalyptic, prophetic oracles
Part of God's plan: To describe nature of God's plan
Key element of God's character: Sovereignty

Malachi at a Glance

Authorship: Malachi
Date of writing: 460 B.C.
Date of events: 460 B.C. and beyond
Purpose: To encourage post-exilic Jews
Form: Prophetic oracles in question-and-answer format
Part of God's plan: To describe the nature of God's plan
Key element of God's character: Sovereignty

Esther at a Glance

Authorship: Anonymous
Date of writing: 400s B.C.
Date of events: 483–471 B.C.
Purpose: To describe God's protection of His people
Form: Narrative
Part of God's plan: To demonstrate preservation of God's people
Key element of God's character: Sovereignty

application questions

1. How else do these books reveal God's faithfulness? His jealousy? His sovereignty?
2. What is one way this information can help you in your personal life?

questions for study and discussion

1. Read Ezra and Nehemiah.
   a. In what ways did post-exilic Israelite society differ from society before the Exile?
   b. Why do you think the Jews had not rebuilt the walls earlier?
   c. Why did Nehemiah include the names of those who returned from exile (Nehemiah 7)?
   d. If God is so interested in saving the Gentiles, why do these books seem so critical of contacts between the Jews and other nations?
2. Read Haggai.
   a. Why did Haggai want the Jews to rebuild the Temple?
   b. Who was Zerubbabel?
3. Read Zechariah 1, 4, 9–14.
   a. Identify ways in which Zechariah's prophecies differ from those of his contemporary, Haggai. What might be some reasons for the differences?
   b. Who was the Joshua referred to in Zechariah 6:9–15?
4. Read Malachi.
   a. Why does Malachi sound so much like a court case?
   b. What do we learn from this book about the "day of the LORD"?
5. Read Esther.
   a. This book contains many examples of irony. Identify some.
   b. What were some of the "coincidences" God used to accomplish His plan?
6. What else can we learn about God's plan from these books?
7. What else can we learn about God's character from these books?

endnotes

1. We know this date thanks to the precise way Haggai dated his messages.

2. The Temple they were building would be heavily renovated by King Herod the Great about the time Jesus was born. It was this second Temple that Jesus would enter.

3. For this reason, many consider Zechariah to be apocalyptic prophecy.

chapter twenty-three

Looking Back
1 and 2 Chronicles

SUGGESTIONS FOR READING 1 AND 2 CHRONICLES

The bulk of 1 and 2 Chronicles is historical narrative, similar to what we found in Samuel and Kings. Like those books, this material was included for theological as well as historical purposes; these stories are part of God's bigger story.

Reading through the opening nine chapters of genealogies requires great perseverance. When tempted to give up, remind yourself that these lists were important for the Jews just back from exile. As a group-oriented culture, their identity had a lot to do with their ancestors. As well, the genealogies taught the people important theological lessons, which we'll explore below.

INTRODUCTION

Of the thirty-nine books of the Old Testament, these two are probably the most neglected and least appreciated. It doesn't help that they begin with nine chapters of genealogies or that most of the material they contain has already been covered in 1 and 2 Samuel and 1 and 2 Kings. But once we understand why these books were written, they will more than repay our attention to them.

OVERVIEW

One of the most obvious things about these books is how much they repeat what we find in the books of 1 and 2 Samuel and 1 and 2 Kings. Why do we

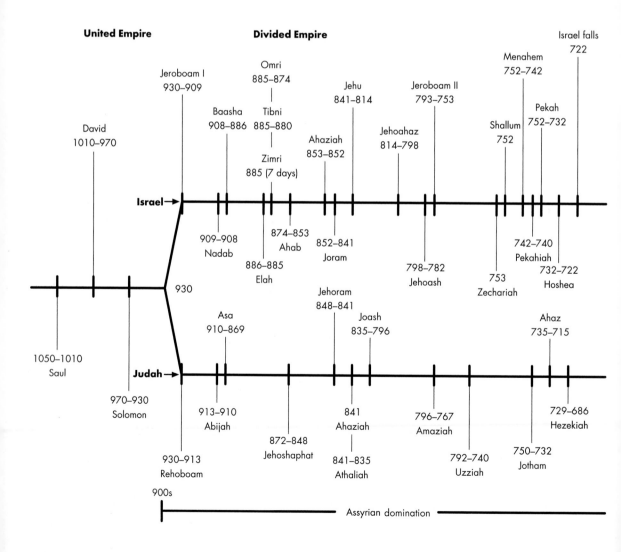

need two versions of the same thing? The anonymous writer of 1 and 2 Chronicles chose to retell Israel's history to meet the needs of the Jews who had returned from exile in Babylon.

After the initial thrill of being back in their homeland, those who returned grew discouraged by the hard work of rebuilding. God used prophets such as Haggai, Zechariah, and Malachi, and leaders such as Zerubbabel, Ezra, and Nehemiah to encourage the Jews. He also inspired the writer of 1 and 2 Chronicles to retell Israel's history from the beginning of the monarchy, through the Exile, and up to the decree from Cyrus that allowed the Jews to return home. Although several sources were used to prepare these books, most of this material probably came from 1 and 2 Samuel and 1 and 2 Kings.[1] Rather than just repeating the earlier information, the author of Chronicles reshaped this material for his own purposes. Some even consider these books the first commentaries on the Old Testament.

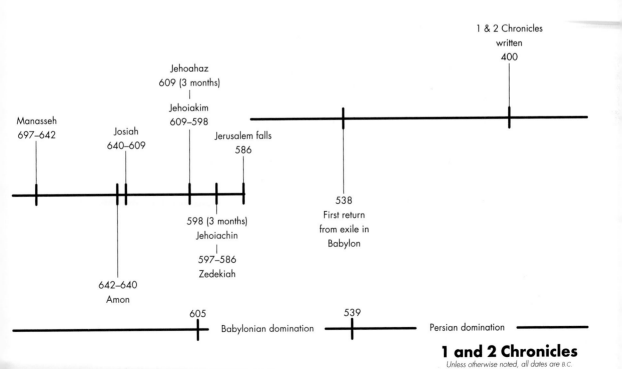

1 & 2 Chronicles
written
400

Jehoahaz
609 (3 months)

Jehoiakim
609–598

Manasseh
697–642

Josiah
640–609

Jerusalem falls
586

538
First return
from exile in
Babylon

598 (3 months)
Jehoiachin

597–586
Zedekiah

642–640
Amon

605
Babylonian domination

539
Persian domination

1 and 2 Chronicles
Unless otherwise noted, all dates are B.C.

Turn Back

This writer had two purposes. First, he wanted to emphasize the need for the Jews to live righteously. Israel's disobedience had brought disaster. To avoid another catastrophe, the Jews must understand what God required and then do it. Second, he wanted to give them hope: God had not forgotten Israel and still had great plans for them. At the heart of 1 and 2 Chronicles we find this promise from God: "If my people, who are called by my name, will humble themselves and pray and seek my face and turn from their wicked ways, then will I hear from heaven and will forgive their sin and will heal their land" (2 Chronicles 7:14). Although spoken to Solomon, this was the formula by which the returned exiles could experience God's blessing. The writer of Chronicles retold Israel's history so the Jews would turn from their sins and humbly turn back to God.

Are 1 and 2 Chronicles historically accurate?

Because these books include details left out of the books of Samuel and Kings and because they leave out details those books include, some doubt the Chronicler's historical reliability. These doubts ignore important facts. First, the Chronicler mentioned several sources from which he drew his material. If he didn't care about accuracy, why mention sources?

Second, since the Chronicler's primary sources had already been written, he probably assumed his readers would know about the details he left out. Third, the Chronicler had a theological perspective that guided his selection and treatment of the facts. Even though he wrote from a particular perspective, we have no evidence that he misrepresented those facts.

Focus on Obedience

We can see this in the emphasis he put on the need for obedience. He presented Saul as an example of disobedience; the reason for Saul's tragic death was "because he was unfaithful to the LORD" (1 Chronicles 10:13). By contrast, throughout these books we learn how obedience brings blessings. David and Solomon prospered as they put God first (1 Chronicles 10–29; 2 Chronicles 1–9). While 2 Kings 18–20 tells us much about Hezekiah's political fortunes, the Chronicler focused instead on his religious reforms and the resulting blessings (2 Chronicles 29–31). Kings are clearly evaluated more on how well they obeyed God and less on their military or political accomplishments.

The Chronicler also emphasized the importance of proper worship as one expression of obedience. Second Kings includes four chapters describing Solomon's construction and dedication of the Temple. Chronicles includes six chapters on the same subject (2 Chronicles 2–7). This doesn't count the seven chapters that describe the preparations David made before Solomon became king (1 Chronicles 22–26, 28–29), material entirely missing from 2 Samuel. Only the Chronicler tells how Hezekiah purified and organized the Temple and celebrated Passover like it had not been celebrated for many years. Hezekiah's obedience in regard to the Temple and the resulting blessing is evident in the Chronicler's summary of his reign: "In everything that he undertook in the service of God's temple and in obedience to the law and the commands, he sought his God and worked wholeheartedly. And so he prospered" (2 Chronicles 31:21).

Focus on Repentance

For those who had been disobedient, repentance had to precede obedience. To emphasize the need for repentance, the Chronicler included details not found in the books of Samuel or Kings. Only in Chronicles do we learn that Hezekiah invited to his Passover celebration those Jews the Assyrians had left behind in the Northern Kingdom. Most of the northerners rejected this invitation, but some "humbled themselves and went to Jerusalem"

299

What went wrong with David's census? Part 2

Although the Chronicler avoided mentioning most of David's failings, he did tell how David, against God's will, counted the people (1 Chronicles 21). The Chronicler probably included this story because it shows how David obtained the land on which Solomon would later build the Temple, and the Temple was very important to the Chronicler.

A comparison of the account in 1 Chronicles with the same story in 2 Samuel 24 reveals a very important difference. In the earlier version, God prompted David to take the census. In Chronicles, Satan prompted him to do so. Apparently, the Chronicler wanted to emphasize that although David sinned by taking the census, it wasn't his idea. God's enemy, Satan, tempted David to disobey.

(2 Chronicles 30:11). By including this account, the Chronicler emphasized how repentance could again reunify the Jews into one nation.

Second Kings 21 describes Manasseh as one of the worst kings of Judah. Again, to emphasize the possibility of repentance, the writer of Chronicles included something the writer of Kings left out: Before he died, Manasseh turned from his sins and was forgiven by God (2 Chronicles 33:10–17)! It took a period of captivity to get his attention, but Manasseh returned home a changed man. What better example to share with the returned exiles?

Focus on the Good

The writer of Chronicles not only got his point across by including material not found in Samuel and Kings, he also left out material those books had included. We read almost nothing in 1 and 2 Chronicles about the Northern Kingdom of Israel; the focus is exclusively on Judah. This may have been, in part, because the vast majority of his readers would trace their heritage back to the Southern, not the Northern Kingdom.[2] Also, the Chronicler probably focused on Judah because this nation had been the more righteous of the two.

The writer of Chronicles didn't mention most of the bad things David and Solomon did. We read in 2 Samuel how David committed adultery with Bathsheba and had her husband killed, but that story is left out of 1 Chronicles. First Kings 11 describes how Solomon turned from the Lord and worshiped other gods; we never hear about this from the Chronicler. This was no high-level cover-up. The Chronicler's audience already knew these stories from having read the books of Samuel and Kings. The writer of Chronicles left them out because they would distract the reader from one of his main purposes: showing how God used David and Solomon to accomplish His will. By selectively using and supplementing the material in Samuel and Kings, and by emphasizing certain details, the Chronicler reminded the returned exiles of the importance of obeying God.

More than Genealogies

The Chronicler also wanted to encourage the Jews by reminding them that God had not forgotten them. The judgment that took them into exile was specifically described as temporary (2 Chronicles 36:21–22). They were still His chosen people and He would accomplish His plan through them. This is why the Chronicler devoted so much space to the genealogies. Notice how they begin with Adam and go all the way to the time after the exile to Babylon. In this way the Chronicler emphasized the unbroken chain that united those who returned from exile with the very beginnings of God's plan. These genealogies also emphasize Judah, the royal tribe, and Levi, the priestly tribe. God had preserved the line of David to lead His people (1 Chronicles 3:17–24) and the Levites to ensure that Israel could always worship God. Although they may not make interesting reading for us, these lists would have encouraged the Jews.

God's Promise Fulfilled

The Chronicler brought encouragement in other ways as well. As mentioned earlier, he specified that the Exile would be only temporary and would end as God promised (2 Chronicles 36:21–23). Unlike 2 Kings, which ended with Israel in exile, the Chronicler included the decree of Cyrus, allowing the Jews to return home.

Encouragement also came to the Jews through the portrayal of David and Solomon. A large percentage of Chronicles is devoted to these two kings. Out of sixty-five chapters, twenty-eight focus on David and Solomon who together ruled for eighty years. The remaining thirty-seven chapters cover a period of almost four hundred years. So much attention is given to David and Solomon because their reigns represent the high point of the monarchy. The two most important moments in the nation of Israel occurred while these men were on the throne: (1) God's covenant with David, and (2) Solomon's construction of the Temple.

Kingly Examples

God promised David that one of his descendants would always sit on the throne of Judah (2 Samuel 7). Although the Exile had ended this succession, the Jews looked ahead to the Messiah, one of David's offspring, who would rule from David's throne. Solomon had built the Temple where God could meet with His people. A look back at the glory days, especially at the beginning of the Davidic covenant and the Temple, would certainly encourage the Chronicler's audience. They would also be encouraged by how these kings were presented. By highlighting only the positive elements of David and Solomon, the Chronicler emphasized the qualities the Jews should look for in the Messiah, the coming "son of David."

Those Israelites who returned from exile needed more than a retelling of history. They needed encouraging, uplifting lessons from their past to guide them in the present. This is what the Chronicler gave them. From his creative yet historical presentation, the Jews would have remembered the importance of obedience and been encouraged by the fact that God still had a job for them to do.

GOD'S GREAT PLAN IN 1 AND 2 CHRONICLES

In spite of their disobedience, God was not finished with His people. He still planned to use them to reconcile all people to himself. God inspired the Chronicler to retell Israel's history in order to convince the Jews that they still had an important part to play in His plan. As well, these books further clarify how God's plan would come to pass. For one thing, the examples selected show how obedience was essential for God's people. For another, the Chronicler's emphasis on the Temple and its worship reminds us that God's goal for His plan is fellowship with His people. Finally, by focusing on David and his descendants, we gain a greater sense of expectation for the Messiah who is to come from the line of David.

WHAT WE LEARN ABOUT GOD FROM 1 AND 2 CHRONICLES

Faithful to His Promises

Among the attributes of God we find in these books, the two that stand out most are His faithfulness and His patience. At the formation of Israel as a nation, God had promised to bless obedience and punish disobedience. First and 2 Chronicles show God faithfully keeping these promises. They contain many examples of the obedient being rewarded. For example, because King Jehoshaphat turned to God for help at a time of military crisis, God gave him a tremendous victory. After that, "the fear of God came upon all the kingdoms of the countries when they heard how the LORD had fought against the enemies of Israel. And the kingdom of Jehoshaphat was at peace, for his God had given him rest on every side" (2 Chronicles 20:29–30). Even a wicked king, if he repented, could experience the blessing of God (2 Chronicles 33:10–13). Those who failed to repent found God faithful to punish their disobedience. Among the disobedient in 1 and 2 Chronicles we read about Saul (1 Chronicles 10), Rehoboam (2 Chronicles 11, especially verse 5), Jehoram (2 Chronicles 21), Ahaz (2 Chronicles 28), and the kings who ruled after Josiah's death (2 Chronicles 36).

303

Untiringly Patient

As we survey the history of Judah, we also can't help noticing how patient God has been. So many times He could have destroyed this nation, but He waited. His people turned to other gods, neglected His Temple, even lost track of the Law. They had broken the terms of the covenant and deserved immediate punishment, but still He waited, giving them yet another chance to repent. He kept sending prophets to call His people back to obedience, though they refused to listen to these prophets and frequently persecuted them. Even after God sent judgment through the Babylonians, we continue to see God's patience. He waited until the time was right, then kept His promise and brought His people home.

---

1 and 2 Chronicles at a Glance

Authorship: Anonymous; traditionally, Ezra

Date of writing: 400 B.C.

Date of events: 1010 B.C.–538 B.C.

Purposes: To challenge and encourage post-exilic community by retelling the history of the Israelite monarchy

Form: Genealogies, narrative, some poetry

Part of God's plan:

1. To emphasize God's continued interest in Israel
2. To describe nature of God's plan: importance of obedience; goal of fellowship with God; insight into coming Messiah

Key elements of God's character: Faithfulness, patience

---

application questions

1. What other examples of God's faithfulness do you see in these books? Of His patience?
2. In what ways has He been patient with you?

questions for study and discussion

1. Skim 1 Chronicles 1–9.
   a. Why might the Chronicler have traced the genealogy beyond Abraham, back to Adam?
   b. Why might the Chronicler have emphasized the tribes of Judah and Levi?
2. Read 1 Chronicles 13 and 15.
   a. Compare this account of how David brought the ark to Jerusalem with the account in 2 Samuel 6. What differences do you notice?
   b. How might these differences have fit the Chronicler's purpose?
3. Read 1 Chronicles 28–29.
   a. Compare this account of the transition from David's rule to Solomon's with the version found in 1 Kings 1–2. What differences do you notice?
   b. How might these differences have fit the Chronicler's purpose?
4. Read 2 Chronicles 6–7. What do you suppose the Jews who had returned from exile thought when they heard or read these accounts?
5. Read 2 Chronicles 20. According to this chapter, how did Jehoshaphat show his obedience to God?
6. Read 2 Chronicles 29–32. Why do you think the Chronicler paid so much attention to Hezekiah's religious reforms, when the writer of Kings all but ignored them?
7. What else can we learn about God's plan from these books?
8. What else can we learn about God's character from these books?

endnotes

1. The book mentions written genealogical records (1 Chronicles 4:33; 5:17; 7:9, 40; 9:1, 22; 2 Chronicles 12:15), letters and official documents (1 Chronicles 28:11–12; 2 Chronicles 32:17–20; 36:22–23), poems, prayers, speeches, and songs (1 Chronicles 16:8–36; 29:10–22; 2 Chronicles 29:30; 35:25), and several other historical and prophetic writings. The only thing we know about these writings is what we read in 1 and 2 Chronicles.

2. Due to intermarriage, most of those exiled from the ten tribes of the Northern Kingdom disappeared among their neighbors. For more on this, see "Whatever happened to Israel?" in chapter 13. Notice how most of the attention in the genealogies in 1 Chronicles 1–9 concerns those from the Southern Kingdom—Judah and the Levites—who were responsible for the Temple in Jerusalem.

chapter twenty-four
The Time Between the Testaments

INTRODUCTION

In most Bibles, the final chapter of the Old Testament is followed immediately by the title page and table of contents of the New Testament. Actually, about four hundred years passed between the end of the Old Testament period and the beginning of the New. Sometimes misnamed the "silent years," these centuries were actually filled with significant moments in human history and important developments in God's plan.

OVERVIEW

The Persian Empire

As the Old Testament period came to an end, the Jews were subjects of the vast Persian Empire. The Persian king Cyrus had allowed the Jews to leave Babylon and return to their homeland, even paying part of their rebuilding expenses. A later king, Darius, expanded the Persian Empire to its broadest extent, stretching from India in the east, to Egypt in the south, to Libya and parts of Greece in the west. After his death in 486 B.C., the empire began to weaken until its defeat by Alexander the Great in 330 B.C.

For the Jews, life under the Persians was tolerable, even if they were no longer an independent nation with their own king. The Persian government efficiently ruled the subjects in its vast empire, allowing them some measure of autonomy. The Jews were permitted and even encouraged to rebuild Jerusalem and their Temple. Perhaps fearful of falling again into disobedience, the Jews of that day became very concerned about obeying the Law of Moses.

Alexander and Hellenism

In 356 B.C., King Philip II of Macedon in northeast Greece became the father of a baby boy named Alexander, who would grow up to change the world. Alexander was tutored by the philosopher Aristotle, schooled in the art of diplomacy in his father's court, and trained for battle in his father's army. When Alexander was a young man of only twenty, his father was assassinated. After securing his political base at home, Alexander embarked upon a decade of military conquests unlike anything the world had ever seen. He battled the Persians across what is now Turkey, finally inflicting the

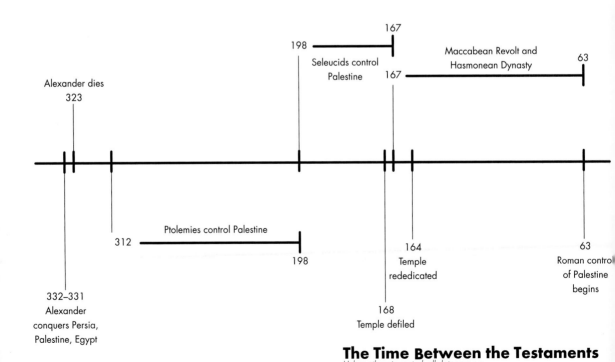

The Time Between the Testaments
Unless otherwise noted, all dates are B.C.

decisive blow against the Persian king at the Plains of Issus, just north of Syrian Antioch.

From there he turned south and proceeded down the coast of the Mediterranean Sea, winning important victories—including the conquest of Jerusalem—on his way to Egypt. He left Egypt in 331 B.C. to travel north then east through the heart of the Persian Empire and as far as Afghanistan, Pakistan, and the Indian Ocean. There his army stopped and refused to go any farther. Reluctantly, Alexander the Great returned to Babylon, where he died of unknown causes at the age of thirty-two.

Even more remarkable than the fact that he conquered so much territory in so short a time at such a young age are the effects of Alexander's conquest on those lands. Everywhere he went, he spread a form of Greek culture known as Hellenism, which put increased emphasis on the role of the individual and on human ability. Alexander's empire also helped to create a common language, a common body of ideas, and a higher level of education in the ancient Near East.

Because Alexander died so young, he was unable to produce an heir who could take over his kingdom. Instead, the territory was carved up among his generals. Ptolemy I was given the land of Egypt and Palestine, thereby assuming control over the Jews. Ptolemy and his successors provided the Jews with peace and security. A significant number of Jews settled in the city of Alexandria, authorized by Alexander but built after his death. This city would become one of the most important intellectual centers of the Mediterranean world. It was here, possibly with the sponsorship of the Ptolemaic government, that the Hebrew Old Testament was translated into Greek starting in the third century B.C. Known as the Septuagint, it became the most popular version of the Bible for the Jews and, later, for the early Christians.[1]

Revolt

Another of Alexander's generals established a kingdom in the territory north of Palestine. This kingdom, known as the Seleucids and centered in Syrian Antioch, sought to extend its influence southward into lands

MAP 19 Travels of Alexander

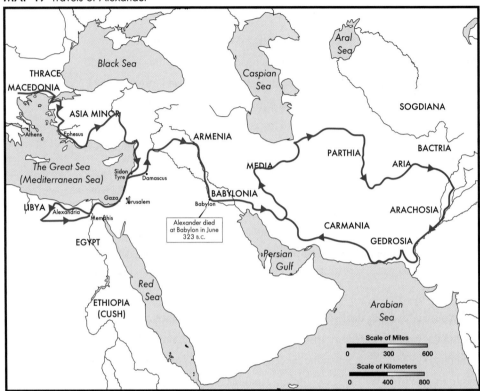

controlled by the Ptolemies. Operating on the principle that the grass is always greener on the other side of the fence, the Jews switched their loyalties from the Ptolemies to the Seleucids in 198 B.C.

Life under their new masters quickly became unbearable. In 169 B.C. the Seleucid king, Antiochus IV, robbed the Temple in Jerusalem. One year later he destroyed Jerusalem's walls, and the next year prohibited the practice of Judaism. Shortly after, he set up an altar to another god right in the Temple in Jerusalem. This was the final straw. Under the leadership of the Hasmonean family, the Jews revolted against the Seleucids in 167 B.C. This family was nicknamed the Maccabees (meaning "hammer"), after their style of guerilla warfare. Under the Maccabees, the Jews reconsecrated the Temple in 164 B.C. an event still celebrated by the Jews during the festival of

310

Hanukkah. Eventually they gained their independence from the Seleucids. For the first time since the Babylonian exile, the Jews were once again free. In 104 B.C., the Jews crowned their first king in nearly five centuries, Aristobulus I.

Unfortunately, Aristobulus and the other Hasmonean kings were too weak to unify the Jews. When the Roman general Pompey arrived in this area in 63 B.C. after having defeated the Seleucid kingdom, he had no trouble extending Roman control over the divided nation. The Romans would remain in charge all through the New Testament period and beyond.

THE APOCRYPHA AND PSEUDEPIGRAPHA

Jewish writers were busy in the centuries between the Old and New Testaments. Thirteen of their books were collected into what is called the Apocrypha.[2] Several were written to supplement Old Testament writings such as Jeremiah, Daniel, and Esther. Others, such as the books of Tobit and Judith, represent short stories about pious Jews, written later but set during the biblical period. Some books sound like Proverbs but have more of the flavor of Judaism during the Hellenistic period. A few of the books retell the history of the Jews. Some describe Jewish history in the post-exilic period (1 and 2 Esdras). Others, like 1 and 2 Maccabees, tell about the Jews who lived during the period of Seleucid rule.

Inspired or Not?

Some Jews believed these books were just as inspired as the books of the Old Testament. They even included them in the Septuagint. Because the Septuagint was the Bible of the early church, a number of Christians also viewed these books as inspired. Other Jews and early Christians recognized them as important but not on the same level as Scripture. The fact that the most widely used Christian version of the Bible, the Latin Vulgate, contained these books advanced their reputation as inspired over the next several centuries. When the Protestant reformer Martin Luther challenged this view, a Roman Catholic council responded in 1546 by pronouncing these books

MAP 20 Rival Powers

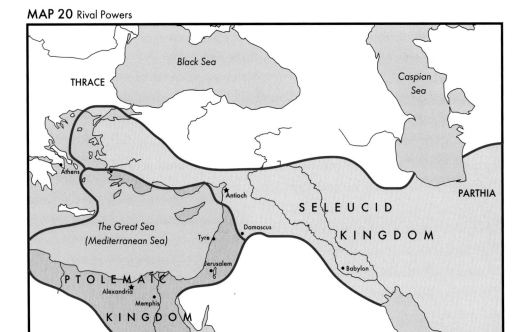

equal with Scripture. This is why Bibles prepared for use by Roman Catholics include the Apocrypha, while Bibles printed for Protestants usually omit the Apocrypha.

A Cultural Window

An even larger category of Jewish writings called Pseudepigrapha was written during the period between the Old and New Testaments. These books are called pseudepigraphal because they claim to have been written by famous figures from the Old Testament. Since the earliest of these books was written about 200 B.C., the claims are necessarily false. No Bibles include them, even though the books claim to be inspired and sound like Old Testament books.

The Apocrypha and Pseudepigrapha are valuable windows into Jewish life and thought in the centuries following the Old Testament period. For example, 1 and 2 Maccabees are a prime source of information on the Jews for the two centuries prior to Jesus' birth. We learn how the Jews were scattered to different parts of the Near East, how they struggled under foreign oppression and sought to maintain their faith in God. We learn how their circumstances changed their relationship with God. Some sought to compromise their Jewish faith with Hellenistic culture. Others resisted that culture, becoming more insistent about being pure and keeping the Law of Moses.

GOD'S PLAN IN THE INTERTESTAMENTAL PERIOD

Preparing the Culture

Although it is difficult to trace the full development of God's plan in this vast and complex period, certain elements seem clear. First, God appears to be preparing the way by which His message could come to all nations. To our knowledge, Alexander the Great never saw himself as God's servant, but he was. By creating a vast empire with a common language and culture, he made it possible for someone to travel thousands of miles—from India to Egypt to Turkey to Greece to Palestine—and communicate in a common language. God used Alexander to create the common culture in which His Word could spread.

God was also at work preparing the way through His people, the Jews. On their own or against their wishes, the Jews were scattered all across the ancient Near East. Many who had been deported to Babylon in 586 B.C. remained there, producing a sizable Jewish community. Jews settled in large numbers in Alexandria and Syrian Antioch. They could be found in western Asia Minor (modern Turkey), in the cities of Greece, and even in Rome. Even though far from their native land, many Jews maintained their ethnic and religious identity, along with the conviction that they were God's chosen people.

God may have permitted this scattering in order to accomplish His plan. Like advance troops in battle, the Jews spread the truth about God, thus preparing the way for the nations to hear, understand, and accept God's plan. When the early Christian missionaries went out to preach the good news about Jesus, they found ready hearers among Jews and those influenced by Judaism.

God used this scattering in another way. Many Jews were living in areas where Greek, not Hebrew, was the predominant language. To be sure that all Jews could understand God's Word, it was decided to translate the Hebrew scriptures into Greek. This translation, known as the Septuagint, was widely used by many Jews and, later, by the Christians. Because God's Word was already translated into Greek, early Christians found it much easier to spread the message of God's reconciling love to a Greek-speaking audience.

Emphasizing the Individual

Hellenism not only provided a common language, it also placed a greater emphasis on the individual than before. Philosophers emphasized the need for each person to care for his or her own soul. Religions began to give greater attention to the questions asked by individuals, questions like where one goes after death. We have seen this emphasis on the individual in the Old Testament period. It receives special attention by Jeremiah, Ezekiel, and Daniel, all of whom spoke of each person being responsible before God. God used Hellenistic influence to advance this trend. By the time of Christ, people were better prepared to understand God's desire to be personally related to each individual.

During this period, God was also at work among His people, preparing them to better understand His plan. For example, He allowed them to become increasingly interested in the coming Messiah or "anointed one." Their concept of the Messiah's role, even His importance, was still undefined, only pencil sketches. Nevertheless, beyond the Old Testament picture, the Jews anticipated that God would send a descendant of David to reward the righteous and punish the wicked.[3] The early Christians began from these sketches and developed the truth about the Messiah in light of what they saw in Jesus.

Clarifying the Afterlife

Also during this period, God further clarified His plan by helping His people understand more about what happens after death. The Old Testament, as we saw, tells us very little about the afterlife. During the intertestamental period, many came to understand that death brought punishment to the wicked and rewards to the righteous. The Wisdom of Solomon, one of the apocryphal books written in the first century B.C., describes the souls of the righteous in the hands of God, beyond torment and at peace eternally. According to Wisdom, the righteous will judge nations, while the wicked suffer punishment.[4] Another apocryphal book, 2 Maccabees, speaks of God raising the bodies of righteous martyrs to eternal life.[5] God wanted His people to understand that His plan included eternity. There He could adequately reward His faithful servants and punish evil.

The years between the closing of the Old Testament and the opening of the New were anything but silent. During these turbulent days, God was at work through a Macedonian general, through godless kings and zealous Jewish guerillas, and in many other ways. He was preparing to execute the most important part of His plan, to reconcile the world to himself by becoming human in the person of Jesus of Nazareth. By offering himself as a sinless sacrifice, He would conquer sin. He would establish a community of Jewish and Gentile believers who would model the reconciled life. He would leave this earth with a promise to return and complete the universal reconciliation He had long desired.

application questions

1. What can you learn about Judaism from 1 Maccabees?
2. In what other ways can you see God working during the intertestamental period?

endnotes

1. The Septuagint, abbreviated LXX, takes its name from the tradition that seventy (or seventy-two) elders were responsible for its translation.

2. This term, meaning "hidden," refers to the content of these books, which contain material only understandable to those with wisdom and insight.

3. An excellent example of this view can be found in the *Psalms of Solomon*, one of the Pseudepigrapha of the first century B.C. Chapters 17 and 18 describe the Messiah as a conquering king who would restore peace to His people.

4. Wisdom of Solomon 3:1–10; 5:15.

5. 2 Maccabees 7:9, 11, 23.

chapter twenty-five

Summary

WHAT WE HAVE LEARNED ABOUT GOD

We began this book by asserting that the most important thing we can take from the Old Testament is a knowledge of God and His plan. Along the way, we have learned much about both. We have seen that God is timeless and eternal, existing before creation. We learned about His power by watching Him create the universe, rescue His people from slavery in Egypt, and redeem them from captivity in Babylon. These accomplishments over the strongest opposition reveal His sovereignty and wisdom.

He Is Holy

We have learned that God is holy. When humans sin, God's holy justice and holy jealousy demand that He punish that sin. He disciplines like a parent punishing a disobedient child, but always patiently and always for the purpose of restoration. His holiness also demands that He not only punish but fix the problem of sin. In the pages of the Old Testament, we see that He provided ways for the sinner to be forgiven, instructed His people how to create a society where sin's social effects could be minimized, and initiated a plan to solve the sin problem finally and forever. Even when His people were faithless, He remained faithful to His promises.

He Loves Us

More than anything, the Old Testament reveals God's love. He created this world and populated it with people because He loves us. When humanity turned against God, He sought for reconciliation. Again and again, He reached out to His estranged spouse through His servants the prophets. But His love extends beyond Israel to all the "Rahabs" and "Ruths" of the world. Our study of the Old Testament has proven true the psalmist's words: "For the LORD is good and his love endures forever; his faithfulness continues through all generations" (Psalm 100:5).

He Is Complex

We have also seen that there is much about God that is hard to understand. Some of His actions seem inconsistent with love, like when He tried to kill Moses (Exodus 4), or when He succeeded in killing Uzzah (2 Samuel 6), or when He incinerated Aaron's sons (Leviticus 10), or scolded the wounded Job (Job 38–41). Much of our perplexity arises because we just don't know enough about what the author was saying and why. But even if we had this knowledge, I still suspect we would find it tough to always understand why God does what He does. God seems to be okay with how He is presented in the Bible; after all, He could have edited out the perplexing parts, but He didn't. Instead, He allowed us to see something of His complexity, how He defies simplistic descriptions. Personally, I'm glad He did.

Because the God I meet in the Bible is beyond my comprehension, I can't reduce Him to a manageable size. Try as I might to make Him fit my world and serve my purposes, I can't do it. I would love to have Him as my personal "genie," granting my wishes and getting me out of tough spots, but He won't fit inside the bottle. I would like Him alongside as my personal advisor, giving me guidance for every decision, or as my personal physician, healing every illness, or as my personal therapist, eliminating life's quandaries—but He refuses to take the job. Of course, there have been times when He has granted my wishes, gotten me out of tough spots, guided me, healed me, and comforted me, but there have been far more times when He has not. This is precisely the picture we see in the Bible. God's behavior is consistent without being predictable, which challenges my tendency to reduce God to Someone simple. It also reminds me of the need to live by faith. Because of God's complexity, I can't predict what He will do; but because God is consistent, I can count on Him to do what is right and loving. It was this faith that gave Abraham the courage to leave his family and home and follow God, without even knowing the final destination (Genesis 12:1–4).

I also find this picture of God quite comforting. Life is complex, full of things that don't make sense. A God I could fully understand would be inadequate to handle what I'm facing. I need a God who is bigger than what I am facing and more complex than life's complexities. But I don't just need a big God, or else how could I be sure He would care enough to help me? I need a God who not only is big enough to help, but also personal enough to care. This is the God we meet in the Bible.

WHAT WE HAVE LEARNED ABOUT GOD'S PLAN

The Bible tells the story of God's desire for fellowship with people. Although created to experience this fellowship, humans were infected early by a virus that made such fellowship impossible. The disease quickly spread to poison interpersonal relationships, physical bodies, and the human spirit. The Old Testament contains ample evidence of this corruption in stories of murder, warfare, conflict, oppression, disease, despair, and death.

The Purpose Is Reconciliation

The Old Testament also describes God's plan to reconcile the world to himself and restore the harmony that once existed. This plan involved the nation of Israel through whom God would reconcile everyone to God. The decisive moment came in the first century A.D. when a young Jewish man was crucified on a Roman cross just outside the walls of Jerusalem. This man was really God wearing a human body, and His death marked God's ultimate step toward reconciliation. His holiness demanded that sin be punished; His

319

holiness then took that punishment on himself. "For this is how God loved the world: he gave his only Son, so that everyone who believes in him may not perish but may have eternal life" (John 3:16 NJB).

The Process Is Personal

Throughout the Old Testament, several aspects of this plan are very clear. First, God sought to restore the fellowship He desired by actually showing up among His people. At first it was periodic, as when God met with Abraham, Isaac, and Jacob at various moments in their lives. Much of the book of Exodus describes God's presence with His people, embodied in objects like the pillars of fire and cloud and the Tabernacle. Throughout Israel's history, God revealed His presence through things (like the ark of the covenant and the Temple), and through people (like prophets, priests, and kings). In the Psalms and elsewhere, the people rejoiced in the presence of God: "The LORD of hosts is with us; the God of Jacob is our refuge" (Psalm 46:7 RSV). When He wanted to describe His judgment on His people, He spoke in terms of leaving them, as He showed Ezekiel in the vision of the throne of God leaving the Temple (Ezekiel 10).

Although the Bible elsewhere speaks of God being present everywhere, He chose to make His presence known in particular places at particular times to emphasize the essence of His plan: God is with us. This is what we celebrate at Christmas: God coming, in Christ, to be with us. The most important thing about heaven—a term that has more to do with a state of reality than a place—will not be the streets of gold and gates of pearl, or even life forever without pain and suffering. The most important thing about heaven is that God will be with His people (Revelation 21:3; 22:3–5). This is what Jesus meant when He prayed, "Now this is eternal life: that they may know you, the only true God, and Jesus Christ, whom you have sent" (John 17:3).

To show that His plan would bring us into perfect fellowship with Him, God let us sample that fellowship on earth. This is not the only way God lets us sample His plan. When God finally and completely reconciles humanity to himself, we will relate to each other in the harmony and fellowship that Proverbs celebrates as the ideal. We will find a truly meaningful existence, the kind pursued by the Teacher in Ecclesiastes. The joyous existence pictured in passages like Isaiah 11:1 — 12:6 hints at the joy to be experienced in heaven. God continues this "sampler" strategy in the New Testament by giving the Holy Spirit, whom He describes as a "down payment" guaranteeing His permanent presence that is to come (Ephesians 1:14).

The Schedule Is His

Reflecting on how God reveals His plan through the Old Testament shows us something else. We see that although God was certainly developing this plan all along, He chose to do so very slowly and in ways that did not always appear to make sense. Who would have guessed that God would begin His plan to create the nation of Israel by calling a man and woman who were childless, and whose son and grandson would also experience the frustration of infertility? When developing a nation that would be the means of introducing salvation to the world, why let them languish in slavery for centuries? If God's goal was to restore fellowship, why forbid the Israelites to create any "sculptured image" (Exodus 20:4)[1] that could remind them of His presence? If God knew that the kings would lead His people astray, why allow Israel to have a monarchy? If "disobedience brings disaster and blessings follow obedience," why do the righteous suffer and the wicked prosper? Why did God wait two thousand years to bring Jesus, only to have Him be born and live in obscurity, then die in infamy? One can propose answers to all these questions, but answers don't remove the glaring truth that God's plan has taken many surprising turns in its long, continuing journey to completion.

This truth reminds us that God is patient. He works steadily and persistently, but never hurriedly. His schedule is not ours. Some in the days of the apostle Peter were scoffing about how long it took God to work. "Where is this 'coming' he promised?" they asked. "Ever since our fathers died, everything goes on as it has since the beginning of creation" (2 Peter 3:4).

321

Peter replied that God took so long because "He is patient with you, not wanting anyone to perish, but everyone to come to repentance" (verse 9). The history of the nation of Israel illustrates God's incredible patience. In spite of all they did to provoke Him to judgment, He proved He really was "a compassionate and gracious God, slow to anger, abounding in love and faithfulness" (Psalm 86:15).

God's plan has been carried out so slowly and so curiously, it is very possible one could completely miss it. Many have, even people who were part of that plan. The prophet Jonah is a good example of someone who forgot that Israel was meant to bring God's "light to the nations." Instead, he ran away.

The Goal Is Relationship

If God knew that people would have a hard time seeing and understanding what He was doing, why didn't He make His plan more obvious? Because He wants His people to walk by faith. In the eleventh chapter of the New Testament book of Hebrews, the writer identifies many Old Testament people who believed, even when they could not see. He speaks of Abel, Noah, Abraham, Isaac, Jacob, Joseph, and others who took God at His word, even though they could not see the end of His plan. Indeed, "without faith it is impossible to please God, because anyone who comes to him must believe that he exists and that he rewards those who earnestly seek him" (Hebrews 11:6).

God has always wanted to have a relationship with each of us, a relationship where our sins have been forgiven and sin's power neutralized. The Old Testament describes how God began the process whereby this could become reality for you and me. In the New Testament, we discover that God intended to accomplish this plan by showing up to remove the penalty and power of sin by dying on the cross. All that remains is for each of us to accept this as God's gift. By faith, we must receive God's forgiveness and allow His Holy Spirit to become our constant companion. Let this God who has longed to be "with us," be with you.

endnote

1. From the *Tanakh: The Holy Scriptures* (Philadelphia: Jewish Publication Society, 1988).

glossary

accommodation: How God works within the framework of different cultures, tolerating people's limitations and reconciling with them, meeting them "where they are" in their understanding.

A.D.: From the Latin for *anno Domini*, "in the year of the Lord"; it has been used for centuries to describe the years since the birth of Jesus.

altar: Primarily a place of sacrifice; a structure on which to present a sacrifice to God.

ancient Near East: The region extending from Egypt in the south to Turkey in the north, and from the Mediterranean in the west to Iraq in the east, as this territory existed during the Old Testament period.

angels: Literally, "messengers," these are created, celestial beings who deliver messages from God to humans and carry out His will in other capacities; sometimes referred to as "sons of God," "holy ones," or "heavenly host." Some scholars suggest a ranking or hierarchy, as evidenced by references to seraphim and cherubim.

apocalyptic: From the Greek "to uncover," it is a genre or type of literature that employs symbolic language to explain a divine intervention soon to take place. The last six chapters of the book of Daniel are considered to be apocalyptic literature.

Apocrypha: A term that means "hidden"; a collection of books written in the intertestamental period and intended to supplement the Old Testament. Although some are considered canonical by the Roman Catholic and Orthodox Churches, the apocryphal books were omitted from the canon of most Protestant churches.

Aramaic: A language similar to Hebrew; spoken by the Jews after the Babylonian exile, as well as by many others in the ancient Near East.

ark of the covenant: The central symbol of God's presence with His people, it was an elaborately crafted rectangular container designed for mobility, carried by priests when traveling, and placed in the Holy of Holies when at rest. Some passages refer to it as God's throne or footstool.

Baal: A fertility god of the Canaanites, understood to manifest himself in storms, using lightning as a weapon and clouds as a chariot.

Babylonian exile: The time between 586 B.C. (when Jerusalem was destroyed and the captives were taken into exile in Babylon) and 538 B.C. (the return of the first exiles from Babylon back to Jerusalem).

B.C.: "Before Christ"; used to designate the years before the birth of Christ.

behemoth: Described in Job, a mighty land animal thought to be anything from a hippopotamus, to a dinosaur, to an imaginary animal possessing the best qualities of all land animals.

Boaz: The "kinsman-redeemer" of Naomi, who married Ruth, ensuring a line of descent for Naomi's dead husband.

Canaan: The land God promised the ancient Israelites as a lasting inheritance; the Promised Land. A bridge of land, Canaan was bordered on the west by the Mediterranean Sea and on the east by the desert, connecting the continents of Asia to the north and Africa to the south.

Christ: The Greek translation of "anointed one."

church: A group of people, both Jews and Gentiles, reconciled to God through the death and resurrection of Jesus. God determined that the church, not the nation of Israel, would be the tool by which God accomplishes His final plan.

circumcision: The removal of the foreskin from the penis. Although some other nations circumcised their males, Israel was instructed to do so when the boy was eight days old. God designated this as a special sign of His covenant with the Israelites, His chosen people.

clean: Undefiled; to be free of impurity physically, morally, or spiritually; able to be reconciled to God; aligned with holiness. An object, type of food, or animal could be designated clean or unclean.

covenant: A solemn agreement or contract between two parties, with each assuming some obligation on behalf of the other. The parties could be equally powerful or one could be more powerful than the other.

Cyrus: King of the Persians who defeated the Babylonians in 539 B.C. He permitted the captive Israelites to return to their homeland and rebuild their society.

Day of Atonement: Also called Yom Kippur, this was the holiest day in the Jewish year and included fasting, confession of sins, and sacrifices to "atone" for the sins of the previous year. In ancient Israel, this was the only day of the year the high priest entered the Holy of Holies.

day of the Lord: The day spoken of by the prophets when God would dramatically and visibly interrupt human history and fulfill His plan.

fear of God: That which characterizes a wise person, one whose relationship to God is based on reverence and obedience.

Feast of Tabernacles: A feast that combined gratitude for the year's harvest and remembrance of God's provision during the Israelites' wilderness wanderings after leaving Egypt. Also called the Feast of Booths, it was held in early fall.

Feast of Trumpets: Also called Rosh Hashanah, this feast included a sounding of trumpets ten days before the Day of Atonement. It was held in early fall and was intended to be a day of rest and sacrifices.

Feast of Weeks: Celebrated fifty days after Passover, this celebration of the barley harvest was later called Pentecost.

Festival of Unleavened Bread: Immediately following Passover, this feast celebrated God's deliverance of the Israelites from Egypt.

Former Prophets: How the Jewish people refer to the books of Joshua, Judges, 1 and 2 Samuel, and 1 and 2 Kings.

Garden of Eden: According to Genesis 2:8, God planted this garden himself and placed human beings there to care for it. It was intended to be a place where God could fellowship with His creation.

genealogy: A list of names; an account that traces the line of descent from an ancestor forward (linear) or presents the development of a single family (vertical).

Gentile: Anyone who is not a Jew.

Hanukkah: Also called the Feast of Lights, this festival celebrates the cleansing and rededication of the Temple after the Maccabean victory in 164 B.C.

Hasmonean: The family name of the Maccabees, who revolted against the Seleucids and established Jewish independence for about one hundred years in the second and first centuries before Christ.

Hebrew: The language of the ancient Hebrews; a member of or descendant of a group of Semitic people known as the Israelites or Jews.

Hellenism: A form of Greek culture spread by Alexander the Great, it put increased emphasis on the role of the individual and human ability. It promoted reason, the arts, the pursuit of knowledge, and established Greek as the primary language of the ancient Near East.

holiness: A characteristic of God, but also a goal set before His people, who were to be holy as He is holy; "to be set apart," spiritually pure, perfect, without sin.

Jews: The people also known as Hebrews or Israelites; members of the tribe of Judah; those who practice Judaism. Before the exile to Babylon in 586 B.C., the Old Testament refers to God's chosen people as Israelites. After the Exile, they are also called "Jews."

Judges: Both the historical book of Judges in the Old Testament and the subject of that book, the men and woman who served as judges or "deliverers" of the Jews. The judges ruled between the time after the death of Joshua until the anointing of Saul as king of the nation Israel.

kingdom of God: Not a nation or territory, it is a collection of people ruled by God; the image of God's rule or sovereignty.

kinsman-redeemer: Best exemplified in the book of Ruth, the kinsman-redeemer was a role designated by God to ensure the continuity of the tribal clan. He was responsible to avenge the death of a blood relative, to reclaim or redeem lost property, and to perpetuate a deceased relative's name and inheritance. The redemption of Ruth by Boaz is often seen as a symbol of Christ's redemption of sinners.

laments: Types of psalms that express individual and communal prayers or cries to God regarding distressful situations.

Latter Prophets: How the Jewish people refer to the books of Isaiah, Jeremiah, Ezekiel, and the Minor Prophets.

Law: In the Old Testament, most often translated "torah"; it can mean a specific commandment or the totality of Hebrew instruction on the proper, godly way to live. The first five books of the Old Testament (the Pentateuch) are also known as the books of the Law.

leviathan: An legendary sea creature that appears several times in Scripture. Some see this creature as a crocodile, dinosaur, sea monster, dragon, or as an imaginary creature possessing the best qualities of all sea creatures.

Levites: Members of the tribe of Levi, one of the twelve tribes of Israel; appointed by God to serve in the Tabernacle and Temple. They were not given an inheritance of land like the other tribes, to ensure their undivided attention to God.

Maccabees: From the word for "hammer," the nickname of the Jewish family that freed the Jews from Seleucid rule and rededicated the Temple in the second century before Christ.

Marduk: The chief god of Babylon.

Mediterranean Sea: Also called "the Great Sea," or "the sea," it is a large body of salt water that extends from the Strait of Gibraltar on the west to Canaan on the east, and from Europe on the north to Africa on the south.

Mesopotamians: Inhabitants of Mesopotamia (from the Greek "between the rivers"), an area that refers generally to the Tigris-Euphrates valley. At times this term applies to the area farther north into Asia Minor and along the fertile crescent into Canaan and Egypt.

Messiah: Literally, "anointed one"; usually refers to a priest or king who was anointed for a divinely appointed role. The term came to describe God's chosen servant who would accomplish His plan of redemption and reconciliation. Christians apply this term to Jesus.

Moab: A country neighboring ancient Israel, located east of the Dead Sea. Its residents were known as Moabites.

monotheism: Belief that there is only one god.

new covenant: The covenant as described by the prophet Jeremiah (31:31–40) and, later, by New Testament authors. It expanded upon the terms of the earlier covenants by making the agreement more personal and internal.

Nile River: Egypt's major river, considered sacred and life-giving in ancient times; it flows north from Lake Victoria in Uganda to the Mediterranean Sea, extending more than four thousand miles in length.

Northern Kingdom: The northern and larger part of the original nation of Israel, which divided in 930 B.C. during the reign of Solomon's son,

Rehoboam. Of the twelve tribes of Israel, ten were located in the Northern Kingdom. Israel fell to Assyria in 722; also called the Kingdom of Israel.

oracle: A message from God delivered to one of His spokespersons, the prophets. The prophet then passed along that message to those God intended to hear it.

parallelism: A predominant feature of Hebrew poetry in which successive lines stand in (parallel) relationship to one another to further amplify or explain the meaning. Among the types are synonymous, antithetic, and incomplete.

Passover: The Hebrew feast commemorating God's deliverance of the Israelites from Egypt by having the angel of death "pass over" them, sparing their firstborn from death. Considered the most important of the Jewish feasts, it was held in early spring.

patriarchalism: A society ruled by males rather than females and in which descent is traced through the males.

Pentateuch: The first five books of the Old Testament—Genesis, Exodus, Leviticus, Numbers, and Deuteronomy.

pharaoh: A supreme ruler of ancient Egypt; another term for the king of Egypt.

Philistines: Enemies of the Israelites first encountered when they entered the Promised Land. They became an increasing threat during the time of the judges until they were held in check by King David. Known as a sea-faring people, they settled along the coast of the Mediterranean Sea, particularly in the southwest section of Palestine.

polytheism: Belief in many gods.

prophet: Someone through whom God spoke messages and gave instructions.

Pseudepigrapha: So called because they claim to have been written by famous figures of the Old Testament, these books were written in the intertestamental period and are not included in the Christian or Jewish canon.

Ruth: A Moabite woman who lived during the time of the judges, followed her Hebrew mother-in-law back to Israel, and accepted her religion. She later married Boaz and gave birth to Obed, who would become the grandfather of King David and an ancestor of Jesus.

Sabbath: The seventh day of the week, the day of rest, the day God rested after creation; literally, "to cease" from work. For centuries, the Jews have celebrated the Sabbath from sundown on Friday to sundown on Saturday.

Septuagint: A term that means "seventy"; one of the oldest and most important Greek translations of the Old Testament, prepared about two hundred years before the birth of Christ. Sometimes abbreviated LXX, it contains several apocryphal books.

sin: The act of disobeying God; the condition resulting from disobedience to God.

Sinai covenant: A formal agreement between God and the Israelites, similar in structure to covenants made between a stronger and lesser king in the ancient Near East. At the heart of this covenant are the Ten Commandments. God made this covenant to reshape the Israelites' self-identity and to guide their behavior as His people.

Southern Kingdom: Also called the Kingdom of Judah, it was the southern and smaller part of the original nation of Israel. Two of the original twelve tribes of Israel were located in the Southern Kingdom. Judah was conquered by Babylon in 586 B.C.

sovereignty: An attribute of God; complete autonomy; of the most exalted kind; total authority. When we say that God is sovereign, we mean that all things come from and depend on God and that He is more powerful than anything or anyone.

Tabernacle: Also known as the "tent of meeting," this sacred, portable tent was where God dwelled among His people, the ancient Israelites. The Tabernacle and its courtyard were the site of worship and sacrifices. It was replaced by Solomon's Temple.

Temple: The sacred place of worship located in Jerusalem. It was called the "house of God" and was constructed by Solomon roughly following the pattern of the Tabernacle. Destroyed by the Babylonians in 586 B.C., the Temple was rebuilt by the returning exiles between 536 and 515 B.C., but on a simpler scale. Herod the Great remodeled this structure considerably, increasing its size and grandeur. It was subsequently destroyed by the Romans in A.D. 70 and has never been rebuilt.

Ten Commandments: Given to Moses on Mount Sinai, these ten laws were meant to help the Israelites live in relationship to God and to one another. They form the heart of the Sinai covenant.

theodicy: The defense of God's goodness and omnipotence in light of the existence of evil.

unclean: Defiled; impure physically, morally, or spiritually; to be in a state such that certain steps would have to be taken to reconcile the unclean person to God. Touching something unclean would make one unclean.

Vulgate: The Latin translation of the Bible by Jerome in the late fourth century A.D. It included the Apocrypha.

wisdom books: A genre or type of biblical literature characterized by attention to life experience and encouragement to fear God; specifically, the Old Testament books of Job, Proverbs, and Ecclesiastes.

Yahweh: Hebrew for "I am," or "I will be," the name by which God revealed himself to the Israelites. This name emphasizes His unique relationship with them.

index

a

k

l

m

n

p

r

S

t